FILMING
POLITICS

Malek Khouri

FILMING
POLITICS

COMMUNISM AND THE PORTRAYAL OF THE WORKING CLASS
AT THE NATIONAL FILM BOARD OF CANADA, 1939-46

UNIVERSITY OF
CALGARY
PRESS

Cinemas Off Centre Series

© 2007 Malek Khouri
University of Calgary Press
2500 University Drive NW
Calgary, Alberta
Canada T2N 1N4
www.uofcpress.com

LIBRARY AND ARCHIVES CANADA CATALOGUING IN PUBLICATION

Khouri, Malek, 1953-
              Filming politics : communism and the portrayal of the working class at the National Film Board of Canada, 1939-1946 / Malek Khouri.

(Cinemas off centre series ; 1912-3094; 1)
Includes bibliographical references and index.
ISBN 978-1-55238-199-1

1. Working class in motion pictures. 2. National Film Board of Canada—History.
3. Motion pictures—Canada—History. 4. Politics in motion pictures. 5. Working class—Canada—History—20th century. I. Title. II. Series.

PN1995.9.L28K48 2007   791.43'652623   C2007-900652-3

The University of Calgary Press acknowledges the support of the Alberta Foundation for the Arts for this published work. We acknowledge the financial support of the Government of Canada through the Book Publishing Industry Development Program (BPIDP) for our publishing activities. We acknowledge the financial support of the Canada Council for the Arts for our publishing program.

This book has been published with the help of a grant from the Canadian Federation for the Humanities and Social Sciences, through the Aid to Scholarly Publications Programme, using funds provided by the Social Sciences and Humanities Research Council of Canada.

Canada

Printed and bound in Canada by AGMV Marquis
∞ This book is printed on acid free paper

Cover design, page design and typesetting by Melina Cusano

CONTENTS

PREFACE AND ACKNOWLEDGMENTS

My first rendezvous with Canadian cinema was in the late 1970s and early 1980s as a young immigrant arriving in Canada from war-torn Lebanon. I remember taking two courses on Canadian film at York University, both of which gave me the impression that this cinema only began to materialize sometime in the 1970s with the making of films like *Goin' Down the Road*, *Paperback Hero*, and *Mon Uncle Antoine*, along with several others. Of course, there were occasional references to a John Grierson and an NFB (National Film Board of Canada), but I do not recall any substantive talk on a serious Canadian cinema that existed before the making of these celebrated films.

As a young film enthusiast in Sidon, a coastline city on the eastern Mediterranean, I had the privilege of sampling all kinds of films, including some shown in local cultural clubs and libraries. This allowed me to view and appreciate documentary films at a relatively young age. Frequently, this also gave me the opportunity to linger after the screenings to listen to some very heated discussions about the films and their social and political significance.

Within a setting engulfed in political strife and a Middle East in constant turmoil, to be directly engaged in politics was part of life, even for a well-pampered middle-class kid like myself. As a result, appreciating how politics unswervingly impacted culture and how culture impacted politics came to me as part of a natural learning process and experience. This politically charged background, however, put me in an awkward position once I began to study film in a Canadian university setting.

One day during a conversation with one of my film professors, James Beveridge – about whose filmmaking background I then knew nothing – I kept ranting about how students in the class had no comprehension of how film interacted with politics, or something to this effect. Beveridge of course alerted me against such quick pronouncements. More importantly, he revealed something that made me very curious. First, he mentioned something about himself being previously involved in making films with the NFB during World War II. Then, he uttered the magic words (for me, at least, coming from a left-wing family background): *Working Class*. I was dumbfounded: did this term even exist in Canada? To my added surprise, he went on to say that making films about the working class, its role in society and in the war was at the front and centre of what the NFB did during that period of its history. Years passed since this conversation but I continued to wonder why no one talked seriously about that era and its films in the same way and with the same passion that Beveridge did. Was it the artistic insignificance of the films, as some suggested? Was it due to their propagandistic and even condescending tone towards their presumed working-class audience, as Peter Morris and Joyce Nelson's (and, to a lesser extent, Brian Winston's) critiques of Grierson claimed, or was it actually because of the politics belied by that unspoken term, *working class* and everything that surrounded it?

The marginalizing of early NFB films in general and the underestimation of their significance to studying social class in particular always raised my curiosity. However, what kept troubling me throughout my later years of studying film was that dignified but subtly bitter tone with which Beveridge expressed his indignation with the fact that the full story about these films was still waiting to be told. Since then, my interest in what cinema signified socially and politically was enhanced with new interest in exploring how cinema impinged on and reflected specific moments in history, particularly those associated with periods of heightened political tension.

This book is driven by the goal of contributing to a rather large and ongoing task – namely the study of the depiction of the working class in Canadian cinema. Workers have been central to this cinema's history, yet the desire among much of the scholarship on Canadian cinema to define a nationalist agenda has concealed some remarkable facets of the way Canadian films portray people from working-class backgrounds. In many ways, this book is a tribute to James Beveridge along with hundreds of other NFB workers and filmmakers, whose exertion during the war offered Canadians a unique perspective on class politics.

My early version of this book came out of a Ph.D. dissertation in the Communications Studies Program of McGill University in Montreal. My appreciation goes to Professors George Szanto and Will Straw for their dedicated support and encouragement, to fellow students for their contributions and insights into the material. In my own Faculty of Communication and Culture at the University of Calgary, I want to thank my colleague and Dean Kathleen Scherf, who for five years now has encouraged my scholarship and been a good friend and tutor. Also thanks to many other colleagues at University of Calgary who are too numerous to mention. A special thanks goes to Bart Beaty and Rebecca Sullivan, whose support and friendship during a difficult period in my personal and career transition I will never forget.

Barbara Rockburn has been a dear friend. She helped me write better by patiently revising my prose. My gratitude also goes to Peter Enman, editor, Scott Anderson, copy editor, and John King, senior editor at the University of Calgary Press for their diligent work on the manuscript.

This book has been published with the help of a grant from the Canadian Federation for the Humanities and Social Sciences, through the Aid to Scholarly Publications Programme, using funds provided by the Social Sciences and Humanities Research Council of Canada.

And a very special thanks to my mother Huneineh and my father Mounir, who, as my first friends and mentors, have so lovingly contributed with their comments, questions, and political commitment to improving my work. I dedicate this book to them.

INTRODUCTION

Responding to the climates of social and political upheavals that prevailed in Canada and around the world in and around the World War II period, many filmmakers from the National Film Board of Canada (NFB) sought new and committed ways to use film as an instrument for social awareness and change. By 1946 these filmmakers produced a major corpus of film which offered a unique outlook on the role of working-class people within Canadian society. This corpus informed and was informed by national and international contexts, and became part of a broader ideological and cultural agenda capable of encompassing wide cross-sections of Canadian society. This book brings to light a wealth of archival material: a range of these films from the initial years of the NFB, films that have either been long forgotten or in fact were never really known. My main objective here is to provide a new reading of these films, by demonstrating the extent to which the Canadian working class was depicted visually for a Canadian film audience during a specific period in Canadian history.

This book avoids detailed assessment of individual films, and favours historicizing and giving an organized view of a broad film corpus. This body of film is assessed in the context of appraising the parameters, and the contextual emergence and descent of the political discourse of the Popular Front and the Communist Party of Canada during the period in which the films were produced. The films are set within a moment that brings them into life: a vast range of interrelated political, cultural and cinematic processes. In this regard, I offer institutional analysis of the NFB during this period; not simply of the politics and personalities who were responsible for the Board's strengths and for its mistakes, but more specifically of the kinds of filmic practices *permitted* to creative artists and administrators who were at the same time independent producers and civil workers functioning under the constraints of wartime society.

I have written this book in the passionate belief that an awareness of intellectual workings of ideological hegemony is indispensable for comprehending not only older film texts, such as the mostly forgotten and sidelined films that this book deals with, but also for understanding cinematic practices of various moments in the history of cinema. Underestimating the relevance of early NFB films to the ideological twists that fostered the entire development of Canadian cinema, and even worse, dismissing them as merely illustrative of authoritarian government propaganda has been endemic in Canadian film studies. Many standard core courses on Canadian cinema customarily continue to ignore these films to the extent that many students are genuinely convinced (as I was two decades ago) that no Canadian film culture of real value or influence existed before the late 1950s, or worse still, before the 1970s. Furthermore, attempts to tackle the issue of class are themselves marred by a similar ignorance of the early NFB films' unique bearing on Canadian cinema's approximation of this issue.

The seven years following the creation of the NFB in 1939 was a seminal phase in the history of Canadian cinema's depiction of working-class people. As they pondered social and political issues such as unemployment, economic prosperity, World War II, democracy, and post-war rebuilding, NFB films were part of a larger cultural practice that advocated a working-class counter-hegemonic political discourse. As such, these films signalled a departure from earlier Canadian cinematic discourse prior to the establishment of the NFB. Furthermore, the discourse of these films drew on a specific propensity within the working-class movement at the time, associated with the Communist Party and its Popular Front strategy. When the Cold War took hold of the country by the mid-1940s, however, the NFB abruptly entered a new phase that represented a reversal in how its films approached working-class and labour issues. The change would consequently alter the ideological purport of NFB films for several years to come.

Throughout its history, cinema in Canada has examined aspects of the lives and politics of working-class Canadians. Hundreds of documentary and feature films have focused on defining what it means to be a worker, assessing the role of labour in politics and in society, and evaluating the significance of the labouring process. Numerous films have also told stories about the unemployed, the poor, unions and union activists. In hindsight, Canadian cinema documented and chronicled a wealth of stories about the struggles, victories and defeats of workers and their communities. These films, however, were never ideologically homogenous. On the one hand, some films tended to idealize, patronize and/or even disparage workers. Through the elision and mystification of the notions of production and work, some films often privileged a narrow understanding of workers, their lives and their struggles. Still, a substantial number of films presented an ideologically different take. Among those were the films produced by the NFB between 1939 and 1946.

Films produced by the NFB during World War II stressed the leading role of workers in society. They contemplated the responsibility of workers in fighting fascism, called for the defence of and celebrated the creation of the world's "first working-class state" in Russia, and pondered forging "a new world order" based on ideas of equitable and collective democratic control and utilization of social and economic resources. As rudiments of a unique moment in Canadian history, these films were an extension of a broader counter-hegemonic movement which placed the working class at the centre of its struggle for "political and social change." As such, the films became active elements within a movement that transcended the partisan limitations of left-wing politics and involved intellectuals and cultural workers and broad discursive counter-hegemonic social and political formations.

Despite the critical significance of the body of NFB films between 1939 and 1946, research on Canadian cinema has largely ignored, or at best presented a narrow view of the ideological workings of these films. Particularly missing from the literature on the NFB and its founder John Grierson is the clear impact made by the labour movement and the Communist Party of Canada (CPC) on the Board's film discourse during this period. The CPC and its Popular Front policy at the time notably informed how NFB films tackled political issues, and virtually patterned the counter-hegemonic philosophical thrust of these films' discourse.

The influence of the movement around the strategy of the Popular Front, initiated by the CPC in the mid-1930s and supported by substantial sections within the working class, expanded beyond the party and the labour movement; it even informed social and political interests that included but also went beyond those of the working class and the socialist left. Indeed, the strength of this movement largely rested in its ability to offer a political perspective that conceived working-class interests as synonymous with those of the majority of society. The discourse of the NFB films itself became an extension of this socially and politically heterogeneous mass movement.

The NFB's film discourse reflected a consensual approach to understanding and dealing with the social and political preoccupations of the day. It offered a constellated perspective which celebrated "new" ideas and values, such as the creation of public social institutions, regulation of market forces, support for cooperative and centralized social and economic systems and plans, solidifying the role of workers in the management of the workplace and society, emphasizing the central labour input into commodity value creation, a new and revamped role for women in society, and measuring economic output based on its linkage to social needs rather than to capitalist profit. Such ideas were presented as commonsensical propositions that were vital to building a modern society.

My reading of early NFB films, therefore, demonstrates how they constituted a valuable element within the working-class and left culture of the period. Concurrently, this reading also demonstrates how a cultural practice and discourse – the loose affiliation of movements and organizations which, in various forms of alliance or sympathy with the communist movement, transformed the NFB's culture. The book examines a corpus of films and discusses how they articulated a counter-hegemonic perspective as an extension to similar views of those adopted at the time by the Popular Front. Here I give clear consideration of historical context as produced out of a dialectic, rather than a single-sided or static element. In this regard, I only briefly deal with questions about possible direct organizational links between specific NFB filmmakers and workers and the Communist Party of Canada, and deliberately avoid questions of a possible communist "conspiracy" within the NFB. To begin with, this fear-mongering approach has had its proponents for several decades within several disciplines of Canadian history. In any case, I think that traditional exaggeration of the role and weight of individuals in shaping history does not serve the goal of understanding the complexity of any discourse, including the one which informed and was informed by the NFB films in question.

Instead, the book chooses to explore historical context and how it broadly impacts, extends and limits film practice. It concentrates on manifestations of counter-hegemonic impulses within the films to demonstrate how they, within the limits of the era and of the institution, articulated the working class as active agents of history. In other words, the book brings the institution and the series of film products together, explaining both why certain subject matter and certain narratives become possible, and – just as important – why others in fact remain absent.

Before I go any further, however, it is imperative to clarify this book's utilization of the term *working class*. Given the ground-shifting events that impacted working-class politics after the collapse of socialism in Eastern Europe in the early 1990s, and considering the expansion of the role of technology in industrial production, which allowed broader and more vigorous multinational capitalist expansions, reference to the term working class certainly needs revisiting.

When it comes to identifying classes, the dominant tendency is to exclude rather than include more people from the working-class category. In most cases the inclination is to delimit this class to blue-collar industrial white males. Consequently, racial and ethnic minorities, women and children are often excluded from this category. White-collar workers, teachers, public servants, the unemployed or the poor are also invariably omitted from the working-class categories. This narrow definition clearly mystifies the notion of class and reinforces misconceptions about social realities in advanced capitalist societies such as Canada; it also reiterates ideological perceptions of these societies as middle-class economic and social havens to which the notions of class divisions, let alone struggles, does not apply.

My use of the term working class includes those who sell their labour for wages. This definition roughly distinguishes as members of this class those who create in their labour and have taken from them surplus value. It also allows the inclusion of those who have no – or relatively little – control over the nature or the products of their work and those who are not professionals or managers. This definition, though admittedly blurred at the edges, gives us at least a reasonable place from which to start.

Equally as important, my utilization of the term working class also benefits from Gregory Kealey's attempt to move beyond the narrow indications that come with the use of the term *labour* as "a category of political economy, a problem of industrial relations, a canon of saintly working class leaders, a chronicle of union locals or a chronology of militant strike actions."[2] My use of the term labour is mainly linked to the labour movement itself, which includes trade unions, workers' organizations and other labour related *institutional* connections. In light of these definitions the parameters of this study become clearer, in that it does not focus on exploring individual or institutional linkages between labour unions and the NFB, but rather maps out a discourse that transcends immediate structural associations and involves broad discursive practices of a working-class counter-hegemonic movement.

Having said that, it is important to point out that the films at hand indeed concentrated on depicting blue-collar industrial workers. Clearly, this corresponded with the numerical strength of this section of workers during this particular period in the development of the Canadian capitalism. The films' focus on industrial workers also reflected the influence of this specific section of the working class in organizing and mobilizing other workers and segments of society. This influence extended to the movements of the unemployed, agricultural workers and farmers, fishing industry workers, as well as intellectuals and groups who supported the policies of left-wing labour organizations, the Popular Front and the Communist Party. For its part, a significant number of NFB films depicted workers in the rural and the fisheries economic sectors. In most cases workers in those areas variously shared organizational and political links with industrial workers. Nevertheless, it is important to note that the context and political preferences of each of the blue-collar worker sectors mentioned above differ, even if there is overlap in progressive goals. The intention in this book is to stress how the counter-hegemonic sentiment of the films from around the World War II period carried weight in connection with commonalities in the outlooks and concerns of various sections of the Canadian working class.

In relation to other terminology and scope, it is important to stress that this book uses the terms *left wing* and *communist* almost interchangeably. There were two influential political currents within the Canadian labour and working-class movement in the period that this study deals with: one dominated by the social democratic Co-operative Commonwealth Federation (CCF), which was created in 1935, and the other by the Communist Party of Canada, which was officially launched thirteen years earlier in 1922 (the party was known between 1943 and 1959 as the Labour Progressive Party). After the establishment of the CCF in 1935, the trade union movement became increasingly divided between supporters from one or the other of these two political tendencies. Of course labour unions included many who were partisans of neither organization. Certainly within the communist faction there were a large number of unionists who were non-party members. The communist-supported group of unions was generally referred to as the left wing of the labour movement. Still, it is imperative to point out that much of the emphasis on ideological differences between the Communist Party of Canada and the CCF during World War II was largely influenced by Cold-War-inflected rewritings of the period's history. This includes much of the material that deals with the ideological and political nuances that separated the CCF and the CPC. As left and labour Canadian historian Ian McKay proposes in his paradigm-shifting article on the issue, there remains a tendency to deny, or at least to underestimate, the similarities in the policies of the two parties during the pre-Cold War period.

McKay suggests that the shift towards a Popular Front policy by the post-1935 Communist Party in many ways resulted in the emergence of a "third period" wave in Canadian socialism, "in which nationalism, the management of the economy, and the restoration of harmony to the international order were seen as paramount."[3] This, McKay suggests, eventually resulted in a "certain convergence within a common formation" between the CCF and the Communists on the question of the socialist state.[4] Aside from sectarian and political differences around issues such as the need for a vanguard revolutionary party as advocated by the Communist Party, and the emphasis on a mass party and coalition as promoted by the CCF, as well as latter party's adherence to "parliamentary Marxism,"[5] both parties shared a common vision of a country "in which capitalist ownership has been replaced by social ownership, and 'the rapacious system of monopoly capitalism' replaced by a 'democratic socialist society.'"[6] The CCF-produced book *Make This Your Canada* essentially celebrated "a specific kind of socialist state: one in which democracy is supplemented by comprehensive and systematic state planning, similar to (at least in general terms) the type of planning seen in both the Soviet Union and wartime Canada."[7] Even on the issue of solidarity with the Soviet state itself, the CCF was far from being anti-Soviet as it later became at the height of the Cold War. In fact the party adopted a similar view to that of the Communist Party, in which it conceived of the Soviet Union as an example of a country where the population was able to embark "'upon a colossal plan of organized social revolution,' which has already given them 'a powerful new system capable of withstanding the onslaught of the world's mightiest armies.'"[8] Overall, the CCF shared at this moment in history almost all the programmatic elements that were proclaimed by the CPC in 1935 in the context of its adoption of Popular Front strategy. Another important element to stress when it comes to influences from other groups which inadvertently enhanced the discourse and influence of the counter-hegemonic movement at the time, is the role played by the cooperative movement in general during this period in Canadian history. For example, the importance of the cooperative spirit – particularly when it comes to Atlantic Canada – was connected to the well-rooted regional priest-led cooperatives and credit unions, which were in many cases decidedly non-communist. In any case, this book concentrates on examining how one of the two major popular left-wing traits within the Canadian working-class movement, the Communist Party, and by extension its Popular Front policies, informed the discourse of NFB films.

An important issue to which this book indirectly alludes is the fact that the NFB during this period paid almost no attention to the cultural and political specificities of working-class concerns and life in Quebec. Both Pierre Veronneau's three-volume book on the history of Quebec cinema, and Gilles Carle and Werner Nold's documentary *Cinema Cinema* (1985) discuss the Quebec team at the NFB during its first twenty-five years. What resonates from these two attempts to tackle this epoch of Quebec cinema is that the embryonic francophone contingent within the NFB during World War II seems to have been largely sidelined or marginalized, at least in its ability to independently tackle Quebec's conditions during this pre-Quiet Revolution period. It is important to note here, however, that recruiting Québécois, who were largely not in sympathy with the war, and "still harboured resentment concerning the conscription laws of World War I," represented a challenge to Grierson and to the NFB. This situation seems to have trickled down to the Board focusing on making soft-sell programs "to persuade these unenthusiastic people to join the war effort."[9]

The only group of films with specifically Québécois themes was Norman McLaren's six film animation series *Chants Populaires*. Five of the six films were produced in 1944 and the last in 1946. The series visualized a group of French Canadian folk songs. Probably the only film of the period to deal with a mainly Quebec-related working-class setting and topic which also involved a filmmaker from Quebec was Jean Palardy's *Gaspé Cod Fishermen* (1944). The film describes how collective effort "brings together the people of Grande-Rivière on the Gaspé Peninsula to catch, prepare, and sell the cod upon which they depend for food and income." Another film with specific significance to depicting life among economically marginalized segments of Quebec was Jane March's *Alexis Trembley, Habitant* (1943), which presented a picture of peasant life within a traditional Quebec family.

While a distinct Quebec film culture did indeed emerge prior to the years of the Quiet Revolution, the emergence of labour film itself in Quebec is probably best regarded as part of this rebellion against existing cultural and ideological limitations in Quebec, which itself did not occur until almost two decades after the end of World War II. This, nevertheless, remains ironic considering that Montreal was where the first and only official communist Member of Parliament ever to be elected won a seat in the early 1940s in the Cartier area, one of the city's most well-recognized working-class districts at the time. Further study of this apparently contradictory manifestation of political and cinematic dynamics within Quebec is clearly needed! Suffice to say, the relocation of the NFB headquarters from Ottawa to Montreal in the 1950s later paved the way for a major evolvement in Quebec (and for that matter Canadian) cinematic interest in the working-class subject in the 1960s and 1970s.

In its first editorial in 1977, the Canadian film and cultural journal *Cine-Tracts* contemplated a critical practice capable of unmasking the ideological character of criticism itself. This goal was to be achieved through a specific theoretical connection:

> In linking together the issues of self-reflexivity, subjective positioning, and hegemonic social structure, we are proposing the outline of a possible theory of culture which embraces both the "critique of ideology" and the problematic of praxis. This work is largely incomplete and thus far, poses far more questions than answers.[10]

Today, finding this theoretical critical connection remains as crucial as it was more than twenty years ago when it was originally proposed by *Cine-Tracts*.

This book's employment of a theoretical framework that brings ideological hegemony to the centre of its re-evaluation of NFB's early films is itself a tribute to the task that *Cine-Tracts* set out to accomplish. The book conceives the depiction of the working-class subject in the NFB's war films as a cultural practice located in historically determined social praxis. By studying film within historically defined terms, this book also attests to the inherent limitations and possibilities of cinematic practice and points out its interactive influence on hegemonic power relationships.

The discipline of film studies continues to contend with seemingly contradictory critical priorities. While theoretical elaborations over the last three decades provided new perspectives for studying cinema, the basis for analyzing film remained variably focused on dealing with the filmic text in relative isolation from its setting within history. Furthermore, while disparate approaches have been useful in untangling a variety of filmic social denotations and the ways in which audiences understand and relate to them, that has not prevented the widening of an arbitrary gap between film studies and social sciences. Therefore, looking at cinema as a social process and consequently assessing its significance based on studying the empirical elements in different areas of film practice is still largely posed as antithetical – or at least as a non-converging parallel – to dealing with the filmic text as the main subject of appraisal.

Labour and cultural historian Steven Ross identifies five components that are crucial for addressing the ideological construction of the working class in cinema. These include: the movie industry, movie audience, historically related political dynamics, the manipulation of state power, and labour relations within the movie industry. While he acknowledges that each of these elements develops in its own unique way, Ross also suggests that they overlap with each other at particular points of their evolution, thereby creating "common fields of intersection." The final film product as seen by audiences becomes an extension of all these elements.[11] Ross's approach echoes propositions made two decades earlier by British cultural critic Raymond Williams.

Williams acknowledges the need to temporarily isolate precise elements within the general framework of cultural analysis, based on specific research priorities. But he also draws a precept of a sociology of culture that lies in the "complex unity of the elements thus listed or separated." This unity, Williams contends, epitomizes the task of the sociology of culture as a distinctive task "from the reduced sociology of institutions, formations, and communicative relationships and yet, as a sociology" makes it radically different from the analysis of isolated forms.[12]

Understanding any cultural intellectual climate presupposes an analysis of the underlying ideas or philosophies characterizing a specific milieu, how they are rooted in material practices and how they circulate within the various parts of the superstructure (the term is based on Marx's allegorical demonstration of the materiality of economic formations as constituents of an infrastructure, and ideology, culture and politics as elements of the superstructure), and how phenomena that might appear unique contain a common ideological nucleus, the substance and function of which may be reciprocally converted or translated from one to the other. As part of historically specific hegemonic relationships, cultural analysis cannot avoid assessing what cultural products most evidently manifest in relation to ideological intelligibilities.

Building on Williams's approach to studying the cultural text as an extension of wider social and historical interactive elements, this book examines the depictions of the working-class subject in the films produced by the NFB between 1939 and 1946 as sites for excavating and untangling the dialectics that have shaped the ideological intelligibilities of the period of which they were part. The films are presented as testimonies to the interacting and overlapping dialectics surrounding the struggle around ideological hegemony during this specific era of Canadian history.

The book concerns itself with examining the discourse of this body of films, and as such explores one aspect of a discursive formation associated with the NFB's interaction with the Canadian working-class movement within a specific historical moment. In this regard, Foucault's approach to identifying discourse as opposed to discursive practice is important to reaffirm. For Foucault, discourses are systems of thought or domains of knowledge that form around certain themes or ideologies, for instance, justice. A discursive practice, in this case the juridical system, would involve institutions (courts, etc.) and technologies (laws, means of enforcing them). Together, discourses, institutions, and technologies interact as the discursive formation of the law.[13] In the case of this book, the emphasis is primarily on exploring the discourse of working-class representations in NFB films within a specific period of the Board's history. Therefore, while I do indeed refer to the institutional and personal related aspects that were part of the general discursive formation in question (i.e., the NFB, NFB films, the Communist Party, and the working-class movement during World War II), my incorporation of these elements is restricted to demonstrating and pointing out their impact on the nature of the system of thought itself (i.e. the discourse) and the context within which it operated.

This study is also theoretically grounded in Antonio Gramsci's articulation of the notion of hegemony (and by extension, counter-hegemony) as it functions through the emergence of historical blocs. Gramsci submits that various social and political forces form material bases for specific hegemonies that in turn give prominence to a more or less hierarchical structure of social classes, as well as broadly consensual cultural, political and ethical viewpoints and philosophies. The hegemony of any given social class is maintained only as long it is able to ensure a broad-based cohesive alliance that by the end reflects the material interests of this class. To counteract capitalist hegemony Gramsci underscores the need to develop strategies for building an alternative proletarian hegemony (or counter-hegemony); this can only be achieved through bringing together a new class alliance or historical bloc between the working class and its own political and cultural views and the interests at its core. Attaining such a counter-hegemonic bloc is crucial before any revolutionary transformation of society can be achieved.

Gramsci's theoretical approach is particularly useful in helping us understand the emergence of the NFB's discourse on labour and the working class, and the class character of this discourse in connection with the struggle around political hegemony in Canada prior to, and after World War II. Gramsci's approach represents a turn away from the concept of monolithic, virtually irresistible ideological determination in favour of exploring dialectical relations between the interests of several classes under the hegemony of one of them. In speaking of spontaneous and active consent, Gramsci refers to the subordinate classes' acceptance of the ruling class's world outlook and its moral and cultural values. The ideology of the capitalist class, expressed through its intellectuals and the institutions developed within civil society in the course of a prolonged rise to dominance (e.g., political parties, churches, schools, the press, etc.) has the effect of moulding the consciousness of people and providing them at the same time with rules of practical conduct and moral behaviour.

Therefore, hegemony goes beyond the restrictive parameters of false consciousness or direct control and manipulation of the masses, an assumption that is largely characteristic of how of the critical discourse on Canadian cinema interprets ideology, as I will demonstrate in the first chapter. Rejecting this form of negative interpretation of ideology, Gramsci recognizes it as a "terrain on which men move, acquire consciousness of their position, struggle, etc."[14] As such, hegemonic ideology provides a relatively coherent and systematic worldview that does not simply influence, mould, or hail people, but serves as a principle of organization of social institutions.

By stating that "structures and superstructures form a historical bloc," and that "the complex, contradictory and discordant ensemble of the superstructure is the reflection of the social relations of production," Gramsci provides a basis for appreciating how social forces are also capable of setting limits to the operation of cultural practices. He also demonstrates that social and cultural realities do not purely reflect or mirror economic class interests, and that they are not predetermined by dominant economic structures or organization of society. Instead, these realities emerge within arenas of interminable struggle.[15]

Since, in their material practice, social subjectivities operate within the structures they inhabit, they are also potentially capable of negotiating their conditioning and of becoming active and creative agents that grapple to break the bounds of a necessity that in the last analysis is only relative. This is what Gramsci labels the moment of catharsis, which "indicates the passage from the purely economic (or egoistic-passional) to the ethico-political moment." This moment designates the passage from "objective to subjective" and from "necessity to freedom,"[16] when "structure ceases to be an external force which crushes man, assimilates him to itself and makes him passive, and is transformed into a means of freedom, an instrument to create a new ethico-political form and a source of new initiatives."[17] Ideology, as perceived in this book, is therefore a "terrain on which men move, acquire consciousness of their position, struggle, etc."[18]

This terrain involves different forms and/or levels of social consciousness, all of which contribute to sustaining or challenging specific hegemonies. While ideology particularly engages "modes of feeling, valuing, maintenance and reproduction of social power,"[19] these conditions also allow for varied levels of ideological self-consciousness among the subaltern. A higher level of ideological awareness could lead to the emergence of social agency that has the potential of playing a role in social and political change. As such, ideology transcends expressing or reflecting entrenched and unconscious set of values and influences. In this book, hegemonic dominance in civil society is seen as enhanced by philosophical consensus around values and ideas. Such consensus, however, is itself in a relentless struggle to reaffirm its dominance within society. Values in any given society are always open to different interpretations; they can be expounded to solidify the consent of the subaltern and its concordance with the interests of the dominant class, or they can conversely be construed in a counter-hegemonic fashion to ideologically challenge the outlook of that class.

Both traditional and contemporary modes of ideological analysis within film studies have an inclination to fetishize and/or isolate the analysis of certain signifying systems within the film. This often occurs at the expense of appreciating the importance of film as a historically grounded cultural process. One result of this tendency, at its extreme, is to become preoccupied by the grammar and language of the film (irrespective of how the notion of language is dealt with in the context of the multiple discussions by Metz to Deleuze and their respective followers) to the extent that the historicity of cinema as a crucial element of how it interacts with audience becomes irrelevant to the discussion. Concentrating on the internal workings of the text (or even on a universalized form of cognitive understanding of the text) traditionally steered away from appreciating film as part of continuum and as an embedded element of a wider social matrix. This is at the core of why film studies rarely deals with certain hegemonic moments where there are manifestations of political challenge and ideological resistance. The emphasis on the internal textual working of cinema virtually lessens the interest in, and the ability to formulate better appreciation of, broad bodies of film (outside of genres, filmmakers, nationalisms, ethnicities, gender, etc.) that specifically relate to various historical moments and settings. Subsequently, filmic practices of counter-hegemonic relevance have been largely oblivious to some Canadian film critics.. By choosing to analyze a body of film in the context of the historical moment of their emergence and death, I am hoping to contribute to the task of seeking a more historically conscious

Canadian film studies. Through its interdisciplinary incorporation of film studies with left-wing political and social history, and through its emphasis on the significance of early NFB films as valuable elements of working-class culture beyond the specific and limited terms of evaluation within traditional film studies (where aesthetic concerns are privileged), this book hopes to broaden both the base of written history on the formation of the NFB as well as our understanding of Popular Front initiatives.

The second consideration is my emphasis on film as constituent of political and cultural process within which ideological effects amalgamate to produce specific visions of life. My reading of the films concentrates on looking at them as excavation sites for political and ideological messages that, if viewed from a relative distance, appear to merge into a hegemonic whole.

In cinema, the question of ideology becomes clearer when a film is looked upon as a practice directed at reforming consciousness. The ideological significance of cinematic practice is most effectively exposed when we prioritize specific points in the filmic narrative where values – moral, political, social, and otherwise – are introduced, challenged and eventually resolved (or, in some cases, are left without a resolution). These points are present and function within complex systems of visual and aural codes, plot structures, as well as absences. These points are explicitly also manifested in the main themes of a film. Thematic components challenge the audience to deal with specific dilemmas, and films present their own ways of settling such dilemmas. Based on how they choose to settle these dilemmas in the context of social, ethical, political, and economical contentions of the period in which they are produced and received, films assume a presence within specific ideological hegemonies.

Since this study's goal is to explore and evaluate a corpus that consists of dozens of films, I have chosen to address filmic content in the context of broader themes. The study, therefore, does not claim to address stylistic elements of the films at hand; instead, it concentrates on categorizing general thematic preoccupations to which these films subscribe and how they interact with working-class politics of the time. To this effect, I present a reading which looks at the films in conjunction with the politics of a significant section of the working class, which at the time projected a counter-hegemonic viewpoint on Canadian politics. This is not to say that specific cinematic strategies are irrelevant to better understand and appreciate how these films worked in a counter-hegemonic fashion. On the contrary, cinematic strategies, such as the heavy-handed dramatization of certain events and stories, the choice of shots and scenes, the "dialectical" montage approach used along with Renoir-like realist techniques, etc., all play a major role in how these films worked on the social and the political levels. Chapter Eight maps out such elements by way of providing critical basis for further assessment of the stylistic aspects of the films' discourse, and perhaps for future detailed textual analysis of specific films.

A critical area for assessing ideological intelligibility relates to the approximation of the notion of change and progress. As in other advanced civil societies, political culture in Canada traditionally regarded change as a sign of vitality and as an antithesis to stagnation – itself associated with the past and with tradition. My reading of the NFB films, therefore, also looks at how they presented a counter-hegemonic ideological perspective on the notions of change and progress, and how they linked achieving these notions to reorganizing the social and economic administration of society and moving it in a fundamentally new direction.

The materialization and fall of a counter-hegemonic discourse on the working class in NFB films was not ideologically predetermined or culturally and politically isolated, nor was it part of a free-for-all cultural public domain. As with any group of films in any specific moment in history, these films informed and were informed by struggles to create hegemonic consensus, a consensus that was constantly and simultaneously marked by incessant political contentions. The discursive surfacing of the NFB's discourse on labour and the working class, and the significance of this discourse in connection with political struggles around hegemony, were all connected with the surfacing of new initiatives within Canadian political culture in the 1920s and 1930s. The book has two main primary sources of investigation: (1) NFB films between 1939 and 1946, and (2) documents on and from around the same period representing the discourse of the Communist Party of Canada, the Popular Front and the Canadian labour movement.

In addressing the films I utilized a discursive evaluation, in the sense that I used a somewhat selective sampling of the material at hand. This sampling, however, was not arbitrary. My broad definition of the term *working class* necessitated an equally broad research strategy. In setting my research parameters I first surveyed the descriptions and contents of all NFB films between 1939 and 1946 for the purpose of identifying those that dealt with labour issues. However, I soon realized that such delimitation would not serve the purpose of a comprehensive evaluation of the ideological significance of the material. Since there were over 550 films produced during this period, and taking into consideration logistical limitations such as the non-availability of many of these films in the NFB or the National Archives, I decided to concentrate on the largest number possible of labour- and worker-related titles. Also incorporated were other films that, even if not directly addressing the topic of labour and workers, nevertheless tackled subject matter with a major impact on working-class politics.

Films from the period between 1939 and 1946, catalogued in the NFB's own list under "Work and Labour Relations" provided the primary source of my research. These films conceived workers as not incidental, but as their key subject of interest. This body of film constituted the core of my screening and evaluation. Other films closely surveyed were those dealing with working-class issues, but which were nevertheless disparately listed under other categories. Those included material under headings and subheadings that directly related to labour, such as child labour, company closures, employment and unemployment, farm workers, job hunting, retirement, strikes, training and vocational rehabilitation, unions and unionization, work and leisure, working conditions, health and safety, women and work, women and non-traditional employment. Yet other supplementary sets of films that were closely examined were found under categories that were not readily related to labour and work. These included films under headings like automation and technological change, career guides, cultural groups, disabled people, discrimination and equal rights, family life and work, historical perspectives, management issues, portraits, and women. My survey would not have been comprehensive, however, without incorporating films that dealt with topics such as communism, the Russian Revolution and the Soviet Union. When early NFB films were produced, discussions around such topics impressed in major ways the ideological thrust of working-class politics both in Canada and around the world. Most films engaging these topics were found in material on World War II and the fight against fascism. In the end I was able to identify a body of films of 180 titles (of 553 films that include redundant footage simultaneously produced under various titles[20]) that involved at least one or more themes relating to working-class and labour politics. Over 150 of these films were eventually screened and assessed and provided the primary source for this book.

My assessment of these films incorporates what Raymond Williams characterized as the most central and practical elements in cultural analysis: cultural formations. As such, my analysis addresses the films simultaneously as "artistic forms and social locations."[21] It accounts for three elements: an overall review of the narrative (the main theme or topic of the film); a test of the film's positioning of the working class within the social and political events and issues of the period (the choice of the area is designated based on the main thematic or topical field of interest of the film); and finally, an evaluation of the ideological significance of the film. The order given here is not necessarily the only order in which films are discussed. In most cases, my access to these areas is interactive; it also overlaps various components that influenced and were influenced by the moment in which the films operated. Issues relating to film structure and style are specifically dealt with in a separate section on stylistic discourse in Chapter Seven.

My analysis therefore goes beyond addressing how the films view themselves and how their role has been customarily identified; instead, it focuses on introducing and interpreting them as social and ideological constructions. This also means exploring the films' social affiliations and ideological choices, which implies situating them within a historical context. In this regard, I incorporate a comprehensive survey of the political and cultural dynamics within which these films came to exist. Specific attention is given to surveying working-class culture and politics, and to their significance to counter-hegemonic cultural practices both inside and outside the sphere of Canada's cinematic culture.

This book incorporates an assessment of the political and cultural dynamics of which the novelty or originality of NFB films came to exist. Examining the filmic discourse on the working class in the NFB films during World War II, and the years which immediately followed, meant exploring social affiliations and ideological choices. A significant amount of research covered material dealing with the history of Canadian political culture in the period between the 1920s and the mid-1940s. Special attention was given to surveying working-class culture and politics, particularly as they relate to the emergence of the communist movement in Canada, and their impact on the formation of counter-hegemonic cultural practices both inside and outside the sphere of Canadian cinema. This research allowed me to locate the origins of the NFB's cinematic discourse, and consequently to determine the counter-hegemonic ideological significance of this discourse.

I have consulted original archival sources that include labour, cultural and political newspapers and journals, trade union pamphlets and congresses' reports, as well as studies on labour, culture and communism in the first half of the twentieth century. Other sources include interventions by two members of the Canadian House of Commons, one a Communist Party supporter and the other a Communist Party member. Citing these two MPs helps clarify unswerving interrelationships between the political discourse put forward through communist Popular Front policies and those found in the NFB's discourse on labour and the working class.

Whenever they exist in film and in many social and political science studies, references to Canadian communist politics are overwhelmingly filtered through second-hand information, sources and interpretations. Indeed the period at hand has been mostly pondered and analyzed based on "polarized opposites – pro and anti-Communist, Trotskyist against Stalinist, the revolutionary Third Period and the reformist Popular Front, the Communist International's Soviet line against native radical expressions."[22]

While I am conscious of various legitimate critiques of various aspects of the role of the Communist Party, I am equally mindful of the problems associated with a generalized and largely anti-party bias in approximating leftist politics as manifested in numerous academic endeavours. In particular, I am cognizant of the tendency to categorically reduce the CPC's practices to mere embodiment of Stalinist politics.

On the one hand, there is no doubt that the orthodox version of Marxism adopted by the Party and the Stalinized Comintern was, to begin with and at best, grounded in a selective reading of Marx. On the other, however, some of the critiques of the party are inclined to underestimate the significance of the party's Popular Front strategy that was adopted between the mid-1930s and 1940s, and to dismiss it as mere epithet to Stalinist dogmatism. Consequently, this approach ignores the impact of the party's own discourse as one viable source for understanding counter-hegemonic cultural practices in Canada in the 1930s and 1940s.

For example, original sources from the CPC are quickly and customarily dismissed in academic studies as naturally biased; hence, they are either ignored or simply supplanted by interpretive (and assumingly non-biased) views by non-party sources. In this book I insist on giving the reader an opportunity to sample first-hand accounts of the CPC's discourse during this critical period of its and the NFB's history. Considering that the book focuses on the interactivity between two discourses, that of the Party (and its Popular Front policy) and that of the NFB films, it makes sense to rely on first-hand sources from both discourses in order to draw meaningful conclusions about possible connections.

Dismissing and/or marginalizing the role played by the CPC in general led to gross undervaluing of policies that represented integral components of labour and working-class political and cultural practice before, during, and immediately after World War II. In hindsight, disregarding these policies and their bearing on Canadian politics was probably responsible for some of the existing gaps in Canadian film studies when it comes to acknowledging the counter-hegemonic ideological working of NFB films during this critical period of Canadian film history (particularly in the work of Morris and Nelson). This in turn resulted in ignoring the major effects of the Cold War on the development of Canadian cinema itself. Whether or not we agree on the extent of the damage on Canadian cinema that resulted from the Cold War, the fact is that most studies consistently downplayed the importance of NFB films during the war and almost ignored that Canada (and Canadian cinema) had its own version of McCarthyist practice, whose role is yet to be properly acknowledged and explored. In this regard, this book also hopes to contribute to the better understanding of how these practices shaped the development of Canadian cinema.

The first chapter of this book provides an appraisal of Canadian film studies literature on NFB's early films. It presents a theoretical evaluation of the general tendency among some Canadian cinema scholars to discount class. This assessment provides a basis for understanding the underlying dynamics behind traditional underestimations of the counter-hegemonic significance of these films.

Discussing pre-NFB Canadian cinematic discourse lays the ground for a coherent appreciation of subsequent shifts in the NFB's discourse and how it informed and was informed by the emergence of a counter-ideological outlook on working-class politics; it also demonstrates how this discourse represented a break from the one that dominated earlier Canadian cinematic culture. Chapter Two specifically addresses the ideological setting of Canadian cinematic culture prior to the creation of the NFB. It maps out the context within which Canadian film culture developed in proximity to an emphasis on the role of cinema as a nationalist educator, and surveys views put forward by the Canadian film industry and cultural establishments, particularly in connection with labour and working-class issues and politics.

Chapter Three outlines the emergence of Communist-based working-class cultural practices in the 1920s and 1930s. It traces expressions of counter-hegemonic practices exemplified in the emergence of the Communist Party's Popular Front policy in the 1930s and its reflection of the increased influence of and interest in working-class-based cultural and artistic practices. After this survey of the formative political, cultural and ideological elements in the development of the NFB's discourse, Chapter Four maps out various institutional and political dynamics that directly impacted the creation of the NFB itself. It describes how the ideological background and interests of some NFB founders and filmmakers, the methods used for distributing NFB films, and the paradoxical role played by the government partly shaped the parameters for the emergence of counter-hegemonic working-class discourse in the films produced by the Board.

Chapter Five explores films produced between 1939 and 1941. This is a transitional period which represents the short phase from the official creation of the NFB to just before its replacement of the Canadian Government General Motion Picture Bureau as the main producer of government-sponsored films. This period also precedes the Soviet Union's entry into war against Germany.

Chapters Six and Seven survey the films produced in the period between 1942 and 1945, where NFB films reflected a largely counter-hegemonic perspective on the role of labour and the working class in society. These films contemplate a central role for labour in the fight against fascism, and celebrate the role played by the Soviet Union both as a war ally and leading fighter against fascism and as a future peace partner. The films also discuss economic and social issues of concern to working people during and after the war, and point out alternative social and political parameters for building Canada in the post-war period. As I discuss how NFB films tackled issues such as the Great Depression, unemployment, fighting fascism, democratic renewal, coordination between labour and management, democracy, the role of labour unions, workers' economic and social conditions, and the role of women in connection with labour, I demonstrate how the NFB's discourse fit into the ideological paradigm of contemporary counter-hegemonic working-class politics. I also address how these films contemplated notions such as building a new post-war social and political order. Chapter Eight gives a brief survey of the stylistic origins and applications that complemented and informed NFB films, and further enhanced their unique contribution to the evolvement of working-class culture. The goal of this chapter is to further and more specifically demonstrate yet another dimension of how films were influenced (this time stylistically) by the left-oriented cinematic discourse of the time.

The final chapter of the book explores another transitional period in NFB's history. This one stretches between the end of World War II and the beginning of the Cold War. Beginning in the year 1945, this phase witnesses the resignation of John Grierson as the NFB's Film Commissioner and the start of a major political shift in depicting working-class issues in the Board's films.

Considering that the book focuses on a corpus rather than on a few individual films, and to situate the films in an easy to follow list that is useful for quick reference, I have included an Appendix which comprises the main pertinent and standard information on the films. The Appendix also includes a secondary list of documentary films that are relevant to the topic of working-class politics and socialism in the first part of the twentieth century.

# 1 SOCIAL CLASS AND THE NFB'S EARLY FILMS IN CANADIAN FILM STUDIES

Images of the working class and issues relating to class in general are present in a wide range of Canadian films. Yet there is evidence of a general failure in most critical/ historical studies to pay proper attention to the role of the working class and class-based issues in Canadian cinema. Until today, there has not been one single book on the working class in Canadian cinema.[1] There has been a Marxist film scholarship in Quebec (visible in an old journal called *Champ libre*) and in occasional monographs about Quebec cinema in French, but its corpus is radically different, it shows the influence of the French academy more clearly, and it dates from the 1970s primarily. While there are some notable exceptions with considerable contributions in this regard, there remains a great need of a systemic effort more specifically on the part of English-language scholarship to fill this important gap in Canadian film studies traditions. The study of the NFB's depiction of class is just one among numerous areas that are still in need of exploring.

Throughout its history, cinema in Canada explored numerous aspects in the lives and politics of working-class Canadians. Hundreds of documentary and fiction films pondered what it means to be a worker, and assessed the role of workers as they evaluated their social, economic and political contributions in Canadian history. Countless films also told stories about the unemployed, the poor, unions and union activists. In this regard there were myriad pioneering efforts by filmmakers such as Evelyn Cherry, Jane March, Stuart Legg, James Beveridge, Tom Daly, Stanley Hawes, Raymond Spottiswoode and later by Allan King, Gilles Groulx, Arthur Lamothe, Denys Arcand, Maurice Bulbulian, Martin Duckworth, Studio D, and Sophie Bissonnette among many others. Efforts by this diverse group of Canadian artists resulted in a wealth of films that variously depicted the struggles, victories and defeats of Canadians of working-class background. Films produced by the NFB between 1939 (the initial year of its creation) and 1946 were among the earliest indicators of a genuine interest in depicting social class by filmmakers in Canada. During this critical phase in Canadian film history, these films deliberated issues such as unemployment, economic prosperity, World War II, democracy and post-war construction.

While cultural studies in the UK were particularly sensitive to class differences in their study of cultural texts, the tendency in the United States and Canada was to effectively downplay class. While a good deal of work in other disciplines such as history, labour studies, and Canadian studies focused on aspects of the representation of labour in Canadian cinema in connection with issues of unemployment, poverty, gendered divisions of labour, work and technology, etc., the depiction of the working class per se mostly remained unevenly scattered across the domain of English-Canadian film criticism.[2]

There is, nevertheless, a body of work that has occasionally appeared over the last two decades which engaged the discussion of class in Canadian cinema. In particular, some writings by Robin Wood, Yvonne Matthews-Kline, Thomas Waugh, Scott Forsythe, and more recently Brenda Longfellow, Janine Marchessault, Susan Lord, John McCullough, Darrell Varga and Malek Khouri among others, made some inroads towards putting class and class analysis on the agenda of Canadian film criticism. Yet, the study of the topic remains largely marginalized in the canons of Canadian film studies, which stays aloof (and at times theoretically prescribing in its approach) when it comes to inscribing class into its corpus.

English discourse on Canadian cinema largely privileges the focus on this cinema's national identity. Over the years this substituted for the examination of social class, and until recently, most other social and cultural identities such as gender, ethnicity, race and sexual orientation. In this chapter I present an overall evaluation of English-Canadian film studies' approximation of the issue of class and then focus on its assessment of the films produced by the National Film Board of Canada during World War II.

The first section of this Chapter examines the general framework of the discourse on Canadian cinema: its history, its theoretical premises, and its main preoccupations. It surveys notions of Canadian nationalism as criteria that had a major impact on this discourse, ever since interest in Canadian cinema began to take shape in the late1960s and early 1970s. It also tackles how nationalism contributed to marginalizing the exploration of issues related to class. The next section deals specifically with English film studies approximation of NFB films of the war period. More specifically, it describes how the underestimation of class eventually led to bewilderment in relating to the centrality of the working-class discourse within these films and the counter-hegemonic significance of this discourse.

THE ELISION OF CLASS IN CANADIAN FILM STUDIES: A THEORETICAL EVALUATION

Theorizing Canadian cinema envisages national consciousness as a distorted reflection of an Other's cultural domination: that of the American mass culture and its overwhelming influence on the Canadian cultural landscape. A pre-eminent example of the application of the notion of ideology in Canadian film criticism is in its assessment of the relationship between the United States and Canada, how this relationship shapes the ideological perspective of Canadians, and how it is ultimately reflected in Canadian cinema. This determinist perception of the function of ideology underestimates how different social and political forces function within the process of ideological stabilization and/or destabilization of any given hegemony.

Interest in Canadian cinema coincided with a growing nationalism that typified grassroots activism in the late 1960s and early 1970s. For many Canadians on the left of the political spectrum, including a growing number of film critics, nationalist anti-Americanism exemplified and shaped in a substantial manner how they analyzed Canadian cinema. This period witnessed growing opposition to American military interference in Vietnam. On Canadian university campuses, students rallied against Canadian industries supporting the war and in opposition to what they conceived of as American control of the Canadian economy, educational institutions, and cultural infrastructures. Within this atmosphere, finding a position that identified with the struggle to develop and define a genuine Canadian cultural identity constituted a central element in how a great number of educators, writers, and critics saw their role and position in society.

Gradually, many English-Canadian film reviewers and critics began to define Canadian cinema through traits characteristic of a so-called Canadian experience. These traits were introduced as embodiments of national identity and were also identified as expressions of resistance against dominant power structures (mainly associated with U.S. economic, political, and cultural hegemony). Within this paradigm, the discourse on Canadian cinema explored variable ontological and epistemological binaries between Canadian and American film models. It also gave priority to examining Canadian culture in conjunction with its unequal relationship with that of the United States. This claimed relationship was also considered a major source of the malaise that dominated the Canadian cultural psyche.

In 1973, Robert Fothergill proposed that a specific "Canadian condition" is systematic in themes of Canadian films. These films, he argued, mostly depicted the "radical inadequacy of the male protagonist – his moral failure, most visibly in his relationships with women." Fothergill equated this "impediment to satisfactory self-realization" by this protagonist with the psychological inferiority that characterizes the relationship between the younger and older Canadian and American brothers.[3] Fothergill's emphasis on the inferior relationship between Canada and the United States essentially shaped early Canadian film studies. It also informed its theoretical application of the notion of ideology in relation to Canadian cinema.

In 1977 Peter Harcourt made one of the most lasting marks on Canadian film criticism. Despite its limited nature and scope, his book *Movies and Mythologies: Towards a National Cinema* became one of the most influential attempts to provide a comprehensive theoretical context for the study of Canadian cinema.[4] Basing his analysis on Roland Barthes' study on mythology, Harcourt focused on the specificity of Canada's "dependence on Europe" and its "proximity to the United States" and how this encourages Canadians to look at themselves as reflected in "other people's mirrors, in terms of alien mythologies."[5]

Harcourt linked Canadian cinema's ability to express the real identity of Canadians to the level by which it articulated the depiction of Canada's own myth. Through his reading of contemporary Canadian films, Harcourt identified recurring themes, all of which, he argued, dealt with the failure of our society to provide meaningful roles to its members.[6] As a result, films repeatedly present stories about adolescence, dropouts, criminals, "or simply about wild and energetic characters" like the protagonists in Pearson's *Paperback Hero* or Carter's *Rowdyman*, both of whom "end up acting destructively because there is nothing else to do."[7] Harcourt proposed specific criteria for analyzing Canadian cinema: a main concern, he suggested, should be how the experiential dilemmas of film characters locates them vis-à-vis their national identity.

Harcourt claimed that film criticism should be able to "un-conceal" the workings of the filmic text.[8] The methodological focus here was on searching the textual tangles of films to locate the specific myth of Canadian national identity. With the text as the main subject of analysis, studying Canadian identity was deliberated as reciprocal to the task of deciphering its metaphoric textual unfolding on the screen. Inadvertently, this meant that bringing into discussion topics that were beyond the issue of Canadian national myth and identity represented an imposition of some sort on the central thematic preoccupations of what were identified as Canadian films. On the methodological level, this approach also implied that evaluating elements that were outside the immediacy of the filmic text risked impressing the critic's own pre-conceived agenda on the reading of films.

In hindsight, Harcourt's critical approach alluded to the relationship between, respectively, concealed and dominant Canadian and American cultures, both of which inhabited ideologically predetermined filmic texts. Consequently, to this approach, the implications, interests, themes, and characters of a specific filmic text including those related to class, essentially became superfluous to critical analysis. With the emphasis on the film text, the task facing film scholars was to apply the prescribed formula of national alienation to an essentially static text which functioned as mere ideological reflection of the unequal relationship which bounded and shaped Canadian entity. As such, even bringing into discussion extra-textual elements relating to history, culture and social dynamics became an unnecessary intrusion of what was conceived as an ideologically pre-determined text. Nevertheless, it is important here to stress that at the time when Fothergill and Harcourt were making their propositions, no one else was substantially taking up the question of Canadian cinema.

The general framework of Harcourt's approach continued to inform the main parameters of Canadian film criticism. A variety of critical forms that stress national identity as an expression of an inferior consciousness, and/or prioritize the filmic text as the main subject of analysis remain constituent of English-Canadian film criticism. In one example, Mike Gasher, two decades after Harcourt, attempts to demonstrate how a Canadian voice has been historically derailed:

> The colonization of the material means of Canadian film distribution and exhibition denies Canadian feature film a mass audience in its own country and contributes to a larger media environment starved of works addressing Canadian themes and Canadian stories, and global issues treated from a Canadian perspective.[9]

In response, Gasher calls for the "decolonization" of Canadian "cultural imagination" by introducing a "self-generated" – rather than externally imposed – Canadian imagination. He argues that Canadian film practice and production could present a challenge to the hegemony of Hollywood cinema in Canada only when it acknowledges that "there is another way of film making and there is another world view."[10]

In another variant of the nationalist trend, an article on genre and Canadian cinema by Jim Leach in 1984 summarizes the main concerns of the Canadian genre as expressions of the gulf between "Canadian reality" and the dreams that underpin American genres: "the measuring of Canadian culture and society against the American standards," Leach writes, "becomes (implicitly or explicitly) a major concern of Canadian genre films." Once again, he refers to Peter Pearson's film *Paperback*

Hero (1973) as a classical story about a Canadian who invests his life in emulating the "glamour drawn from American westerns that is hopelessly at variance with the drab reality of his small-town existence in Saskatchewan."[11]

In a comparative reading in 1989 of the endings of two films, one American and one Canadian (George Lucas's 1973 *American Graffiti*, and Sandy Wilson's 1985 film *My American Cousin*, respectively), Joanne Yamaguchi illustrates the dissimilarity between the sensibilities of the two cultures that they reflect:

> The epilogue of *My American Cousin* is warm and positive (Mom was right, boys are like buses). Even its negative aspects are without a bitter edge (never saw my American cousin again), since no news is good news in the sphere of epilogues. By contrast, the *American Graffiti* epilogue is tainted with an underlying resentment, a cynicism implying that people and situation of great promise inevitably fall from grace (a promising student becomes a car salesman).[12]

Ironically, posing it against the nihilism of its American counterpart, Yamaguchi concludes that the Canadian experience is more hopeful.[13] As she refers to differences between the two national cultures, the writer reverses Fothergill and Harcourt's earlier pre-conception of the Canadian protagonist as lost and pessimistic, and attributes it instead to the protagonists of the American film. However, as it suggests an optimistic approximation of what constitutes a Canadian experience, Yamaguchi's reading, in a similar manner to what was proposed by other nationalist critics, continues to prioritize an assessment of a dichotomy between two fixed sets of cultural and ideological frameworks: one for the dominating, and another for the dominated.

This influential, albeit not necessarily any more dominant approach in English-Canadian film studies, basically favours a deterministic understanding of ideology, which underestimates social, political and cultural dialectic. It relegates ideology to a static and predetermined function, which in itself results in adopting an ahistorical reading of Canadian cinema. It also confines to marginality the role played by contradictory political and cultural forces within Canadian society and emphasizes, instead, a generic Canadian subject that stands above heterogeneous social identities including those based in social class.

As it explores variable ontological and epistemological binaries between Canadian and Hollywood cinemas, and as it isolates the assessment of those binaries from their broader historical context, the nationalist tendency remains confined mainly to assessing the dichotomy between Canadian and American cinematic models. As such, it tends to favour assessing a victimized Canadian social subject who is conceived as a passive object on the receiving end of the negative impact of a dominant ideology. On the one hand, this form of ideological determinism, similar in its critical limitations to various forms of social and economic determinism, de-historicizes the study of Canadian cinema. On the other, it discourages the assessment of diverse social representations – including the representation of class.

I am certainly not suggesting that addressing issues of national identity has no relevance to Canadian film criticism; to simply dismiss the question of national identity does not lessen its ideological relevance to critical discussions on Canadian cinema. However, histories of national cinema also need to be assessed as histories of crisis and conflict, of resistance and negotiation. Dealing with issues of ideology and ideological dominance as they impact national consciousness also has to account for the contradictory social interests and values that underlie it.

As they premise their reading of Canadian cinema on a static nationalist textual perspective, some critics fail to address how, for example, the main protagonists in the 1970s film classics *Goin' Down the Road* (Don Shebib, 1970), as well as *Rowdyman* and *Paperback Hero*, among others, all happen to come from working-class backgrounds. They also ignore that the dilemmas faced by these characters are inflicted by a specific socio-political moment in Canadian history. Viewed as analogies to Canada's inferior relationship with the United States, the protagonists of these films are prescribed as alienated individuals incapable of belonging or having an identity of their own. In the end, such fatalistic acceptance of dominant ideology becomes characteristic of these characters' behaviour ... as Canadians! Under these terms, as Robin Wood points out, defining Canadian identity becomes synonymous with negative descriptions such as "less confident, less assured, more tentative, more uncertain, less convinced, etc."[14] As a result, the social background of characters as well as their place and temporal settings become non-issues for the film critic. This, however, is not the only context within which the marginalizing of class occurs in Canadian film studies.

In some cases the neglect of class takes the form of direct rejection of the mere relevance of the discussion on social representation. Still, this usually relates to the general emphasis on national identity to which I alluded earlier. Basing his argument on the assumption that Canadians are inherently passive on the political level, John Hofsess, for example, argues as far back as 1975 against incorporating the theme of social and political resistance into the reading of Canadian films. Even during the socially turbulent period of the Great Depression, he argues, Canadians always maintained a fatalistic attitude towards politics.[15]

Ironically, Hofsess grounds his argument in letters written by R.B. Bennett, the Canadian Prime Minister whose policies between 1930 and 1935 encountered fierce and broad working-class resistance, leading to one of the largest protest campaigns in Canadian history, better known as the *On-to-Ottawa Trek*. The campaign involved workers and the unemployed in a cross-country mobilization going to Ottawa to protest against government policies of creating what amounted to forced-labour camps for the unemployed. The protest was eventually halted after the RCMP intervened. Clashes in the streets of Regina in 1934 resulted in one death and several injuries. Hofsess nevertheless dismisses these events "as one or two exceptions" to the more prevalent Canadian attitude that shows "astonishing deference to authority." Precluding Peter Harcourt and other nationalist film critics, Hofsess says:

> This mental habit, suggesting Canadians have many moods, their most resonant one being despair, persists in many of our novels and films. Think of *Goin' Down the Road*, *Wedding in White*, *Mon Oncle Antoine*, *The Rowdyman*, *Paperback Hero*: good stories, fine acting, profoundly poignant moments, but nowhere a character with the brains, balls, will or gall to master life as it must be lived in the twentieth century.[16]

This passivity, Hofsess argues, represents the feature of Canadian cinema and therefore any critical assessment of it is unaffectedly bound to focus on the state of despair that domineers Canadians. Hofsess's clearly reflects a classic nationalist rationale for the elision of class. But his approach by no means predominates Canadian film studies' approximation of class-related issues.

Over the years, there emerged several areas of exploration that have affected discussions on class and social change in Canadian cinema. One important example is the discussion on cinematic form and its relevance to addressing the representation of class and class-related issues in Canadian cinema. Michel Euvrard and Pierre Véronneau, for example, examined the contradictions inherent in using specific formal strategies. As they discussed the impact of these strategies on addressing the politics of class, they critiqued the role of the *cinéma direct* movement that emerged in Quebec in the late 1950s, and how it was not able to advance a socially committed cinema. They stressed that clarity of political perspective remained the most crucial element in determining the significance of cinema as a socially radical art form:

> The [cinéma] direct allowed certain filmmakers to conceal their ideological haziness, or even their reactionary ideologies, by confusing the means with the end and by turning the direct into an ideology itself. On the other hand, some were

able to exploit new possibilities offered by the direct, in order to give their analysis of social reality greater effectiveness, by drawing closer links with life.[17]

Euvrard and Véronneau disputed that the overemphasis of form was the determining element in shaping a socially interested cinema. Similar caution against relying on alternative formal techniques as a means to forward social and political messages was raised by Seth Feldman in connection with the 1970s NFB's program *Challenge for Change*, a series that stressed the use of film as a tool for discussing issues of social justice. Feldman questioned the legitimacy of the program's celebrated emphasis on giving a direct voice to those who are incapable of articulating their own concerns. He argued that thinking of this practice as a prerequisite to dealing with the concerns of Canadians of working-class background was based on erroneous assumptions and would lead to wrong conclusions.[18]

Another area which relates to social class was the discussion on Quebec filmmakers of the early 1960s to late 1970s. In an anthology on filmmaker Jean-Pierre Lefebvre, Susan Barrowclough focuses on his rejection of "naturalist mimeticism" and discusses the constraints of linear narrative. She also spotlights his preoccupation with creating cinematic social commentary "which goes beyond the tangible to concentrate on the dreams, the fears, the historical make-up of people and the personal apprehension of a collective experience."[19] Barrowclough then discusses how the interest in class in Quebec cinema blends with other social and political concerns. She argues that in Lefebvre's films, for example, the specific interests of working-class women are depicted in connection with patriarchal domination, particularly as they relate to issues of "managing house and suffering the constraints of rather traditionally-minded men."[20]

Similarly, Euvrard and Véronneau point out how filmmakers such as Lamothe, Groulx, and Dansereau examine the conditions of working-class communities in urban and suburban Quebec. They describe how they used film as an instrument for social action, and by way of encouraging broad discussions on labour strikes, factory shutdowns, and unemployment; they also demonstrate how these films eventually contributed to mobilizing forces of resistance among striking workers and unemployed Quebecers.[21] They also point out that these filmmakers succeeded in convincing groups "such as people on welfare, construction and textile workers, lumberjacks and miners" to appear on screen, and in giving them the "right to speak out."[22]

Euvrard and Véronneau focused on the politics that characterized Quebec cinema beginning in the late 1950s and how this intersected with the direct emphasis on social activism. They argued that the subsequent flourishing of Quebec cinema between

1968 and 1973 was directly linked to the rise of nationalist consciousness in the late 1960s and increased resistance to national oppression.[23] But while the emphasis here was on dealing with a politically conscious Quebec national identity – as opposed to presumably an ideologically alienated Canadian nation – and on tracing connections between class and national oppression, issues relating to social class by other critics were presented as mere peripheries to the discussion on the Quebec national question.

In yet another take on Canadian cinema's incorporation of class, this time comparing Quebec and English Canada, Piers Handling discusses direct cinema.[24] He states that in spite of their good intentions, filmmakers in the NFB's English Unit B were never able to present tangible political analyses of class:

> One can trace a strong line developing from *Paul Tomkowicz*, through *The Back-Breaking Leaf*, to *Goin' Down the Road* (1970) Don Shebib's landmark feature, and other English-Canadian films of the seventies. Each has a strong sense of realism and a social conscience, yet none broadens its analysis onto a political level, although the subjects seem to point them in this direction. While the Québécois filmmakers were living, and making film, in their own peculiar social, economic and political environment, the English filmmakers were separated from their roots and from a similar context of development.

In a variation on a similar theme by earlier nationalist critics, Handling identifies yet another manifestation of Canadian ideological passivity, this time in relation to cultural rootlessness that he prescribes as the basis for English-Canadian filmmakers' neglect of social and political analysis.

Contrasting Quebec and English-Canadian cinemas, James Leach similarly suggests that Quebec filmmakers are distinguishable by their ability to identify social sources of oppression. Filmmakers in English Canada, on the other hand, function in "an environment in which psychological pressures are real but political solutions are difficult to envisage."[25] Leach sees the tendency by English-Canadian filmmakers to place their characters outside of social antagonisms as a reflection of the pacifying ideological reality that dominates the political landscape of their film characters. He goes on to say that "characters are prevented from attaining a political consciousness by the illusions created by the prevailing ideology."[26]

In hindsight, what appears to usher much of English-language studies on Quebec cinema and its interest in social class is its reflection of a national consciousness of Quebec society. In this regard, ideology is once again perceived either as one's own, in which case it becomes liberating and capable of allowing us to become conscious of social dichotomies, or as that of an Other, where it tends to dominate and deprive its carrier from recognizing the dynamics of social relationships and political antagonisms. In both cases, there is an underestimation of the significance of ideology as an element of hegemony and as a dialectical process which is open to resistance and to social and political contest.

Another variation on the theme of national cinema relates to the polemic proposed by another prolific Canadian film scholar. In his essay "The Cinema that We Need" Bruce Elder expounded on the need to overcome the critical preoccupation with the "distinctiveness" of Canadian culture. However, his idea for overcoming such a preoccupation was through unmasking "how events come to be in experience, that is, the dynamic by which events are brought into presentness in experience."[27] This can only be articulated through creating an alternative to Hollywood's classical narrative structure, he argues. While Elder disagreed with Harcourt on what constituted a Canadian cinema (Harcourt emphasized narrative thematic content, while Elder accented textual form), both stressed the filmic text as the main viable subject of analysis. In other words, it was the *authored* text that remained at the core of cultural processes. In the end, both versions of the Canadian-based discourse on Canadian cinema forced a detachment between the socio-historical context and the function of the film as a text. Two conclusions can be deduced from this critical logic: either that the text is a fixed ideological construction, and accordingly there would be no point in alluding to its relationship with specific social and historical moments; or that history and social structures themselves are fixed phenomena of which a text can only mirror eternal essences – which calls the entire notion of history into question.

Harcourt and Elder's variations on the theme of Canadian cinema evolved over the years, and took new forms. Furthermore, new critics revamped the general criteria that characterized these two approaches, sometimes by stressing different social identities and the multiplicity of voices within Canadian culture (specifically through emphasizing gender, ethnicity, race, sexual orientation, and class), and other times by finding formal niches to contest the Hollywood model both ideologically and stylistically (postmodernism has been a major attraction over the last couple of decades). What remains invariable in much of the newer discourse on Canadian cinema, however, is the reductionism in interpreting ideology and ideological workings.

A significant push towards a new outlook on Canadian cinema as part of broader aesthetic, cultural, social and political processes has been taking place over the last two decades. Important advances have been made in addressing this cinema's treatment of race, ethnicity, gender, and sexual identity. These readings enhance a socially conscious outlook on the depiction of marginalized identities. But even as they diverted from earlier nationalist perspectives, and as they attempted to invoke a much needed refurbished appreciation of heterogeneity within Canadian society, some of these writings remained entangled within a form of reductionist understanding of ideology and ideological working; within this reductionism a near elision of class continues to mark the canonical parameters of Canadian film studies.

In an effort to identify with the realities and struggles of marginalized social subjects, some of the more recent readings of Canadian cinema (such as in some of the work of Christine Ramsey)[28] position these subjects in a stationary dichotomy with a static centre of power. In most cases, this centre continues to gravitate around the United States. Even when the identified centre is not simply perceived as the United States, there remains an underestimation and mystification of the poignant dialectics that inform relationships between a dominant centre and dominated margins, including, for example, the dynamics of social struggle and resistance. By viewing Canadian national consciousness as a mere reflection of unequal relationships, some English-Canadian film criticism prescribes a specific critical task: studying how films depict Canadian inferiority in relation to various sources of ideological domination. This task replaces the contemplation of the dynamics of cultural and political hegemony. It also relegates social and cultural subjectivity to the confines of pre-assigned attributes and functions. The result is under-appreciation of the liberating possibilities inherent within and without social, political and ideological power structures. For that matter, locating and assessing counter-hegemony and counter-hegemonic practices, a topic at the centre of this book's endeavour, becomes at best a non-issue or an area that is not worthy of exploration. Eventually, by underestimating historical specificities and how they inform and are informed by non-static ideological workings, critical analysis reduces ideology to an eternal essence of political and social domination.

Both nationalist and non-nationalist models appear to share similar elucidations of ideology in connection with film: (1) both models account for the specificity of the film text as the basis for their critical analysis. Clearly, given the fact that films (or bodies of film) are the main subjects of analysis, this point of departure is natural and crucial. But as they tentatively acknowledge the social and political conditions within which a filmic text exists and operates, their reading of the text still tends to undervalue the significance of the film text as one among several other structural elements in the social body, or structure, of the cinematic text. Instead of conceding and incorporating diverse super-structural (e.g., legal, political, philosophical, ethical, religious, educational) and infra-structural (e.g., social, historical, economical) elements of analysis as structural overdeterminants, both critical models reduce the affectivity of ideology in film to the textual and/or narrative determinants. (2) These models conceive of ideology as a reflection of sameness. Rather than accounting for ideological working as the functional and operational similarity between two autonomous spheres (e.g., ideology as an element of the superstructure *and* the social and economic base) the main critical focus is on unmasking what is hidden in the mirror/text as an ideological reflection. Eventually the main task of the critic is centred on restoring or unmasking the authenticity of the national or social subject. (3) Authorship is confined to its original and/or originating textual source. The social author function of the subject/spectator and/or reader is reduced to passive audience receptiveness. In the end, looking at social and political subjectivities without appreciating how they enforce, reinforce and resist ideological hegemonies and how they potentially enunciate counter-hegemonic alternatives, lessens the interest in studying films that might possess non-normative ideological functions.

CLASS, POLITICS AND THE STUDY OF NFB WAR FILMS

Despite the significance of the body of NFB films produced during the World War II period in assessing and analyzing the development and historical dynamics of Canadian cultural and cinematic discourse, English-Canadian film criticism has largely presented a limited view of the ideological workings of these films. Among the prominent works in this area are Gary Evans's *John Grierson and the National Film board: the Politics of Wartime Propaganda* (1984) and *In the National Interest: A Chronicle of the National Film Board of Canada from 1949 to 1989* (1991). Another is D.B. Jones's *Movies and Memoranda* published in 1981. These books provide overviews of various episodes in NFB history and elaborate on interactions between the development of the NFB and its founder John Grierson's documentary aesthetic. Peter Morris's 1971 book *The National Film Board of Canada: The War Years* includes few contemporary articles on the NFB, and a select index of the films. Graham McInnes and Gene Walz's more recent book *One Man's Documentary* (2005) is an excellent memoir of McInnes's own experience as screenwriter within the NFB during its early phases of existence. Other writings focus more specifically on John Grierson. These include *Grierson on Documentary*, a collection of his writings published in 1966. Edited by Forsyth Hardy, the book contains a chronologically organized selection of Grierson's writings, speeches and interviews. In 1984, *John Grierson and the NFB* was prepared by the John Grierson Project (a project initiated by McGill University) and brings together a large collection of remembrances by people who knew and worked with the NFB founder.

John Grierson: A Guide to References and Resources (1986) is an extremely helpful book in pointing out the origins of Grierson's philosophical associations and ideas. Joyce Nelson's book *The Colonized Eye: Rethinking the Grierson Legend* (1988) presents a revisionist approach to the work of Grierson and its impact on Canadian cinema – one I will deal with separately later in the chapter. Gary Evans's latest Grierson book is *John Grierson: Trailblazer of Documentary Films* (2005), which presents a novel-like approximation of Grierson's contribution to documentary filmmaking.

The NFB and the role played by John Grierson is also among the subjects in three anthologies on Canadian cinema: *The Canadian Film Reader* (1977), edited by Seth Feldman and Joyce Nelson; *Take Two*, edited by Seth Feldman (1984); and *Self-Portrait: Essays on the Canadian and Quebec Cinemas* (1980), edited by Pierre Véronneau and Piers Handling. Other studies assess various aspects in Grierson's legacy with even more specific attention made to his concept of film as contributor to social change. Two examples are Peter Morris's articles "Backwards to the Future: John Grierson's Film Policy for Canada" in *Flashback: People and Institutions in Canadian Film History*, and "After Grierson: The National Film Board 1945–1953" in *Take Two*. Grierson's interest in documentary as a medium for promoting social and political change was also the subject of numerous articles. Of particular interest are Jose Arroyo's "John Grierson: Years of Decision" in *Cinema Canada* and Peter Morris's "Praxis into Process: John Grierson and the National Film Board of Canada" published in the *Historical Journal of Film, Radio and Television*.

Other more recent work from outside Canada on Grierson include the 1990 *Film and Reform, John Grierson and the Documentary Film Movement* by Ian Aitken, *Claiming the Real, the Griersonian Documentary and its Legitimations* (1995) by Brian Winston, *John Grierson: Life, Contributions, influence* (2000) by Jack Ellis and *From Grierson to the Docu-soap* (2000) by John Izod and Richard Kilborn. The last four titles appeared over the last decade and reflected renewed interest in Grierson's work from the point of view of revisiting its influence as well as its confines on documentary filmmaking practices. Pierre Véronneau's third of his three-volume collection on the history of Quebec cinema, *L'Histoire du cinema au Quebec, III. Resistance et affirmation: la production francophone a l'ONF – 1939–1946*, published in 1987, offers the only serious attempt to deal with the role and function of the NFB in relation to Quebec during the war period.

Most of the above-mentioned writings provide a positive assessment of Grierson's efforts to use film as a socially conscious educational tool (aside from the work of Nelson, later articles by Morris, and Winston's book). They are largely sympathetic to his views on the role of government in supporting documentary filmmaking. Some of these studies describe Grierson's background as a film commissioner in England, his fascination with early Soviet cinema and its emphasis on social and political issues, and his interest in dealing with issues relating to labour. They also appraise his emphasis on cinema as a nation builder. Studies on the NFB and Grierson remain an important source of information for assessing the complexities of the period. They particularly provide extensive data of Grierson's political and personal history as well as his writings, speeches, and actual film work in Britain and in Canada.

However, by overemphasizing the personal drama of Grierson's life, some of these studies, particularly the Canadian studies, tend to underestimate the discursive dynamics that ushered in the work of the NFB during its early years of existence and within which Grierson functioned as Commissioner. In general they tend to present Grierson's legacy – and consequently the whole NFB history during the war years – in a largely narrow biographical or/and filmographical fashion. More importantly, a crucial aspect of their critical shortcomings is in how they overwhelmingly ignore the role played by oppositional social and political forces of the left. As such, these studies ignore the function of counter-hegemony in influencing the ideological and practical parameters of early NFB films, and consequently only marginally address them as extensions to the discursive social, political and historical setting within which they were made. Furthermore, these studies tend to only footnote the NFB war films as evidence to understanding the social and political dynamics of the period. No studies have so far attempted to provide an elaborate assessment of the films themselves as social and political signifiers of the war period or in connection with their depiction of social identities. M. Teresa Nash's 1982 McGill University dissertation on how these films represented women remains the only and most comprehensive attempt to exclusively deal with the films in terms of their social significance and impact.

In the late 1980s, Grierson's politics, aesthetic and formal interests, as well as his emphasis on propaganda as an educational tool, all came under vigorous re-examination. A critique of Grierson is found in Peter Morris's "Rethinking Grierson: The Ideology of John Grierson" published in *Dialogues* and originally delivered in a lecture at the 1986 conference of the Film Studies Association of Canada. Morris revisits Grierson's writings and suggests that his traditionally celebrated organic approach and thinking have certain affinities to the philosophical roots of fascism. For her part, Joyce Nelson in *The Colonized Eye: Rethinking the Grierson Legend* (1988) presents an important reassessment of what she considered as negative impact of Grierson on the development of Canadian cinematic culture.

Nelson's watershed book was the first Canadian effort to polemically engage the ideological impact of Grierson's work during the period of World War II. In her assessment of the NFB's work Nelson rejects the characterization of Grierson's interest in documentary as an expression of left-wing or even liberal political orientation. She argues that film to Grierson merely represented a public relations arm for emergent multinational capitalism, and that NFB films made during the war were based on aesthetic and political strategies that were obnoxious and repressive. Even the anti-fascist films, she stresses, were authoritarian in their tone.

As she acknowledges the importance of assessing the historical context of the films, Nelson all but ignores the presence of left or communist social and political forces, let alone the presence of a counter-hegemonic discourse at the time. She also does not acknowledge the role or views of left-wing labour unions, parties and movements and their impact on shaping the discourse of NFB war films; instead, she summarily claims that these films reinforced workers' submission to capitalist ideology. In one example of how erroneous conclusions are drawn from de-historicized reading of films is Nelson's assessment of the role of the Labour-Management Committees (LMC) during the war, a role that was depicted sympathetically in NFB war films.

The LMCs were created in the early 1940s by way of developing a social and political partnership, which in addition to labour also involved the participation of management and government. This partnership was to help improve working and living conditions for workers, and in the process meet the urgent demands of wartime industrial production. An important aspect of the NFB's discourse on the partnership between workers and business related to the role of these Committees. Nelson argues that the emphasis on the role of the Committees by these films proves their anti-labour views.[29] She does not however account for the position taken by labour itself and by its left-wing supporters. In hindsight, her analysis dismisses the role played by these forces in pushing for the creation of these committees; it also ignores the discourse within which labour conceived of the creation of these committees as an indication of its own success, first in uniting forces in the war against fascism, and second in achieving a higher level of a coequal relationship in the management and decision-making process within the workplace. Later, after the end of the war and the beginning of the Cold War, those committees became among the first casualties to be targeted for abolishment by big business and the government.

Nelson's analysis is largely informed by the nationalist discourse on Canadian cinema, which paints a mainly passive depiction of the Canadian social subject. Tom Daly, a veteran editor and filmmaker in the NFB who worked closely with Grierson during that periods responded to Nelson's critiques by pointing out their narrow historical perspective:

[Nelson] wrote very well when putting things together to make her case, but if you go back to the sources, you see that she left out lots of key stuff in the dot-dot-dots that would undermine her case. And she was always reading in hindsight with her present-day attitude towards things, as if everyone should have had that attitude back then.[30]

Clearly, the lack of a multifaceted reading of cultural politics and the politics of culture during this period of Canadian history essentially leads Nelson to erroneous conclusions as to the actual significance of NFB war films. This brings us back to the importance of incorporating an inter-textual approach to reading film.

As Raymond Williams would argue, opening a film text to a broader context traces relation between the different signifying systems of a culture.[31] As I discussed earlier in the chapter, the passive approximation of Canadian subjectivity and of history is itself based on a deterministic understanding of ideology as an all-encompassing domination. This essentially leads to sentencing to virtual insignificance or failure any attempt to pose counter-hegemonic alternatives to the status quo. In this regard, it comes as no surprise that Nelson, along with some film-studies scholars of the NFB, tends to ignore even the mere possibility of influences from outside the hegemony of the upper classes during that period in Canadian history.

Particularly missing from the Canadian material dealing with the NFB and Grierson is the role played by labour and the Popular Front policy, which was promoted both before and during the war by the Communist Party of Canada. Studies on this period's NFB and Grierson tend to neutralize the varied political and cultural dynamics that were part of the process of shaping Canadian hegemony. They particularly ignore references to the role played by the oppositional social and political forces of the left. As such, these studies, for all intends and purposes, actually erase the function of counter-hegemony in informing the ideological and practical parameters of the work of the NFB during this period. Indeed, they have taken for granted that John Grierson was either a social progressive or a minion of a new industrial establishment, often with little supporting research.

Over the years, however, there have been some studies that show a different appreciation of the role played by the NFB during the war. Indeed, some of these studies even addressed the issue of the depiction of class in intersection with the historical moment that surrounded the creation of the NFB. Of particular note is Barbara Halpern Martineau's article "Before the Guerillieres: Women's Films at the NFB During World War II" published in the *Canadian Film Reader* (1977).

Martineau examines the work and impact of Canadian women filmmakers during the war. She traces how their films address working-class concerns, and emphasizes the need to provide an analytical outlook which goes beyond the limitations of gender-based criticism. Martineau suggests that "as for women's films of the past the pressing need [for feminist film critics] is for rediscovery and description." As she analyzes the work of contemporary filmmaker Jane March and her effort to document the social difficulties faced by working-class women, Martineau criticizes the inability of some feminist film critics to recognize March's and other contemporary filmmakers' work simply because these filmmakers did not "conform to the expectations of conventional phallic criticism."[32]

Charles Acland's work on Canadian cinematic culture in the period after World War I and just prior to the establishment of the NFB is also of particular significance to the re-assessment of the work of this institution. Acland's articles "National Dreams, International Encounters: The Formation of Canadian Film Culture in the 1930s" and "Mapping the Serious and the Dangerous: Film and the National Council of Education, 1920–1939" (respectively published in 1994 and 1995) bring forth issues that are useful to assessing the development of Canadian film discourse of the period. Equally as important, Acland brings to light arguments which are critical to understanding the hegemonic significance of the development of Canadian cinema during World War II. For its part, Manjunath Pendakur's work on the political economy of the film industry in Canada (1990), and Ted Magder's assessment of the history of the relationship between the Canadian government and Canada's film community (1993) both represent examples of an interest in studying the discursive dynamics of Canadian cinematic culture. These studies also provide important grounds for further assessing how Canadian cinema deals with social class and the role of class in Canadian culture.

An important feature in the history of left-wing and communist culture and politics in Canada in the 1930s and 1940s resulted from the international communist movement's major changes in its political strategy. The Comintern, the organizational link between communist parties around the world, re-examined its policies in 1934, in order to take into account the new political situation and the experiences of communist parties. In Canada, communists and social democrats (members of the CCF) within the Trade Labour Council were moving toward unity and cooperation within the Canadian trade union movement. Changes also involved building a united workers' and Popular Front in the struggle against fascism. Popular Front strategy patterned the philosophical base of the counter-hegemonic discourse during this critical period of Canadian and NFB history. The movement associated with the front expanded its influence beyond the Communist Party and the militant working-class and labour movements. Indeed, the strength of this movement enabled it not only to put forward a working-class perspective on contemporary issues, but also to present it as that of an emerging counter-hegemonic historical bloc.

The discourse of NFB films was itself similarly informed by this same socially and politically heterogeneous mass movement. While it incorporated a loosely defined working-class perspective outlook based on the ideas of the Popular Front, this discourse sought a consensual approach to dealing with social and political issues of the day. It also offered a counter-hegemonic perspective which supported and celebrated ideas such as: cooperative and centralized social and economic planning, an increased and equal role for labour in social and political administration of society, an appreciation of the role of labour in production value creation processes, new outlook on the role of working women, and the linking of economic production to social needs rather to capitalist profit. All these ideas were offered as commonsensical alternatives that were integral to building a modern progressive society.

2 CANADIAN FILM CULTURE BEFORE THE NFB

EARLY CANADIAN CINEMA: THE BUSINESS CONNECTION

The early control by American capital over the Canadian film production industry in the 1920s shaped how cinema, as a new cultural medium, came to be perceived among the Canadian public. Despite the high level of domestic control and ownership over mushrooming exhibition theatres, and in conjunction with the explosion of film production in the United States, Canadian film distributors and theatre owners had very little to offer in terms of Canadian-made films. This eventually led to a unilateral flow of American influence over Canada's cinematic culture and practice at least up until the late 1930s.[1] Aside from non-feature tourist and advertising films and a few narrative features, film activity in Canada before the creation of the NFB was fragmentary and limited; when the NFB was later created, it filled a major gap in Canadian filmmaking and allowed for a significant shift in the way Canadians looked at film as a cultural practice.

The year 1917 was an important one in Canadian film history. It saw the creation of Canada's first private and public film production facilities and institutions. The province of Ontario became the first government in North America to create a public film board, the Ontario Motion Picture Bureau (OMPB). 1917 was also the year when the first and at the time busiest Canadian film studio opened in Trenton, Ontario, and when the federal government created the Exhibits and Publicity Bureau of the Dominion Department of Trade and Commerce. In 1923 the Bureau was renamed the Canadian Government Motion Picture Bureau (CGMPB), and remained the principal government film production vehicle until the creation of the National Film Board in 1939. The CGMPB survived, at least as an official agency, until 1941.

On another level, the Canadian film industry's development coincided with the launching of active publicity campaigns by the Canadian Pacific Railway (CPR).

The company's management was astutely cognizant of the need to capitalize on the "potential of the new medium of motion pictures" as well as the "public's fascination with trains and motion."[2] The way the CPR saw itself using the new medium to advance its own interests was echoed by other major players in the Canadian economy as well as by the Canadian government. The consensus within the business and government communities was that, when it comes to producing and using films, the interests of the private and public sectors were complementary and, therefore, should be maintained that way. The interests of the capitalist class were considered as one and the same as those of the entire society, and film was to play the role of a tool to promote this motto.[3]

When it comes to the government's own plans, they seemed to coincide with, and complement, those of big business; these plans also enhanced, albeit not necessarily defined, the way they both viewed the role of the new medium. In fact, even before cinema assumed the role of a new communication medium both the CPR and various levels of governments saw mutual benefit in using photography:

> The CPR in cooperation with the federal and provincial governments and with the Hudson's Bay Company, developed plans to encourage immigration and settlement to western Canada and the development of agriculture, mining and forestry. In order to meet these objectives the CPR developed an extensive system of promotion which included the use of still photographs, illustrated lectures and testimonial pamphlets.[4]

Later the CPR contacted both British and American production companies to make films about Canada. In one case, the company produced a series of 35 film shorts in 1903 and 1904 entitled *Living in Canada*. Many of these films feature scenes that depict immigrant workers in various Canadian locations. In one of the shorts, there was even a series of scenes of a Labour Day Parade, despite CPR policy, which was not known to encourage the participation of workers in trade union activities.[5] In 1910, the company produced a series of ten-minute films about workers, each of which presented a romantic melodrama about a worker who comes to Canada as the land of opportunity and ends up achieving economic success as well as finding lost love.[6]

Soon after World War I, the CPR and the federal government launched promotional campaigns to encourage returning veterans and British immigrants to help in the development of the Canadian west. Film was deemed an effective tool for these campaigns. Considering their previous experience in using photography, senior officials at the CPR decided that it would be more economical and more effective to produce films in-house, as the CPR had done before when it produced still photographs and publicity posters. By 1920, the company would establish an independent motion picture production unit, in which the company maintained the majority of stock. Associated Screen News, would become the major driving force and facilitator in the development of Canadian film.[7] In light of the later mid- and late 1920s American domination over the feature film production industry, these early documentary roots of filmmaking in Canada would later become the epithet through which Canada began to mark and define its own independent association with cinema.

As the influence of the American feature film industry increased, private and public sectors of Canadian film production shifted their interest to the area of non-feature filmmaking. By the late 1920s, the Canadian film industry's capacity to survive in the shadow of the successes of American production moguls was coming to an end. Eventually the one area within which Canadian capital was still able to sustain some high level of control was in theatre exhibition. With Conservative Prime Minister R.B. Bennett's introduction of the first Canadian broadcasting legislation in 1932 the future of Canada's featureless film industry was now secured. The fact that "Canadians were selling American movies and watching American movies" and that they were no more "making many of their own" became a well-acknowledged reality.[8]

WORKERS ON FILM

One of the official objectives behind the establishment of Canada's first public film board, the Ontario Motion Picture Bureau (OMPB), was to "carry out educational work for farmers, school children, factory workers, and other classes"[9] The Board was created a little less than two years before the outbreak of the largest mass working-class revolt in Canadian history: the Winnipeg General Strike of 1919. It also occurred around the same time the Russian Bolshevik revolution shook the world, and set in motion a new phase in the development of working-class politics, organization and discourse. This gives an indication of the social and political setting within which the creation of the OMPB took place. In the same context, the federal government was itself becoming more conscious of the propagandistic possibilities of creating its own film production facilities. In hindsight, with brewing social and political instability, both provincial and federal governments could not have been motivated solely by promoting Canada's film production interests. Social instability was creating an atmosphere where cinema's role and function was opening to new political frontiers.

As I demonstrate in the next chapter, federal and provincial governments were responding to a situation where the first Red Scare was taking hold in the aftermath of the 1917 Russian Revolution. As this revolution began to make sympathetic reverberations among industrial workers both on the local and international levels, and as organizing labour unions and associations became an even more highly politicized feature in working-class life, particularly in major Canadian urban centres, the business and political establishment's fear of communist influence among workers also seemed to be on the increase. The Canadian Reconstruction Association, a big-business group, sponsored a film called *The Great Shadow* (Harley Knoles, 1920).

The film was also "supported by the CPR and other major employers"[10] and depicted an infiltration of a labour organization by Bolshevik zealots. Several companies in Toronto were so impressed by the film's message that they made major contributions to the actual production of the film. The film was mostly shot in the new film studios in Trenton, Ontario. Scenes with workers were shot at the Vickers factory in Montreal where "union members were recruited to serve as unpaid extras."[11] Upon its release, *The Great Shadow* received rave reviews in major Canadian magazines and newspapers, and employers handed out free tickets to their workers to attend the showings. The film became one in a series of at least nine films that "depict[ed] the insidious, and immediate, Bolshevik threat to the American way of life."[12] Peter Morris quotes *The Motion Picture World*'s review of the film:

> [The film] told the story of a union headed by Jim McDonald (played by Tyrone Power) struggling with a gang of Bolsheviks led by Klimoff (Louis Strene) "planning to wreck the government and society by poisoning the mind of organized labour." In sympathy with the reasonable demands of his men is capitalist Donald Alexander (Donald Hall) whose daughter Elsie (Dorothy Bernard) is in love with a secret service agent (John Rutherford). The propaganda of the Bolsheviks sweeps aside McDonald's reasoned arguments and a strike is called. Incendiarism and sabotage follow and McDonald's child is killed. Elsie is kidnapped by the Bolsheviks and rescued by her lover who captures the agitators. Public opinion is stirred and at a union meeting, McDonald wins over the men and "an armistice between capital and labour providing no strikes for twelve months is arranged."[13]

Another, lesser known, film of the time was *Dangerous Hours* (Fred Niblo, 1920). The film presented a similar cautionary tale but this time about a young American university graduate who is seduced into a violent class struggle by a female Bolshevik agitator. There are several flashback scenes about the Russian Revolution, most of which depict the destruction of churches and the "nationalization" of women.[14]

Referring to the period prior to the establishment of the NFB, Ted Magder points out that the need to promote the government's views on issues affecting Canadians, including those related to unemployment and labour problems, could have been behind the interest in creating a federal government film agency. He suggests that the creation of the Canadian Government Motion Picture Bureau in 1923 was directly connected to the rationale of providing a basis for stronger government and business control over an emerging working-class political culture:

> The films produced by the Bureau in its early years of operation clearly fit into the reconstruction plans of the Canadian state. Government officials and private business people were particularly concerned over the prospect of a post-war depression. Moreover, an increase in labour strife and growing ethnic and regional tensions, including the rise of protest parties, suggested a very unstable post-war climate.[15]

To begin, the government had no clear notion of how to foster a politically effective action that could eventually use film for the national interest of all Canadians. A less inconspicuous objective, however, was the government's interest in tackling the more pressing problems of the rise in labour activity and the growing signs of pre-Depression economic problems. The manner in which the government packaged its intent to manage potential social unrest was manifest in its increased emphasis on the notion of national unity. The government sought the use of cinema not only as means to "attract new investment capital and hard-working immigrants," but also as a tool to "nurture that illusive sense of 'national unity and pride' that the politicians of the centre so desperately sought." Only then such an investment would be "worthwhile indeed."[16]

As labour tensions increasingly became a feature of Canadian politics, and fearing the volatility of the social and political situation among working-class people both locally and internationally, the Ontario government began to increase its involvement in the production of films, particularly those dealing with labour issues. The context within which the government became involved here was through producing educational films that addressed the situation of industrial workers. However, as Shelley Stamp Lindsay's study on the 1921 Ontario Provincial Board of Health production *Her Own Fault* shows, the government's interest in labour education basically boiled down to maintaining social and cultural control.

As it dealt with problems facing Toronto's working-class women and their "work and leisure habits" in the early part of the twentieth century, *Her Own Fault* stressed personal inadequacies, inefficiencies and unhealthy habits of workers as major causes behind the degradation of their quality of life. The film demonstrated how the different habits of two morally and ethically dissimilar women workers affected their lives:

> Eileen, a model employee whose sensible habits make her a productive worker and ultimately place her in line for a promotion; and Mamie, a slacker whose unwholesome lifestyle lands her in the hospital with tuberculosis, unable to work. Each embodies a different attitude to the new urban, industrial environment in a structural opposition governed by the patterns of the work day. Beginning as each rises and readies for work, parallel editing contrasts the workers' activities outside the factory; later, two-shots of the women at work on the same factory bench demonstrate the impact that each worker's lifestyle has on her productivity.[17]

In contrast to the way NFB films would later stress ideas about social and collective responsibility, *Her Own Fault* argues that the individual responsible behaviour of workers represents the first step in solving their social and economic problems. Equally as important, the film implicitly emphasized labour and working-class problems as non-political issues and inadvertently warned against seeking political solutions to problems of workers' alienation and class exploitation. In a broader context, this reiterated a hegemonic common-sense outlook on workers' issues as personal issues in need of personal solutions. It also affirmed the image of the woman worker as an inferior Other who is in need of nurturing and guidance.

Clearly, the government was essentially using film as a viable tool to neutralize potential instability both inside and outside the workplace. Equally as important, film was inadvertently utilized as means to combat the radicalization of working people, and more specifically, to stem the growing tide of union and socialist influence among them. As such, film as a potential discursive political practice at the time reflected the confluence of interest between the capitalist class and the government.

Unlike later NFB's screening practices – particularly its emphasis on screening films in community and union halls, as well as its effort to encourage audiences to discuss the topics dealt with in the films – earlier government-sponsored screenings basically built upon and encouraged the passivity of the spectator. In the attempt to promote their own political agendas, and even as they officially despised the way commercial theatres were prescribing to public immorality, federal and provincial governments stressed the use of private film exhibition and distribution outlets. Even when films were screened in factories and for a targeted working-class audience, the setting was still chosen by way of controlling the audience's reaction as to not allow any possible discussion of the politics of these films.

Along with their paternalistic educational messages, government and privately supported films effectively reaffirmed the passive receptive practice of the spectator vis-à-vis events and views that were presented on the screen. Groups of workers were encouraged to see specific films, such as *The Great Shadow* and *Her Own Fault* as part of company-controlled special screenings. As such, the establishment's definition of educational cinema meant instructing people on ways of dealing with their problems while discouraging them from discussing and voicing their own views about them. As Lindsay asserts, "by exploiting motion pictures and the field of commercial amusements, even to such a limited degree, the government show[ed] its willingness to exploit new technologies for the purposes of social control."[18]

> With *Her Own Fault* the [Ontario] government interven[ed] in the entertainment sphere, hoping to sway the behaviour of Toronto's working women. It appeal[ed] to factory workers whom it most [sought] to address not simply by locating screenings in working class areas, but by presenting its message on the movie screen, that consummate symbol of urban pleasure in the early twentieth century.[19]

Considering that up to the early 1920s cinema was itself still conceived of as a lower and working-class form of entertainment, the government's use of commercial outlets represented a rewarding and effective tool to reach and influence its target audience.

CONNECTIONS TO NATIONALIST IDEOLOGY

Aside from occasionally documenting adventures by Canadians to explore and conquer their rough environment (such as the 1928 film *In the Shadow of the Pole*) or paying tribute to Canada's participation in World War I (including *Lest We Forget* in 1935 and *Salute to Valour* in 1937), most Canadian Government Motion Picture Bureau (CGMPB) films from the late 1920s to the mid-1930s focused on celebrating the beauty of the Canadian natural landscape. Even after the introduction of sound, the Bureau's films "'continued to portray the same golden wheatfields, the same leaping salmon and tumbling waterfalls as in pre-sound days, except that now they were accompanied by spoken dialogue and music'."[20]

The period between the wars witnessed the rising influence of Canadian nationalism. This occurred in conjunction with a growing interest in educational and cultural organizations and institutions, and several groups were set up by upper and middle-class professionals and educators. These included the National Council of Education and the Federated Women's Institutes of Canada (formed in 1919), the Canadian Authors' Association (1921), and the Canadian Historical Association (1922). Other groups included the Young Canada movement, the Banff School of Fine Arts, the Radio League, and the Workers' Education Association. In 1935, three important cultural institutions were created: the Canadian Broadcasting Corporation, the Canadian Association for Adult Education, and the National Film Society of Canada.[21] All these groups functioned within the parameters of broader political and cultural discursive formations that invariably accentuated nationalism (particularly national unity and national education), as an ideological alternative to what was considered as the degradation of culture and identity. By understanding the hegemonic nature of the nationalist discourse advocated by sections of the Canadian economic and political elite in the period before World War II – including the National Film Society and the National Council of Education – we inadvertently begin to comprehend the depth of counter-hegemonic significance of the NFB's later emphasis on class. As we will see later, the NFB films contrasted the nationalist discourse with one that focused on class identity.

In his essay on the shaping of Canadian film culture of the 1930s, Charles Acland argues that this culture became the "crucible" which enhanced "the formation of the question of national culture as one of national education." He also suggests that the 1930s became symptomatic of the "contradictions [that were] inherent in the designs of [Canadian] national culture."[22] In this context, semi-official cultural institutions such as the National Film Society (NFS) were essentially preoccupied with discussions of how Canadians were to emerge as national citizens "with the desired characteristics."[23] However, it was the class background and interests of the members of these institutions that ultimately designated the scope and the limitations of these groups' activities as well as the realm of their cultural influence:

> [The groups'] class specificity meant that voluntary organizations were structurally restricted to those who had the cultural capital to participate, who had free time, and who shared in a particular taste formation that would encourage them to attend, say, a lecture about Eisenstein's *October* rather than a Hollywood film. A country-club atmosphere prevailed, with a small group of individuals (mostly white, Anglophone males) forming what would be the defining moment of Canadian cultural nationalism.[24]

The notion of national unity, however, originally began to evolve as a buzzword in the establishment's cultural rhetoric throughout an earlier period of the twentieth century.

Hegemonic discourse since the early 1900s stressed forging a Canadian culture that reflected the national identity of Canadians. In this regard, the English-Canadian power establishment looked in suspicion towards what it regarded as foreign cultural influences and intellectual movements. As Maria Tippett points out, supporters of an authentic Canadian culture in the first forty years of the twentieth century did not appreciate what they regarded as symptoms of an unhealthy national spirit:

> They felt that the "cultural and creative life of Canada" was inhibited by "timidity; staticness; a sense of inferiority; a lack of confidence." And most significant... by "a wholesale looking outwards for ready-made standards or complacent acceptance of existing things as good enough."[25]

Clearly, the quest for a nationally authentic culture essentially meant a search for a cultural identity for those who inherited British background and traditions. More to the point of this study, the emphasis on national culture during this period also meant denial of class specificity and identity and consequently of contradictory class interests and divisions. It epitomized the Canadian elite's discursive emphasis on the myth of a classless society and the pre-eminence of a nationalist Canadian identity.

As Ian McKay suggests in his analysis of Helen Creighton's work on the politics of anti-modernism, the emphasis on national authenticity has roots in nineteenth-century romanticism and twentieth-century irrationalism, "most notoriously under fascism":

> Since the nineteenth century, many nationalists have argued that the culture of the unlettered peasant folk encapsulated the natural "cultural core" before it was complicated (and perhaps corrupted) by society. The "lore of the folk – their ballads, sayings, superstitions, and so on – could be seen as a treasure transcending all division of class and ethnicity, and binding the nation together. Cultural "authenticity" was often defined to mean faithful adherence to a supposedly "original" form.[26]

The assumption among many of those who advocated a national identity between the wars was that Canadian society is originally based on a certain "organic unity."[27]

The establishment of the National Council of Education (NCE), the National Film Society (NFS), and later, of the Canadian Association for Adult Education (CAAE), came in conjunction with the rise of Canadian nationalist rhetoric in the aftermath of Britain's official declaration, which relieved Canada's colonial status. Charles Acland discusses how Canadian film history traditionally ignored the influential role of the NCE in the development of Canadian film culture, and as part of the Canadian business establishment. The NCE, Acland argues, promoted a specific version of nationalism by emphasizing the need to "improve popular taste," and strengthening the trilateral connection between government, business, and educational instruments of society.[28] Ironically, this ideologically loaded connection originated in none other than 1919 Winnipeg, the time and site of Canada's first major working-class uprising. Acland describes some of dynamics behind the creation of the NCE:

> [...] the NCE began as a direct response to recommendations from the 1919 Winnipeg conference on "Education and Citizenship," organized by the Canadian industrial Reconstruction Association to discuss national unity in the service of industry. The conference delegates agreed upon the need for a national organization for education and Canadian citizenship. When the NCE emerged the following year to fulfill that purpose, much of its support came from those same business interests, including Sir Edward Beatty, President of the Canadian Pacific Railway, who later become the council's Honorary Vice-President.[29]

Irrespective of the irony of this organization's creation around the same time and place as Winnipeg's infamous General Strike, the policies advocated by the NCE implied some diametrically different concerns from those advocated by working-class people at the time.

As striking workers in Winnipeg were being branded as foreign subversives, since a sizable number of the participants in the general strike movement were of Eastern European and Russian origins,[30] the NCE for its part was advocating the reaffirmation of the British character of Canada. In the minds of the NCE's membership, British and Christian traditions were what defined the qualities and ideals of the Canadian national identity. But equally as important, the NCE had a relatively clear view vis-à-vis what was expected from labour. In a letter by the council's "most influential member," Major Fred J. Ney urged workers "to combat softness, slackness, indifference and indiscipline, and stimulate discipline and a sense of duty and alertness through national life."[31]

In hindsight, Ney echoed the previously mentioned film *Her Own Fault* and its ideas of dealing with working-class problems. His emphasis on individual discipline carries striking resemblance to the film's views about the behavioural characteristics of "soberness," "naturalness" and "hygiene" as fundamental elements to workers' success, safety and happiness. Ney's ideas on discipline were viewed as the hallmark of national identity and dignity, and as recipe for all Canadians to follow, irrespective of their class background. According to the NCE, the individually responsible citizen was prescribed as the cornerstone of a proud and prosperous nation. This inter-connection between nation and individual comprised a critical component in the NCE's rhetoric and enhanced the development of the nationalist discourse:

> The implications of this articulation are substantial, for if we are going to speak of the emergence of a discourse of cultural nationalism in this country, we also need to understand the conjuncture which produced particular formations of what this means. The historical instance demonstrates particular imaginings about the workings of the individual moral will and a related biological claim that someone must choose for "the people ..."[32]

Finding its cinematic translation in the NCE's subsequent denouncement of the "foreignness" of certain films that threatened the "upward march of civilization,"[33] the nationalist discourse became largely symptomatic of the ideological core of the ominous rhetoric of fascism. The nationalist rhetoric was originally promoted by government and mainstream intellectuals alike. Gradually, however, and as it began to show more explicit sympathy for fascism, the government establishment began to distance itself from the NCE's pronouncements. This allowed mainstream politicians to adopt new approaches that did not necessarily agree with the NCE's approach.

Outside of the nationalist discourse, other influences in the early part of the twentieth century were simultaneously having their own impact. These influences were also contributing to the creation of an alternative outlook on the role of Canadian cultural practice. Maria Tippett draws a picture of how foreign stimulus played a critical role in expanding the horizons of Canadian cultural practices beyond narrow nationalist discourse:

> Whether, then, English-Canada's cultural activity was influenced by imitating foreign models, affiliating with foreign organizations, associating with movements based abroad, or taking up residence outside the country, the process was a very important factor in its making for it ensured that work would not be provincial

and narrow, and able to do no more than meet the standards of a small and closed community. By moving it onto the international stage, that process at once fostered the growth of cultural activity in English-Canada, giving it a quality and finish it would not otherwise have had.[34]

The influence of socialist and working-class cultural practices in the early twentieth century had a clear resemblance to these foreign cultural influences that Tippett talks about, the least of which is how they subscribed to an ideology that was self-proclaimed as internationalist. Yet it was the dynamics of working-class involvement in radical and socialist politics within Canada itself that later gave rise to the broadly based counter-hegemonic cultural movement in the 1930s, which in turn paved the way for a new discourse on this class within emerging Canadian cinema.

3 THE DEVELOPMENT OF A WORKING-CLASS COUNTER-HEGEMONIC MOVEMENT: A HISTORICAL SURVEY

The depiction of working-class people within a specific body of film and a precise moment in history is informed by cultural intelligibilities that are drawn from a complex historical process. This process brings together various social, economical, political, and cultural elements. It also constitutes a framework within which certain cultural practices, such as cinema, acquire their ideological significance. Evaluating the ideological and hegemonic significance of the depiction of the working class in the NFB films during World War II requires an appreciation of the political and cultural history within which these films were made. Without assessing this history it is easy to draw conclusions that do not necessarily correspond with the ideological nature of these films and how they impacted the social and political environment within which they operated.

Leftist social and political opposition played a major part in developing the discourse on the working class during the early years of the NFB. By examining elements that have contributed to the development of this discourse, we realize that the NFB's portrayal of the working class largely complemented the views put forward by the Canadian left, particularly through the Communist Party and its Popular Front policy.

There are two major challenges to reading a cultural discourse from a historical setting that is different from ours. On the one hand, there is the temptation to impose a set of ideological assumptions that are products of our own historical time-frame rather than those of the period being addressed. This tendency underestimates the fact that what is ideologically commonsensical in a specific historical moment might not be as such in another. Critical evaluation here becomes burdened by values, norms, criteria and standards that are mostly incompatible with those belonging to the moment in question. The reading in this case is predisposed to inflict ideological input on the subject that belongs to the analyst's own historical setting.

The second inclination does take into consideration the specific and immediate historical setting within which a precise cultural discourse took shape, yet it falls into the trap of underestimating the less-than-immediate setting from which this discourse has emerged. This leads to a reading that is historically static and non-dialectical. Not taking into account that ideological hegemonies are historically responsive, this inclination mystifies the ideological working of a specific discourse, particularly in relation to what preceded it and to its significance as part of a historically grounded dialectic. A corollary to the methodological shortcomings of the above-mentioned tendencies is that they ultimately derail our ability to map the manner in which specific discourses inform, and are informed by, contentions around ideological hegemonies.

The immediate discursive formation that finally embodied the NFB's discourse on the working class crystallized around the mid-1930s when the Communist Party of Canada adopted its Popular Front approach towards working-class politics. The NFB films' discourse on the working class between 1939 and 1946 was itself part of a process that took shape over a period of more than three decades before the creation of the Board.

Since the late nineteenth century, and particularly over the first three decades of the twentieth century, that is to say the period immediately prior to the establishment of the NFB, there had been a major shift in working-class politics in Canada and around the world. As a result of complex internal and external developments, resulting in an increased level of political class militancy and unionization within the working class, a mass counter-hegemonic movement was beginning to emerge in Canada. This movement took shape within a trilateral connection that achieved a zenith by the mid-1930s when it succeeded in incorporating the core of a relatively broad socialist alliance that was largely, but not exclusively, centred around the Communist Party of Canada, with a growing militant working-class movement, and with an emerging group of progressively-oriented organic intellectuals and artists. This Canadian counter-hegemonic historic bloc materialized in what came to be known as the Popular Front.

The policies put forward by this Front constituted a discursive base for the development of a new intellectual formation, which became most influential between the mid-1930s and the early 1940s. Eventually, this helped constitute a loose confederation of intellectuals and critics who had thoroughly analogous objectives, and who developed a body of polemical cultural practices to justify their opinions. It is within this intellectual formation that the NFB's counter-hegemonic discourse on the working class finds its roots.

THE RADICALIZATION OF THE WORKING CLASS: COMMUNISTS AND THE LABOUR MOVEMENT

Antonio Gramsci's writing became known inside and outside socialist circles in Canada and in North America only in the late 1960s. Yet his ideas – which stipulated an alternate, autonomous, and well-disciplined Marxist political organization with the working class at its centre, and the role of such an organization in bringing together various social forces seeking to change the existing order and to replace it with a new and eventually a socialist order – essentially defined how the working-class-based communist movement in Canada during the 1930s and early 1940s interacted with Canadian social and political culture. This movement exerted an organic political and cultural influence that transcended the immediate realm of the Communist Party and the working class and in many respects functioned in a similar way as a Gramscian *historical bloc*.

The materialization of a broadly based counter-hegemonic bloc by the late 1930s interacted with the earlier formation of a new trilateral connection. This involved the development of an organic link between an increasingly militant and well-organized labour movement, an influential political avant-garde (the socialist movement in general and the Communist Party in particular), and finally, a small but growing number of intellectuals and artists who associated themselves with the working class and with the party.

In the early 1930s, the Communist Party of Canada (CPC) and its militants within the labour movement exerted a very narrow influence among larger sections of Canadian society. The party was not yet capable of exerting a political and intellectual leadership within a wider social and political alliance. The linkage between three elements – the party, the labour movement and left-leaning intellectuals – constituted the critical base for the materialization of a left-wing counter-hegemonic movement in the late 1930s and early 1940s; it also provided the ingredients for developing a wider relationship between the CPC and larger sections of the working class outside of the trade union movement, as well as with other classes and segments of the population. These changes began to take shape shortly after 1935, largely as a direct result of the shift in CPC's policy. However, before I deal with this period in CPC history I will first discuss an earlier critical phase that resulted in solidification and radicalization of the working-class movement itself in Canada. The protracted development of the workers' movement during this period provided the material base for subsequent expansion in the role of the Party and opened the way for the emergence of the Popular Front.

THE WORKING CLASS, THE RUSSIAN REVOLUTION
AND THE EARLY SOVIET STATE

For the greater part of the twentieth century, labour politics have been influenced largely by the Marxist perspective on the role of the working class in overthrowing capitalism, and in relation to a revolutionary socialist transformation of society. The attempt to apply Marxism to practical revolutionary politics found its first connection in the 1917 Russian Revolution, and in the establishment of the Soviet Union as the "first working-class state in history," although some consider the 1871 Paris Commune to be the first attempt to establish such a state.

In Canada, Marxist politics finds its roots in home-grown developments associated with the restructuring of industrial capitalism in the early part of the twentieth century. A major event in the history of the development of the Canadian working-class movement, which also contributed to its political radicalization and organizational growth, was the 1919 Winnipeg General Strike. Other elements, such as the upsurge in labour militancy and the consolidation of a broadly based militant trade union movement, the creation of working-class political parties including the Communist Party of Canada in 1921, the Great Depression, and the mobilization to fight against Fascism in Spain, all accelerated the birth and coalescence of the socialist movement in Canada.[1]

Earlier organized attempts to create socialist organizations resulted in small formal groups such as the Canadian Socialist League (founded 1901), the Social Democratic Party (founded 1911), and the Socialist Party of Canada (founded 1905).[2] Other groups included the Industrial Workers of the World and the Western Federation Miners, both of which made major impact on the development of working-class culture in Canada in the period before 1914.[3] The early attempts to form what later became the largest self-proclaimed revolutionary Marxist party in Canada occurred in the period between 1917 and 1935, which witnessed one of the twentieth century's most severe crises of capitalism. According to Ian McKay, there were "scores of revolutionary groups" that mushroomed before the solidification of the CPC, but the "most lasting and memorable monuments to the period came from the Communists especially from *The Worker*, the party's newspaper, wherein a discourse of heroic revolutionary praxis was richly developed."[4]

Working-class politics in the first half of the twentieth century were also significantly affected by discussions and contentions about the nature and role of the Soviet Union as a working-class state. As our analysis of the NFB war films will later show, an important aspect of how these films approached issues relating to labour and the working class also involved evaluating the role played by the Soviet state in world politics, as well as in relation to issues of social, political and economic progress.

Appraising the Soviet Union became the subject of fierce debates within the working class – both in Canada and around the world. As early as 1919, militant Canadian workers from Vancouver, Toronto and Montreal expressed solidarity with the Russian Revolution. In earlier manifestations of this solidarity, workers demanded an end to Canada's involvement in the military intervention by western powers against the newly established Soviet state. During the British Columbia Federation of Labour ninth annual convention, its president, Jack Kavanagh, moved a resolution expressing the Federation's refusal "to assist in the forwarding of the men, money and materials intended for use against the workers of Russia and that the executive committee of the organization carry on a system of propaganda with this in view."[5]

Solidarity between workers and Soviet Russia represented a critical topic in the period prior to the establishment of the NFB. The policy of supporting the Soviet Union attracted positive as well as negative reactions from leading members and organizers of the early Canadian labour movement. To summarize the rationalization of the support for Soviet Russia during the early days of the revolution, I quote a delegate to one of the major labour conventions, which ended up sending messages of solidarity to the Bolsheviks, the Soviet Government and the Spartacists in Germany:

> I don't think that we should fail to understand that when the working class over in Russia is being oppressed by the capitalist class of the world, that is our oppression and whatever we can do to assist our fellow workers in those countries it is up to us to do it and to put our ideas into operation, which are identical to those of the workers there and not in our own capitalist class.[6]

During the early years of its creation, the Communist International had a twofold purpose – to bring about socialism in capitalist countries and to defend the Russian Revolution from military and ideological attacks. This policy dominated much of the discourse of the militant working-class movement both internationally and locally. However, as the Soviet state began to recover from the civil war and external intervention by the early 1920s, its government began to encounter numerous internal political and economic difficulties.

The death of Lenin in 1924, compounded with the failure of several revolutionary attempts to create other working-class states in Europe, added to the difficulties facing the Soviet government and presented it with new challenges. Internal schisms within the leadership of the Communist Party of the Soviet Union, which resulted in the exile of one of the revolution's most senior and respected leaders, Leon Trotsky, also had a major political impact on the unity of communist and labour movements inside and outside the Soviet Union, including in Canada. All these issues variously affected how the world perceived the Soviet Union, its politics and its role in working-class politics. They also meant that support for communist parties, both within and without the working class and the labour movements, could not be taken for granted anymore. In Canada, this resulted in changes in the dynamics of radical working-class politics. It also presented challenges to the Communist Party, forcing it into accommodating pro-Soviet policies that in many cases were hard to defend. Even as early as the 1920s, the emergence of splinter communist groups sympathetic to Leon Trotsky, for example, affected and weakened the support the party enjoyed within the labour and working-class movement. In hindsight, however, the Communist Party was largely able to weather these early political storms and move into the 1930s with relative strength and confidence.

The development of the labour and the unemployed movements during the years of the Depression helped create sympathy for working-class-based socialist politics in Canada from the late 1920 to the mid-1930s. Later, the role played by the communist movement in Canada and in Europe in supporting the Republicans' side in Spain and in creating the anti-fascist Popular Front, the image of the Soviet Union as an ally during World War II, all helped forge the working-class counter-hegemonic discourse in Canada in the early to mid-1930s.

THE GREAT DEPRESSION

With the market crash of 1929 a long period of deep economic crisis dominated the world capitalist economy. Capitalist crises of overproduction have always been accompanied by high unemployment, and consequently, a tremendous drop in the standard of living for the working class. The acute crisis of relative overproduction was at the heart of the layoffs of hundreds of thousands of workers around the world, and in particular in advanced capitalist countries in Europe and in North America. The ferocity of the situation was reflected in some of the social statistics about the period. While unemployment figures were not kept before World War II, economist A.E. Safarian estimates that about one-fifth of the work force in Canada was unemployed in 1933 when the crisis reached its worse point.[7] By that year, personal disposable income was almost half that of 1929. In turn, agricultural recovery was painfully slow. Since the overwhelming majority of the workers had no alternative source of income, a large portion of the domestic market all but ceased to exist, thus exacerbating and then prolonging the crisis. In 1937, the personal disposable income still remained substantially below the 1929 level.[8]

The worsening economic situation resulted in widespread poverty and even frequent cases of starvation. For many families this also meant the humiliation of going on the welfare lines and of depending on charity to make ends meet. Hundreds of thousands of unemployed workers had no idea when, where, or how they and their families would eat their next meal or whether they would continue to have a roof over their heads. The Depression forced as many as one million people onto the welfare rolls, and in most cases deprived them of most of their personal possessions. Seizure of people's goods, evictions, and foreclosure of mortgages on farms and homes became common and widespread practices during the Depression. With this crisis at hand, an intensified series of social and political upheavals began to rock most advanced capitalist countries, including Canada. Those upheavals resulted in an increased militancy and political consciousness among people of working-class backgrounds. It also led the government to react in an increasingly violent manner to working-class resistance. As we will see later, NFB films looked at this period as an example of how old and chaotic economic management could lead to major social upheavals. The films would also promote increasing the role of the government in economic and social planning as the only reasonable alternative that could help build a prosperous future for all Canadians.[9]

A two-pronged strategy characterized the work of the militant elements of the labour movement, particularly those connected with the Communist Party during the Depression. On the one hand, they launched a massive effort to organize the unemployed through campaigns demanding jobs and descent wages. They also organized solidarity and relief groups with those forced into poverty by the crisis. The other aspect in the strategy of labour militants was to launch major campaigns to organize industrial workers and to defend their interests against company policies.[10]

A major event took place during this period. In January 1930, as the economic and social situation worsened and labour actions and strikes intensified, communist militants within the trade union movement forged a new labour body: the Workers' Unity League (WUL). The League's stated goal was to persuade less militant unions of the need to set up industrial unions based on class-struggle policies:

The aim was to win the membership to militant policies. Communists in these unions had to struggle for trade union democracy, against the expulsion of militants and for the development of unity from below around specific issues. Their function was to fight for the immediate demands of the workers, expose the class collaborationism of the reformist leadership and contest union election on a program of workers' demands.[11]

As a trade union centre basing itself on the idea of class struggle, the WUL set for itself the task of organizing the unorganized – particularly in mass-production industries.

The WUL undertook the task of organizing militant and mass-based industrial unions under rank-and-file control. As such, it advocated creating unions capable of mobilizing the workers for the defence and improvement of their living and working conditions and ultimately for the overthrow of the capitalist system.[12] On another level the WUL initiated a new strategy in labour organization. The WUL's constitution entrenched the concept of accepting as members all wage workers "regardless of race, creed, color, sex, craft or political affiliations."[13] As we will see later, the emphasis on the equal role and rights of workers of all national backgrounds and the role of women in the work force would become a critical component in the discourse of NFB films during the war.

Six years into the Great Depression the crisis was reaching another high point. Among the most significant developments during this period was the grassroots effort to demand work for the unemployed and higher wages for workers. The campaign would later become known as the On-to-Ottawa Trek. Responding to increased social and political tensions across the country, the federal government, headed at the time by Conservative Prime Minister R.B. Bennett, proposed a plan to force single unemployed men into relief camps under military control and in isolated locations throughout the country. The unemployed were to be interned, and to observe military rules. They were also to receive twenty cents a day for their work in the camps. The actual implementation of the plan resulted in exploding strife inside the relief camps themselves.[14] In reality, these camps also became the focus for militant action and organization around the country. The level of militant activity grew within the camps and so did the demonstrations organized by the unemployed in areas outside the camps. The mobilization for the On-to-Ottawa Trek sought to bring together working people from across the country to take trains to Ottawa to place their demands before the Federal Government. Maurice Rush, a witness and one of the participants in the mobilization for the Trek, describes the organization of the campaign:

Recognizing the need for organization and united action, the Workers Unity League (WUL), the Canadian trade union centre led by communists, decided to establish the Relief Camp Workers Union (RCWU). Subsequently, RCWU branches were set up in every camp. Between the time the relief camps were established in 1932 and the On-to-Ottawa Trek of 1935, the RCWU led many struggles for the unemployed, often coming into cities and towns to stage protests.[15]

The role played by the Communist-led WUL was expanding. Even though the League membership did not exceed that of the less-militant trade union federations, the Trades and Labour Congress (TLC) or the All-Canadian Congress of Labour (ACCL), the WUL quickly became the most influential Canadian trade union centre. Whereas the other two centres lost tens of thousands of members during the early half of the decade, the League reached a membership of forty thousand in its first four years of existence. Between 1933 and 1936 the WUL initiated and led 90 per cent of labour strikes in Canada, and in 1933 alone "it led 181 of the 233 strikes which took place. Of this number, 111 were won."[16]

On another front, while most farmers were involved in bitter fights to save their farms, and workers were struggling to save their jobs and lessen the impact of the Depression on their lives, hundreds of thousands of others had neither farms nor jobs. In 1930, the Unemployed Councils, created earlier by the Communist Party, merged with the National Unemployed Workers' Association. Later those councils officially declared their affiliation with the WUL.[17] The mobilization of the unemployed and the workers during the On-to-Ottawa Trek campaign in 1935 epitomized the Communist Party's coming of age. It demonstrated the ability of the party to initiate, organize and lead mass working-class-based actions.

The Trek met a violent end in Regina on July 1, 1935 after an attack by the Royal Canadian Mounted Police. The events shocked the country and moved Canadians to support the demand for legislation of an official act to guarantee social security. While some CPC supporters claim direct linkage between today's system of employment insurance and several other social reforms and the fight associated with the Trek events, what is more certain is that the demands put forward by an increasingly powerful and well-organized WUL in support of alternative work policies, ideas about guaranteed wages and farm income became very popular among a wide cross-sections of workers, farmers and the unemployed. Such ideas helped mobilize a protest movement that surpassed any other previous working-class protest in Canada in its popularity and the clarity of its demands.[18]

The protest actions, strikes and activities led by the WUL, including the On-to-Ottawa Trek, became symbols of a widespread rejection of Prime Minister Bennett's response to the country's social and economic crisis. This sentiment played a major part in bringing about the resounding defeat of the Bennett government in the 1935 general election. Under the leadership of William Lyon Mackenzie King the Liberals gained 132 more seats than the Conservatives.

One of King's main campaign policies was his promise to abolish the Relief Camps, which were finally closed in June 1936. The role played by the WUL, the Communists, and the newly established social democratic party known as the Co-operative Commonwealth Federation (CCF) in mobilizing action against the relief camps widened the political base and the respect for the labour-based socialist movement in Canada. Another manifestation of the new atmosphere was one of the points in King's election platform, which promised to repeal Section 98, a law under which communists were detained and imprisoned on the charge of advocating the violent overthrow of the government. The law was also used by the government to suppress attempts to organize workers and trade unions.[19]

Equally important, the new successes of labour enhanced support for a new approach in dealing with the issue of unemployment. It particularly promoted government intervention as an alternative. Later, the two earliest NFB films, *The Case of Charlie Gordon* and *Youth is Tomorrow* – officially produced in 1939 under the auspices of the Canadian Government Motion Picture Bureau – would stress social collective planning and government coordination as the preferred' framework for dealing with the problem of unemployment.

THE EMERGENCE OF WORKING-CLASS CULTURAL PRACTICE

Various influences affected the cultural discourse on the working class prior to the establishment of the NFB. They include international as well as Canadian-based cultural practices, both of which helped set the paradigm for political and formal approaches that became widely associated with alternative labour and working-class culture.

INTERNATIONAL INFLUENCES IN THE PERIOD OF *CLASS-AGAINST-CLASS* POLICY

Between 1929 and 1934 the policy of the Communist International emphasized militant class struggle as the main component of its political strategy. Communist parties advocated direct class struggle in their propaganda and agitation work. For communists, the outbreak of the Depression made the goal of the revolutionary overthrow of capitalism seem more feasible than ever before:

> During the depression, when the workers of the capitalist countries were rapidly organizing and becoming increasingly class conscious, and when the differences between crisis-ridden capitalist economies and socialist construction were all too obvious, socialism seemed just around the corner. The truth scarcely needs to be explained, although it certainly bore repetition. The working class – and its cultural leaders – could well afford to scorn the bourgeoisie and everything associated with it. The working class was able, for a time at least, to ignore its potential allies.[20]

The Canadian Communist Party's policy towards intellectuals was almost one-sided. It based itself solely on gaining their support for the working class in the revolutionary effort to overthrow of capitalism. What in fact was being advocated was a class-against-class approach in which the role of the intellectual would be to help raise class-consciousness among workers in favour of revolutionary socialism. The question of what was in the revolution for the intellectuals themselves seemed almost irrelevant.

Nevertheless, on the international level there was a clear growth of interest among intellectuals and artists in expressing solidarity with working-class and socialist politics. This directly complemented earlier efforts in support of the new Soviet state. Establishing the Workers' International Relief organization (WIR) represented one important example of these efforts.

The WIR was originally created at Lenin's instigation in Berlin in 1921 to help in the effort of famine relief in the Soviet Union in the aftermath of the Civil War. With the end of the famine crisis, the WIR, which had numerous branches in several countries, became an international support force for strikers and workers and their families around the world, providing them with food, clothing and shelter. The leader of the German section of the WIR, Willi Muenzenberg, was also interested in the role of cultural propaganda, particularly the role of cinema.

Muenzenberg, who was also the representative of the Communist International in the WIR, proposed that communists change their dismissive and often patronizing attitude towards film and cultural struggle in general. He declared that "in the main, labour organizations and even Communist Parties and groups have left this most effective means of propaganda and agitation [i.e., film] in the hands of their enemy." He then argued that the urgent task facing communists at this point was to re-conquer "this supremely important propaganda weapon" which at this point was under the monopoly of the ruling class.[21] Subsequently, the WIR extended its activity into several mass-media and cultural practices. By the early 1930s, groups of intellectuals and artists who expressed support for labour and socialist ideas began to function in several countries including Germany, the Soviet Union, Britain, France, Switzerland, Czechoslovakia, Austria, the Netherlands, and Japan.[22]

In the United States the history of working-class cinema goes back to the early days of filmmaking. In his study on silent cinema and its effect in shaping working-class culture in America, Steven Ross illustrates how movies and the working class became intertwined for "nearly two decades after the first nickelodeon opened in 1905." Ross identifies three elements that characterized the link between early cinema and workers: workers became the industry's main audience; they also became "the frequent subjects of films;" and finally, workers themselves became makers of movies not only as studio labourers but as independent producers. The emerging industry included a wide range of producers including the American Federation of Labor, the Ford Motor Company, the National Association of Manufacturers, the Women's Political Union, and the National Child Labor Committee. Among those, "working-class filmmakers were the most ambitious and persistent."[23] American working-class filmmakers produced films that reflected new ideologically counter-hegemonic alternative to dominant bourgeois values:

> As early as 1907, workers, radicals, and labour organizations were making movies that challenged the dominant ideology of individualism and portrayed collective action – whether in the form of unionism or socialist politics – as the most effective way to improve the lives of citizens. Over the next two decades, labour and the left forged an oppositional cinema that used film as a medium of hope to educate, entertain, and mobilize millions of Americans.[24]

Among other means of communication, cinema in America clearly became the most effective political tool for workers to publicize their views and unite their effort. Pre-Hollywood cinema (i.e., mainly before the early 1920s) became the poor man's amusement. As Ross suggests, this cinema turned the previously hidden and "private realm of factories, mines, and fields into highly visible parts of public culture."[25] By the early 1920s, however, the growth of American film production "signalled the rise of a new type of film industry and the birth of 'Hollywood' as a metaphor to describe it."[26] As we saw earlier in our survey of the same period in Canadian cinematic culture, among the issues stressed by private film producers in Canada was finding ways to fight against the dangers of Bolshevik intrusion into the ranks of the working class.

The second wave of working-class cinema in the United States occurred after several WIR sections became increasingly involved in areas of cultural agitation and propaganda. In the early 1930s the WIR organized revolutionary drama groups, dance groups, symphony and mandolin orchestras, bands, choirs and art workshops. Brian Neve's book *Politics and Film in America* presents a detailed account of the creative ferment that enlivened both the theatre and the left-wing political milieu in New York during the 1930s. The innovative work of collective enterprises such as the Group Theatre, the Worker's Laboratory Theatre, the Red Dancers, The Living Newspaper, and the Yiddish Artef shaped the political consciousness of many future Hollywood luminaries and created a cultural climate that was generally sympathetic to socialist ideas and to working-class politics.

Among the more active elements within the working-class cultural movement in the U.S. was The Workers' Film and Photo League (known after 1933 as the Film and Photo League). The league became part of a broad movement sponsored by the WIR and was active in providing visual coverage of working-class events and concerns for the left-wing press.[27] On another level, socialist-oriented filmmakers in the United States established Frontier Films, a collective that sought to balance ideological ties with the Communist Party with the interest in the material produced by Soviet film and theatre artists such as Stanislavsky, Pudovkin, Vertov, and Eisenstein.[28]

CANADIAN INFLUENCES AND *CLASS-AGAINST-CLASS* POLICY

Before the Russian Revolution and before the outbreak of the Great Depression, the role of the intellectual as a socialist activist or critic was largely unheard of in Canada. Aside from periodic and dispersed intellectual activism associated in Quebec, for example, with the Catholic Church, or in English Canada with the Mechanics Institutes or the Knights of Labour, Canada had few sites of organized working-class cultural practices.

According to Michiel Horn, "few intellectuals questioned the institution of private property, the dominance of capital over labour, or the benefits of a market economy."[29]

He suggests that "probably the great majority of [intellectuals] shared the prevailing ideas and beliefs without thinking much about them. It was the safe, sensible, natural course."[30] However, the advent of the Russian revolution provided an incentive for the organizational and ideological enhancement of a working-class-based culture.

In 1921, the Communist Party initiated an organization called the Canadian Friends of Soviet Russia, which soon joined the previously mentioned World International Relief (WIR). The Canadian branch was headed by prominent party leader Florence Custance.[31] No documented evidence points directly to the link between the Canadian branch of the WIR and the development of local progressive cultural organizations or with the successive emergence of what later became the most active communist-related cultural groups, the Progressive Arts Clubs. The official platform of the two groups, however, as well as their goals, activities, and the manner in which they were both led by Communist Party members all offer indications as to a consolidation of an active circle of Canadian artists and intellectuals with close ties to the working-class and with socialist ideas and politics.

It is important to note here that the early communist movement in Canada included very few intellectuals within its ranks. Since its very foundation in 1921 the Party's membership and leadership had come overwhelmingly from people of working-class background – a healthy indication for a self-proclaimed working-class party, but not as healthy for a movement that was also interested in building alliances with other sections of society, including intellectuals. According to the Party's own organizational reports, of a total party membership of 4,500 in 1925, "800 were miners, 800 lumber workers, 400 railroad workers, 800 to 1,000 farmers, most of whom also worked in the mines or the lumber camps, and most of the remainder were city workers employed in the needle, leather and metal trades."[32] During the first ten years of its establishment the party gave low priority to recruiting writers, artists, professionals, university graduates, or students. However, when the party began to experience substantial growth in the 1930s, it also became more willing to accept a greater variety of members. As noted earlier, by the early 1930s radical socialists, particularly communists, were beginning to build links with the more active and militant sections of the Canadian working class. But the party was also beginning to create a nucleus of support among other segments of the population.[33]

The new radicalism was finally beginning to take root among a small but nevertheless growing number of intellectuals. While it never rose to prominence in the early years of the Great Depression, the transported genres of proletarian literature and socialist realism – including poetry, novels and other art forms, some of which were brought from abroad by Russian, Jewish and Eastern European socialist and communist working-class activists – all became familiar features among working-class people as well as a growing number of intellectuals. More and more radical artists and writers were expressing pronounced and bold sympathy for the plight of the underprivileged and their own anger against prospering capitalists.[34] In 1932, Canadian communists initiated organizations that became active in the fields of arts and culture and in support of several working-class causes. According to Ivan Avakumovic:

> To begin with, there emerged a nucleus of young intellectuals who identified themselves publicly with the CPC.... Those intellectuals who were not wholly involved in the party apparatus or the Communist-led trade unions were active in the Progressive Arts Club... Communist influence among intellectuals also increased when the CPC made a determined effort to gain the sympathy of a broad spectrum of non-Communists who were disturbed by certain developments at home and abroad.[35]

Further, Avakumovic points out that "attempts to curtail the civil rights of communists in Toronto... brought party members into contact with Protestant clergymen, professors at the University of Toronto and pacifists grouped around the Fellowship of Reconciliation." This broadening group of intellectuals became involved in mass public events that supported all kinds of activities by striking workers and the unemployed, and opposed the actions of the government against workers. Later, those intellectuals also "provided a nucleus of intellectuals who were prepared to join forces, or sympathize with the communists when party members organized a Canadian congress against War and Fascism in Toronto in October 1934."[36] With some of its roots found in the cultural activities and meetings in the home of Abraham Nisnevitz – an immigrant poet who wrote both in Yiddish and English and whose house became the centre of a variety of cultural activities and events that were deeply committed to supporting working-class causes – socialist oriented intellectuals were slowly coming to the fore of a Canadian progressive artistic movement.

In 1932 a group of thirty-five people comprised of mainly blue-collar workers and a few students was established in Toronto as the Progressive Arts Club (PAC). The club was divided into subgroups of writers, artists, and theatre workers. Later, new sections were created in Montreal, Winnipeg and Vancouver as well as smaller industrial communities in Ontario. The club printed its own journal, *Masses*, which published members' articles, poems, and short stories. They also published material in *Always Ready*, a magazine dedicated to children; in the Communist Party newspaper *The Worker*; and in *The Labour Defender*, the organ of the Canadian Labour Defence

League. Among the writers contributing to these journals were Maurice Granite, Oscar Ryan, E. Cecil-Smith (who later commanded the Mackenzie-Papineau Battalion fighting on the side of the Republican forces in the Spanish Civil War), Dorothy Livesay and Stanley Ryerson.[37] The group also included several artists:

> Among the artists were the sculptors Helen Nelson and Sam Dagan, who made busts of workers and Party members, and the cartoonists Avrom Yanovsky and "RIC" (Richard Taylor, who later became a cartoonist for the *New Yorker*). The pictures and cartoons in Masses were all done by the painstaking process of linoleum block printing. It was considered a proletarian medium because of its cheapness and accessibility. Moreover any printing house which offered to do engraving for *Masses* was subject to police raids. The artists' group also designed, drew and printed posters and handbills for numerous demonstrations and rallies, all of which had to be done in complete secrecy.[38]

In its effort to drum up further support for proletarian culture *Masses* became one of the more important journals read by progressive intellectuals around the country. The journal published full scripts of agitation and propaganda plays, order slips for workers' songbooks, commentaries and publicity material on progressive art exhibitions, theatre productions, and other PAC, labour and socialist public events and activities. Between April 1932 and April 1934 the journal published twelve issues.

Masses concentrated on Canadian events concerning workers such as strikes, police brutality, arrests of workers and the struggle against the implementation of repressive government legislation. In an effort to stress the goal of international communism, *Masses* regularly drew parallels "between the character and actions of both local and international capitalists, fascists and workers."[39] The journal also covered developments in the Soviet Union and expressed its solidarity with it. As we will see later, an important feature in the NFB films' discourse about a new role for workers and farmers in the political and administrative leadership of Canada was similarly based in pointing out the achievements of workers in the Soviet Union.

The radicalization of the working-class cultural movement in Canada was also manifest in the rise in influence of a number of women artists and writers. In his study on the role of women in the communist culture of the early 1930s, Douglas Parker draws attention to what he considers a watershed in the development of the radical women's movement and its contribution to Canadian culture in general and to socialist political discourse in particular.

Parker suggests that the increased participation of women in left-wing groups shifted the focus away from a "rigidly defined proletarian literature," and towards a literary and artistic aesthetic that incorporated broader and more gender inclusive themes and concerns.[40] Within the same context, other progressive artists were becoming part of Canadian artistic scene. Paraskeva Clark added a new dimension to the circle of painters in Toronto during the 1930s and later in the 1940s. Her paintings, largely influenced by cubism and her years of training in the Soviet Free Studios between 1917 and 1921, offered an alternative perspective to the influential Group of Seven and helped instigate new artistic movement that emphasized organic links with the social and political struggles of the day.

In theatre, it is suggested that the first Canadian example that deserves consideration in the discussion of documentary theatre emerged out of the tradition of the Agitprop Theatre, and particularly the production of the Communist-Party-inspired play *Eight Men Speak* in 1933.[41] The Agitprop was originally created in the 1920s by workers' theatres in Britain and the United States. It derived from the revolutionary theatres of Germany and the Soviet Union. The Agitprop presented polemical statements on political developments and depicted the ideological significance of events rather than the events themselves. *Eight Men Speak* indirectly dealt with an event that became the subject of a widespread protest movement in Canada.

In August 1931 the RCMP raided the offices of the Communist Party and the homes of party leaders. The authorities arrested eight communist leaders, including its general secretary Tim Buck and Tom McEwen, the leader of the Workers' Unity League. This was done under the authority of Section 98 of the Criminal Code which was used to link the Communist Party to professing violent overthrow of government. The trial of the eight Communist leaders and the attempted murder of Tim Buck in the Kingston Penitentiary prison inspired the production of *Eight Men Speak*.

The campaign launched in solidarity with the leaders of the CPC and the WUL and other communist and labour leaders during their internment was of critical importance. By November 1933 the campaign became the subject of a petition that was later officially presented to Prime Minister Bennett. The petition, which bore 450,000 signatures, demanded the release of the eight prisoners, an investigation into the attempted murder of Tim Buck and a repeal of Section 98. The welcome rally later organized to celebrate the freeing of the communist and labour leaders in the Maple Leaf Gardens in 1934 was attended by 17,000 people, while 8,000 others had to be turned away for lack of space.[42]

By the time the play *Eight Men Speak* was staged, the wide support for the political cause that it advocated was already largely established. The launching of the play, however, did not only reflect this grassroots support but also contributed to building the campaign to free labour and communist leaders from jail and to repeal Section 98 of the Criminal Code. This was indicative of the way the influence of a working-class cultural discourse was beginning to transcend the confines of an intellectual avant-garde to assume an influential position in creating a new form of popular culture.

The four authors of *Eight Men Speak*, Oscar Ryan, E. Cecil-Smith, Frank Love and Mildred Goldberg, took care to disguise any details that could lead to libel suits. The day after the resounding success of the first performance of the play, which attracted a capacity crowd of 1,500 people, the police threatened to revoke the theatre's license. The virtual outlawing of the play spurred the left-wing cultural movement to launch a political campaign in defence of working-class culture.[43] The play's success in attracting the attention of the general public also signalled the emergence of a new kind of a cultural current. This current organically linked between the organized socialist movement, the grassroots working-class movement, and an emerging group of intellectuals. This took place as the labour movement was strengthening its own organizational base, and in conjunction with the solidification of the role played by socialist militant elements within this movement.

The emergence of a working-class-based cultural practice in Canada in the 1930s owed a great deal to the way communist intellectual activists saw and stressed their own role as part of a broad movement for social and political change. These intellectuals sought ways through which their artistic production became relevant to the struggles that were taking place around the country and the world. Consequently, they saw a need to be accessible – both formally and in terms of content – to wider sections of the population and particularly to their intended working-class audience, and they consciously attempted to do so without patronizing. As such, many of these intellectuals became popular and celebrated figures among workers. Despite their idealistic, hyperbolic, and in many cases erroneous evaluation of Soviet achievements, and their disregard of the critiques of abuses that were beginning to take place in this "worker's state," these intellectuals' contribution to Canadian cultural and political life was mainly innovative, genuine and more importantly, effective. Their input also translated in a qualitatively dramatic shift from the elitism that characterized the work of many other artists and intellectuals of the same and earlier periods.

In many cases, such as that of *Eight Men Speak*, the successes of these intellectuals in building direct links with workers and grassroots sections of Canadian society became a major element in the development of the socialist and the working-class movement itself. Equally as important, they provided solid grounds for the subsequent production and dissemination of a broader based working-class cultural and artistic practice that went beyond the immediate circles of this class and its supporting intellectuals, to become part of an emerging counter-hegemonic discourse.

As the Communist Party shifted away from its isolationist class-against-class approach to the more inclusive Popular Front strategy, the already-built alliances with the working-class movement and a core of organic intellectuals formed a nucleus for even wider cultural and political connections. The integration of three major components of working-class political culture – the militant labour movement, the Communist Party, and supporting organic intellectuals – comprised the base for the further labouring[44] of Canadian cultural discourse. NFB films constituted an important example of how this discourse became manifest in various areas of Canadian cultural practice.

For communist militants, advocating unity in the fight against Fascism gradually provided the link between the short and long-term objectives of the working-class movement. The struggle for democracy and social justice was considered as a prerequisite for the subsequent struggle for socialist transformation. In this context, the Communist Party was essentially engaging in a protracted struggle against bourgeois ideological hegemony, a *war of position* of sorts, to cite Gramsci's famous analogy. Within this prolonged struggle, the left would forward its own common sense ideas and philosophy.

FROM CLASS-AGAINST-CLASS TO THE POPULAR FRONT

A critical moment in the development of the socialist movement in Canada in the mid-1930s relates to the formation of the Co-operative Commonwealth Federation (CCF). Although originally intended as a federation, the CCF eventually became a membership organization based on clubs. Many workers flocked to join the new social democratic party that broadly declared itself in favour of a new social order. Clearly, communists were faced with the task of defining their relationship to this new player on the Canadian left-wing scene. The predominant view at the time within the Communist International was that social democracy was equivalent to "social fascism" and therefore "would have to be rejected and ultimately defeated if socialism were [*sic*] to win out over fascism."[45] In Canada, as well as in other countries, this attitude towards social democracy isolated communists from wide segments of the non-Marxist left. It also contributed to depriving the working-class movement of the potential of becoming a leading element within a historical bloc capable of incorporating larger sections of the population, let alone an effective transformational force in politics.

Faced with the dangerous rise of fascist movements in Europe, particularly in Spain, Italy and Germany, the 1935 Seventh Congress of the Communist International (CI) denounced its earlier position toward social democracy. The CI called for the unity of the two movements in the goal of defeating fascism and preventing war. It also advocated the creation of united fronts in defence of democracy. These fronts were to include ideologically diverse workers' organizations, middle-class groups and even anti-fascist capitalists. A statement by Georgi Dimitrov the leaders of the CI declared:

> Joint actions by the parties of both [Communist and Socialist] Internationals against fascism, however, would not be confined to influence their present adherents, the Communists and Social-Democrats; it would also exert a powerful influences on the ranks of the Catholic, anarchist and unorganized workers; even on those who had temporarily become the victims of fascist demagogy. Moreover, a powerful united front of the proletariat would exert tremendous influence on all other strata of the intelligentsia. A united front would inspire the wavering groups with faith in the strength of the working class.[46]

Dimitrov characterized fascism as "the open terrorist dictatorship of the most reactionary, most chauvinistic and most imperialist elements of finance capital."[47] The new policy argued that while fascism was a capitalist-based ideology, capitalism itself does not necessarily equate fascism.

NFB films during World War II would later present a synonymous interpretation of the need to ally Canada's and western fighting resources with those of the Soviet Union. Some of those films would also clearly argue for the creation of a common front between anti-fascists of different ideological and social backgrounds. For example, the films dealing with the Chinese resistance against the Japanese invasion would explicitly emphasize the United Front between Chinese communists and nationalists as an example of the effective way of fighting fascism. A similar approach would be taken vis-à-vis the communist-led resistance movement against the Nazis in the Balkans and Greece, which also included in its ranks a wide range of political and social ingredients.

As communist parties continued to support short- and long-term working-class demands including the revolutionary overthrow of capitalism, they were persuaded that the effective struggle against fascism necessitated linking their work with broad-based social and political movements. The United Front policy (the term *United Front* was used interchangeably with the term *Popular Front* by CI Marxists at the time) resulted in a qualitative change in the political stature of communist parties. The new policy created parameters for an innovative relationship between, on the one hand, working-class and labour militants, communist parties and socialist intellectuals, and on the other, non-Marxist socialists and progressives, and even liberal minded intellectuals – both within the rank and file of the working classes as well as among other classes and sections of society.

Popular Front policy also offered revamped interpretations of the involvement of communists in the fight for democracy. This played an important role in the left's subsequent expansion of influence. The struggle for democracy and social justice was proposed as synonymous with – and even a prerequisite to – the struggle for socialism.

On August 4, 1943, two Communist Party members, J.B. Salsberg and A.A. MacLeod, were elected from Toronto ridings to the Ontario Legislative Assembly. Successes at the provincial level were quickly followed by other accomplishments in municipal elections across the country. During the same year the Labour Progressive Party (the party under which the CPC operated at the time) elected its first and, up to today, only member of Parliament. The party's candidate, Fred Rose, won a by-election in the Montreal working-class federal riding of Cartier. Rose became the only Communist Party member ever to be elected in a federal election in the United States or Canada. In one of his speeches a few years later in the House of Commons, Rose summarized how his party reconciled democracy as a constituent element in the fight for socialism:

> The issue to-day is not what these [anti-Communist] people call free enterprise versus socialism; the issue is democratic progress versus chaos and insecurity. Our party, the Labour Progressive Party, stands for socialism, but we are realistic enough to know and to understand that the vast majority of Canadians are to-day not yet ready for it. We consider that at this time the fight for social progress is a fight in which the people will learn, through their own experience, whether or not they want socialism. The essence of socialism is democracy, and it will not come until the majority of Canadians learn through their own experience that socialism is the system they need.[48]

Rose's discourse exemplified how communists rationalized their Popular Front policy. It also reflected how communists at the time looked at the struggle against capitalism as a protracted battle rather than as a revolutionary overthrow of government.

The new CPC approach provided vital enhancement to labour and communist action around the country, and helped the party reach out successfully to wider segments of Canadian society throughout the war period. The Front's interpretation of the struggle for democracy became central in the NFB films' discourse on the fight against fascism as well as its approximation of Canada's post-war future. The issues of struggle for social and economic justice, equal opportunity, collective participation in the political process and for workers' equal share in managing the workplace, all became synonymous with these films' interpretation of the struggle for a democratic future.

UNITY WITHIN THE TRADE UNION MOVEMENT

The adoption of Popular Front policy in 1935 was accompanied by closer cooperation between the communist-led Workers Unity League and other labour unions. Earlier, the labour movement was marred by passionate inner fights that resulted in major divisions, splits and reorganizations. The Popular Front approach promoted by the Canadian CP after 1935 ultimately helped the party strengthen its position in the rank and file and leadership of the Canadian trade union movement.

By the mid-1930s the Workers Unity League was the centre of most major union organizing campaigns, particularly within larger labour unions and the natural-resources-based industries. WUL and communist activists became the principal and most active organizers in the major industries of Canadian forestry, mining, steelworkers and fishing industries, as well as among workers in construction and building, painting and carpentry, garment and clothing factories, and electrical and machine industries.[49] As communists increasingly focused on new United Front policies, the WUL advocated support for a united Canadian trade union centre. The proposal was positively received by most sections of the less militant TLC (Trades and Labour Congress) and the ACCL (All-Canadian Congress of Labour). A year after the WUL made its official appeal for "full organization [labour] unity" the constituent unions of the WUL finally merged with their TLC counterparts.[50] The merger increased the membership of the Canadian trade union movement by 30 per cent between 1936 and 1937 and allowed communists to play a leading role in both the grassroots and leadership levels of the labour movement.[51]

The merger between the WUL and TLC also had a significant effect in developing an organizational and political link between Canadian and American labour unions. Although it was considered a regrettable development by some Canadian labour historians (Irving Abella's *Nationalism, Communism, and Canadian Labour* characterizes it as symptomatic of the Americanization of the Canadian labour movement), the majority of Canadian union members "saw the American connection as both necessary and beneficial."[52] In this regard the merger also complemented the left-wing anti-nationalist perspective within the movement. The left's position on the issue of nationalism was later echoed by John Grierson and in NFB films.

Considering our earlier discussion on the views on nationalism within the circles of Canadian cinematic culture, the left's position clearly contrasted with that of the Canadian National Council on Education and the National Film Society prior to the establishment of the NFB. Indeed, the view in favour of international solidarity later constituted a critical component in the discourse of NFB war films. Support for this solidarity would also be demonstrated in these films' emphasis on the need for internationalist labour unity. Furthermore, the activities of the Board would involve producing films in cooperation with American labour unions, such as 1943's *Coal Face, Canada* (Robert Edmonds).

The shift in the position of the communists and their labour supporters towards a more accommodating relationship with their social democratic rivals was not without its negative effects. The WUL advocated a grassroots-based structure and emphasized recruiting on a shop-focused basis, in contrast to the craft-dominated approach of the traditional trade union centres at the time. This allowed for a wider involvement by workers in the affairs of the unions. It also allowed for the more active involvement of women workers, at least within the industries that represented a major section of the work force. In her study of the work of the Communist Party within the Industrial Union of Needle Trades Workers (IUNTW), Mercedes Steedman suggests that as the WUL merged into other union centres, several aspects of the earlier progressive features of the union organizing receded. Steedman argues that the changes in the union structures might have contributed later to the gradual re-marginalizing of women within labour.[53]

Despite these setbacks, the WUL policy of labour unity contributed in the long run to the development of a less divided and more inclusive trade union movement. Later during the war the unity of the movement would play a more major role in building stronger links with other segments of society including women, racial minorities and intellectuals from different social classes. It would also enhance a less sectarian discourse and practice on labour and working-class issues, including on the role of working-class women. As I note later, the depiction of women in NFB war films would reflect a higher level of sensitivity in connection with the role and rights of working women as well as those of racial minorities.

THE SPANISH CIVIL WAR AND THE EXPANSION
OF THE ROLE OF PROGRESSIVE INTELLECTUALS

A significant expansion in the organic role of militant working-class activists and intellectuals after 1935 took place in the context of supporting the Republican's cause in the Spanish Civil War. The fascist revolt against the newly elected left-wing government in Spain led to a major international campaign of solidarity with its loyalist supporters. By the end of the war in 1939 the campaign involved around 60,000 volunteer participants from 53 countries who served in the International Brigades of the Republican Army.[54] The campaign had a major impact on the realm of cultural discourse and practice in Canada and around the world. New links were created among local and international grassroots labour activists and with a considerably larger number of artists and intellectuals. Some of the artists involved in the campaign would later constitute a large section of the filmmakers and technicians of the NFB during its early years.

Internationally, many intellectuals who were unwilling to accept Marxism or militant working-class politics were, on the other hand, vehemently opposed to fascism and war. From the outset, many professionals and artists eagerly joined hands with an increasingly better organized and united working-class movement. Leftist and labour-oriented activists reached out to anti-fascist writers, poets, artists and theatre groups. Leading and influential intellectuals such as George Orwell, Stephen Spender, Arthur Koestler, André Malraux, Louis Aragon, André Breton, Lillian Hellman, Ernest Hemingway, Dorothy Parker, and John Dos Passos; artists such as Pablo Picasso, Man Ray and Diego Rivera; and filmmakers such as Luis Buñuel, Jean Renoir, Jean Cocteau, and Alberto Cavalcanti, among many others, were drawn to support a cause widely seen as a front-line struggle to prevent fascism from spreading and endangering world peace.

In Canada, the communist-led League Against Fascism and War was comprised of more than 250,000 Canadians by 1937.[55] The movement in support of the Spanish Republicans stressed short and long-term links between the interests of working-class Canadians and the fight against fascism, and sought to forge a new alliance between this and other classes and sections of Canadian society, as well as with groups of intellectuals and artists.

When the Spanish Civil War broke out in July 1936 members of the Communist Party of Canada, with the help of leading trade unionists, were already involved in activities in support of peace and against the rise of fascism in Europe. In its mobilization in support of the left-wing Republican government in Spain, the CPC launched the Mackenzie-Papineau Battalion (MPB). The group included a wide cross-section of socialists and a significant number of labour activists, independent leftists and anti-fascists. As it grew, the Battalion began to enlist scores of office workers, students, professionals, intellectuals and artists. Most supporters of the MPB made their decision to join based on political solidarity, not necessarily or only on the imperatives of working-class or socialist politics. All in all Canada sent 1,200 men and women volunteers to Spain to fight against fascism at a time when the Canadian government "did everything in its power to stop the volunteers from going."[56]

The anti-fascist movement gained currency throughout left-wing and liberal Canadian political circles. Merrily Weisbord gives a moving account of the atmosphere within which a significant number of intellectuals committed themselves to the fight against fascism in Spain:

> Embattled Spain had become the symbol of world freedom, and young people from many countries set out to fight for the Republicans. They were housed for several weeks in a center in Paris, then taken in covered trucks to the Spanish border, where they crossed the treacherous Pyrenees on foot.... It was as if the future of the world was decided on the barricades in Spain. "Madrid will be the tomb of fascism! Shouted the Republicans. "They shall not pass! No pasaran! A "Lettre du Front" from members of the Mac-Pap Battalion, published in the Canadian communist paper *Clarte*, May 1937, read: "We can already see that the cause of democratic Spain is the cause of humanity. If the fascism is victorious here, there will be a generalized attack against the democracies of Europe.... We call on all Canadians who cherish peace and democracy to launch an appeal to save humanity from the barbarism of fascism."[57]

The shift in focus from the class-against-class policy towards the more inclusive Popular Front affected the way Canadians from different class backgrounds conceived of the notion of democracy. In other words, questions relating to what democracy implied and what political players it involved became prominent, particularly in light of the rise of fascism in Spain and the political forces that were involved both in supporting it and in fighting against it. The defence of democracy, for that matter, was now being associated with defending a democratically elected left-wing government. The pronounced neutrality and silence of several western governments in relation to what was taking place in Spain, and the explicit determination of some, including the Canadian government, to try to derail the grassroots efforts to support the legitimate elected Spanish government, threw into doubt the sincerity of their commitment to democratic values and to peace. For Canadians such as doctor Norman Bethune, Spain became the place where "the real issues of our time [were] fought out" and where "democracy [would] either die or survive."[58] A new political and cultural movement was clearly taking shape, and a growing number of Canadians were becoming involved in it.

On the one hand, Canadian intellectuals who supported the anti-fascist cause in Spain became the focus of a mass movement that galvanized major sections of the working class and a sizable segment of the middle class. On the other hand, involvement in support of this cause also helped raise the stature of numerous intellectuals and professionals. People like Norman Bethune, painter Fred Taylor, and scientist Raymond Boyer and other middle-class teachers, scientists, and professionals "worked tirelessly as fund-raisers and as committed leaders of the broad-based, united-front organizations, such as the Committee to Aid Spanish Democracy, the Civil Liberties Union, and the League Against Fascism and War."[59] Over a relatively short period of time, groups led by these individuals became well-entrenched influential organic intellectual features within Canadian society:

> Specific interest groups organized by these individuals reached further into the community; the Artists' Group; the New Theatre Group; and Norman Bethune's group for the Security of the People's Health – an organization of doctors, nurses, and social workers of various political leanings who addressed the problems of health-care for the poor and the unemployed, studied health-care systems in other countries, and made concrete proposals to the government and professional associations for more equal distribution of medical services. Fred Taylor would become an officer in the Federation of Canadian Artists, and Raymond Boyer would become president of the Canadian Association of Scientific Workers.[60]

The organic role played by these intellectuals and groups enhanced the organizational and ideological emergence and solidification of the counter-hegemonic formation and its discourse. This discourse would particularly stress the interrelationships between fighting fascism and the struggle for democracy, social justice and labour rights. NFB war films would incorporate a largely analogous approach in their analysis and outlook on the events of World War II and working-class related topics.

THE ROLE OF WOMEN AND THE DEVELOPMENT OF A NEW HISTORICAL BLOC

By 1921, women were highly visible participants in the Canadian labour market. Half of all single women in Ontario, for example, were employed outside their homes, and women in Toronto comprised close to one-third of the work force. Even in Ontario's industrial manufacturing plants that were not typically associated with female labour, women held one position in every five.[61] Despite the overwhelmingly sexist and patriarchal atmosphere of the early twentieth century, women made major contributions to the development of the Canadian labour movement as well as to the building of working-class political and cultural consciousness. Women also played major roles in the actual development of Canadian socialist and communist organizations.

Several leading labour and communist organizers between the 1920s and 1940s were women. Among those were Florence Custance, the first secretary of the Canadian Friends of Soviet Russia; Bea Colle, the secretary (leader) of the Friends of the Mackenzie-Papineau Battalion; Beckie Buhay, the editor of the early Communist Party press and a leading member of the party; Florence Theodore, leader of the Party in Saskatchewan; Jeanne Corbin, an organizer of bush-workers and miners in Northeastern Ontario and Quebec; Lea Robak and Madeleine Parent, both leading Quebec organizers in the needle trade and the electrical industries; and Annie Buller, an organizer for both the Industrial Union of Needle Trades and the Workers' Unity League, and leader in the Estevan miners' strike of 1929. These leaders were among the first Canadian women ever to gain prominence in the arena of Canadian politics, let alone among the largely male-dominated industrial sectors of the working class. With the federal elections of 1940, Dorise W. Nielsen, a candidate for the Labour Progressive Party in Saskatchewan running under the banner of a leftist coalition, became the first communist-supported candidate to be elected to the House of Commons and the only woman to be voted in during those elections.

However, the large role played by women within the Communist Party and within the labour movement as a whole was by no means indicative of an incorporation of a women's agenda per se in left-wing politics. Many current feminist historians would even claim that, if anything, such involvement by women in labour politics might even have inadvertently helped rationalize or even legitimize marginalizing women's issues in leftist politics during this period.[62] In any case, it is impossible to imagine how the role played by these pioneer working-class women activists could have enhanced anything but a major challenge to patriarchal attitudes towards women during this masculinized era in Canadian history. If anything, these women, in multiple ways, helped open the way for a better understanding of the interactivity between different types of oppression that affect society, including those based in gender. What is also certain is that the participation of women in socialist and working-class politics in the late 1920s and early 1930s also informed their subsequent partaking in and their major role in materializing counter-hegemonic Canadian cultural practices in the late 1930s and early 1940s. In the words of Douglas Parker:

> Not only did women artists and writers involved with the cultural left in Canada significantly affect the representation of women, but they also left a profound effect on Canadian culture as a whole. They were, in fact, more successful practitioners of social commentary on the 1930s than were men. Few contemporary novels capture the plight of the unemployed worker in Canada during the Depression better the Irene Baird's *Waste Heritage* (1939). Dorothy Livesay's award-winning *Day and Night* and *The Outrider* are still considered the quintessential, and most technically successful, poems of social protest from the Depression era. Anne Marriott's *The Wind Our Enemy* characterizes the hopeless optimism of the prairie farmers; Michiel Horn referred to it in his introduction to *The Dirty Thirties*. Significantly, the front cover of Bryan Palmer's *Working Class* features Paraskeva Clark's Petroushka, a painting done in 1937 and part of the permanent collection of the National Gallery of Canada.[63]

The communist-based cultural journal *New Frontier*, which succeeded *Masses*, reflected the emergence of new and more inclusive Canadian progressive politics. Of specific importance was the new journal's conscious effort to encourage and "pursue the examination of women's special oppression under patriarchy."[64] *New Frontier* exemplified an important episode in the history of the participation of women in Canadian cultural discourse:

> The brainchild of Jean "Jim" Watts, who invested her inheritance to finance the journal, *New Frontier* served as a model of equity between the sexes. At the administrative level, Jocelyn Moore served as the business manager, while the four chief editors included social worker Margaret Gould and social worker/poet Dorothy Livesay along with Leo Kennedy and J.F. White. Watt's husband, William Lawson, was given the job of managing editor. During its short life, from April 1936 to 1937, no other magazine in Canada published as many articles, poems, short stories and plays written by women, not even *Chatelaine*.[65]

The publishing of *New Frontier* represented a qualitatively critical development in the history of Canadian women's cultural practice. Equally important, it provided new perspectives on the role of women in society. While much of the earlier liberal-oriented discourse tended to de-politicize and de-class the struggle for women's liberation and equality, the new discourse injected a vigorously polemicized outlook on the interactivity between women's liberation, social change, fighting fascism, and democracy.

Popular Front policies enhanced the creation of a social movement that challenged fundamental aspects of hegemonic political and cultural discourse in Canada. In this context these policies provided viable discursive mechanisms for building a counter-hegemonic historical bloc in Canada. They also became part of an organic intellectual practice, which enhanced the emergence of a counter-hegemonic cultural discourse. Building on vibrant connections with the working class since the 1920s, labour and socialist activists in the mid- to late 1930s sought to make art more relevant to the major political issues of the day. With the help of favourable domestic and international political conditions, the Popular Front and its political and organizational outlook on Canadian and international politics helped reshape the cultural dynamics of Canadian society. Many writers, poets, theatre workers and actors, as well as workers in other fields of culture, became convinced of the need for an alternative stance on politics and culture. In turn, the movement enhanced the development of a new cinematic culture which itself remains a unique feature in Canadian film history. The films produced by the NFB in the early years of its creation interacted with this movement's counter-hegemonic and working-class-based ideological, aesthetic, and political outlook.

The next chapter locates the third source of the emerging counter-hegemonic discourse in the NFB's own working context: the formation of a group of organic intellectuals within the National Film Board of Canada itself. While there are very few indications or evidence of direct organizational linkages between the Communist Party – or any Popular Front organizational affiliates for that matter – and specific workers and filmmakers of the Board during the early years of its establishment (no doubt, this would be an important subject for future investigation), the body of film produced by the NFB had the undeniable signature of an intellectual group collective that was clearly informed by the views put forward by the Popular Front – particularly in connection with the role of the working class in Canadian society.

4 THE ESTABLISHMENT OF THE NFB: A POLITICAL AND INSTITUTIONAL OVERVIEW

In addition to forging what later came to be pronounced as the symbol of "Canada's cultural particularity and creative potential,"[1] the 1939 establishment of the National Film Board of Canada (NFB) also spawned the first Canadian motion picture framework to advance a left-oriented estimation of the role and position of labour and the working class in society and politics. This role found its roots in the increased levels and multiple forms of working-class and leftist political and cultural activities during the 1920s and 1930s. The NFB's film discourse, however, came to life also as a direct result of the role played by a group of organic intellectual filmmakers and artists, who were able to bring to fruition a new cinematic practice in connection with working-class politics.

This chapter surveys the history of the establishment of the NFB. It points out elements in the Board's early working practices and how they contributed to the shaping of its discourse on labour and working-class issues. This includes a brief survey of the transfer of power from the Canadian Government Motion Picture Bureau to the NFB, the artistic and political background of some of the key NFB founders and filmmakers during its early years, the NFB's method of film distribution, and the paradoxical role played by the government and how it allowed for this discourse to materialize.

While several Canadian artists working in areas such as writing, painting, and theatre were already part of the cultural climate that emerged during the years of increased social and political activism of the late 1920s to the late 1930s, there were no indications that a similar group was forming in the area of filmmaking. Irrespective of the reasons behind this lack of direct involvement of Canadian filmmakers or film practices in the cultural activities of the left during the earlier years of Canadian cinema – we should not underestimate the extent to which the marginalized position of Canadian film production itself in this period might have contributed to this lack of involvement – the fact is that before John Grierson began to put together the NFB's production team, there were no signals of any Canadian filmmakers or artists using film to deal with or promote a labour or working-class perspective on the issues of the day. However, as we saw in earlier chapters, the NFB was created at a historical moment when a working-class-based and socialist-oriented political and cultural environment had already taken hold among important groups of Canadian intellectuals and artists. The influence of Popular Front policy pronouncements – particularly its emphasis on uniting the effort to fight fascism, to defend democracy, and to support workers and their role in advancing the cause of social change – added a further ingredient to the front's role as a new mass working-class-based and led historical bloc.

There is no doubt that the changing political priorities of the Canadian government vis-à-vis the war in Europe, and its eventual support for mobilizing workers for the war effort against fascism (clearly, the government saw this mobilization as serving its own political agenda on the war), played a major role in giving legitimacy to a fundamental ingredient of a Popular Front policy. However, the NFB's own institutional dynamics were variously and increasingly influenced by the radicalization of many intellectuals both inside and outside Canada. The new cultural atmosphere in the country shaped how NFB films dealt with working-class politics, and eventually how those films became informed by the discourse of the Popular Front.

FROM THE MOTION PICTURE BUREAU TO THE NFB

Originally, the National Film Board was established as a coordinating and supervising agency. While the Act that founded the Film Board, and which Grierson helped to draft, did not give the Board any given production role, there were in fact no official constraints imposed on the NFB against the institution's own ambitions in this regard. What happened is that the NFB had no authority over the actual production of films; film production remained the responsibility of the twenty-year-old Canadian Government Motion Picture Bureau (CGMPB), headed at the time by military Captain Frank Badgley. The transfer of responsibilities between the two agencies occurred in 1941 after a struggle from which John Grierson, the appointed head of the NFB, came out the clear winner.

Although the CGMPB was an operation of the Ministry of Trade and Commerce, various film projects were determined greatly by other government bodies such as the Department of Agriculture. Later, John Grierson cited the effects of such bureaucratic hurdles and complications among the reasons behind his push for the centralization of government film production. His recommendation was to create a committee that would become the National Film Board of Canada. This committee would reinforce government filmmaking beyond the current limitations of the Motion Picture Bureau. The Board eventually assumed responsibility for the government's dissemination of wartime information as a government agency and as a film production unit. It also replaced the Motion Picture Bureau and absorbed its staff members.[2]

The transfer of power from the CGMPB to the NFB had its own political significance. It signalled the economic and political establishment's recognition of the Board's relative autonomy. This autonomy gave the NFB a certain leeway, which later allowed it to produce a body of films that largely offered a Popular Front vision, rather than solely the government's take on issues relating to working-class politics. However, the transfer of power between these two government agencies did not occur without a major battle. During this battle, Grierson offered a letter of resignation to the Chairman of the Film Board. In a letter dated November 27, 1940, Grierson complained that bureaucratic mentality presented a major obstacle to the goals set for the war mobilization:

> Most governments are finding it necessary to use increasingly such media as radio and film, and everywhere one notices the same tug-of-war. On the one hand, the Civil Servants with their formalities of government regulation; on the other hand, the creative people protesting that Civil Service procedure weakens the vitality and paralyzes the initiative which are necessary for good work. One notices that wherever the weight of influence has lain with the civil Service, the spark has gone out and the use of the creative media has not been remarkable.[3]

Eventually, Grierson retracted his resignation, and the outcome of the battle was finally determined when, on 11 June 1941, the federal government issued an order in council converting authority over the Motion Picture Bureau to the National Film Board of Canada. Grierson's success in this initial confrontation set the stage for his relative autonomy over the NFB's operations and allowed him significant creative and administrative control over the publicly funded agency. Coincidentally, Grierson's victory in getting the government's nod of approval occurred within a few days of Hitler's launch of Operation Barbarossa against the Soviet Union on June 22, 1941.

This event signalled the emergence of the new Soviet-Western alliance, particularly after Churchill came to power in Britain and eventually declared that anyone who fought Hitler was an ally. It also helped end the first phase of the war, which was largely labelled as the "phony war." Today, the phrase "phony war" commonly refers to the Western Front from September 1939 to May 1940, when Anglo-French and German forces faced each other across fixed lines and almost no military activity occurred while the Germans were busy in Poland then later Norway. Germans, in a rare moment of levity, referred to this period as the "Sitzkrieg." However, and as far as the left at the time was concerned, this phrase described what it saw as the lack of seriousness in how the west was conducting its battle against fascism. As we will see in our later analysis of the Board's films, the involvement of the Soviet Union in the war would enhance the propagation of a Popular Front view on the role of labour in fighting fascism, including an implicit verdict of the west's earlier lack of seriousness in fighting fascism.

An important aspect of Grierson's own difference with the CGMPB was his dismay at the agency's reluctance to recognize its acute responsibility in fighting fascism. For Grierson, CGMPB's head Frank Badgley represented "a recalcitrant bureaucrat who didn't seem to realize there was a war on."[4] In hindsight, this was neither a far-fetched accusation by Grierson, nor, for that matter, a politically innocent one. For many activists on the left, Canadian and western political establishments were conceived as phony in their fight against fascism. By 1940, the term *Phony War* was widely used by the left to refer to what they saw as the non-serious manner in which the West was conducting its war against Germany. Describing how the British establishment conceived of its war against Germany up until that point, Basil Wright for example writes:

> It was the period of the phony war, and the so-called Ministry of Information [in Britain] was being run by hard-nosed, soft-headed Conservative bureaucrats who were determined to do nothing to help the war effort. They also put a memorandum to all government departments saying that everybody in documentary was a communist.[5]

However, the newly created alliance with the Soviet Union became critical in changing the NFB's film discourse both on the war and on labour. It became an important framework within which this discourse complemented the ideas of the Popular Front on a wide range of social and political issues including those related to the working class. Grierson's assumption of control over the CGMPF signalled a symbolic victory over the more conservative members of the Canadian cultural establishment, some of whom (as we saw earlier in our discussion of the film institutions of the mid-1930s) might have had a soft spot as far as their feelings towards fascism were concerned.

THE GRIERSON TEAM AND
THE POLITICS OF SOCIAL ACTIVISM

There is no evidence of any direct influence by left-wing activists in the arena of Canadian film production activity prior to the establishment of the NFB. Yet, the creation of the NFB occurred during a period of increased artistic and intellectual involvement in working-class and left politics in Canada. Furthermore, the importation of a mostly foreign group of intellectuals and filmmakers to help set up the NFB's operation – many of whom had variable levels of familiarity and sympathy with, and in some cases direct involvement in left-wing politics – could not have been a neutral element in how NFB films eventually perceived the local and international politics of the late 1930s and early 1940s.

In 1938, at the invitation of the Canadian government, documentary filmmaker John Grierson was brought to Canada to assess the government's film production activity. His report became the pretext that led to creation of the NFB. By 1939, the Canadian House of Commons voted on an Act defining the new agency's purpose as the making and distributing of films "designated to help Canadians in all parts of Canada to understand the ways of living and the problems of Canadians in other parts." Grierson was appointed as Canada's first Film Commissioner.[6]

There are, however, paradoxes associated with John Grierson's politics and ideology and his role within the NFB. For example, while Grierson's position as an administrator of a government agency influenced his method of work and made him at times appear heavy-handed in his control, his vision of the NFB as a tool to address social issues became a positive factor that contributed to the agency's function as a collective and as a bearer of grassroots-oriented political discourse.

The Act which initiated the creation of the NFB complemented Grierson's own emphasis in respect to issues of social responsibility. It provided a base which supported Grierson's interest in social problems and modified the government's earlier preoccupation with battling American influence over Canada's national culture and values.[7] In fact, Grierson had no qualms about making his views clear on the issue of nationalism. As far as he was concerned, it was "the curse of the nations that every one of them should be so insistent on its own unique and special virtues."[8] For Grierson, rejecting nationalist views comprised an important aspect of political thinking. It was also an element of tension in his relationship with the Canadian political establishment. As we will note later, while this tension was not allowed to surface during the initial years of the NFB, it certainly became one of the points which haunted Grierson during his later unceremonious departure from Canadian public service.

Grierson's views on national identity, and on defining the role of the NFB in the context of a cordial relationship with the United States, have been the subject of some the criticisms by Canadian film scholars including, as we earlier saw, Joyce Nelson. Once again, it is the kind of criticism that mainly stems from failing to appreciate the historical moment within which Grierson and the NFB were operating. What such criticisms fail to acknowledge, for example, is how the subject of nationalism in the 1930s played politically in conjunction with the rise of fascism. The main argument by people on the left against fascism was that it accentuated nationalism as a basis for oppressing people and to substitute for social protest. In this regard the left argued that the nationalist rhetoric itself was a tool in the hands of the ruling classes to combat the rising influence of the working class and its political parties.

The battle against fascism shifted the focus of the left away from what might have been, under different circumstances, a more accommodating attitude towards the positive aspects of the national question, for example, in connection with issues of anti-colonial struggle and national self-determination. But, the liberation potential of national struggles during this particular period was more or less largely limited to combating colonialism in underdeveloped countries (the 1937 Japanese invasion of China constituted one example of such struggle), while attempts to use nationalist rhetoric in the context of advanced capitalist societies (most of which were basically imperialist countries themselves) seemed problematic. Furthermore, nationalism for the most part was already a political domain that was being used by fascist parties and groups in many advanced capitalist countries as a pretext for fomenting racial and ethnic hatred.

The political agenda of labour and the political left in Britain and Canada focused on the social aspect of fighting fascism and its nationalist rhetoric. In this context, people like Grierson were uncomfortable with the idea of stressing national identity. Instead, their interest lay in addressing social problems and concerns including those relating to the working classes. While the NFB's output under Grierson was aimed at nation building, these films' perspective vis-à-vis the idea of nation building did not subscribe to narrow royalist chauvinisms. Instead, NFB films conceived of Canada's national identity as one in process. In one of his speeches Grierson discussed his outlook on this issue:

> Canada is a young nation which has not yet found herself but is to-day in the
> exciting process of doing so. I like to think that the breathless reception given the

King and Queen for the first time a ceremonial opportunity of raising her young national face to the sunlight.[9]

But what contemporary artists and social activists admired most about Grierson was what they saw as his ability to venture beyond intellectual ivory towers and get closer to the day-to-day problems of average people. Grierson's work in Britain, particularly his work at the General Post Office, became an example of his capacity to use film to depict the working-class subject. In 1937, citing Grierson's role in the production of *Industrial Britain, Coalface, Housing Problems,* and *Night Mail* among others, filmmaker Alberto Cavalcanti expressed esteem for Grierson's contribution to forging a neo-realist movement in cinema:

> In England, Grierson, who bore the full moral responsibility of the [neo-realist] movement on his shoulders, began quite simply by trying to be useful; and Marxist doctrines certainly supported him. The sad history of the avant-garde's errors cannot be rehearsed here: Grierson had his entourage make documentaries on fishermen, or craftsmen, on subjects taken at last from reality.[10]

Under Grierson's leadership within British film circles of the 1930s, the role of the filmmaker assumed a new dimension: that of the social activist. As Jim Beveridge points out in reference to the climate within which Grierson developed and worked, filmmakers were "informed and impelled by a feeling of obligation to 'put things right' – the 'things' being problems such as social and economic injustice, those wrongs within society the continuing existence of which became more and more galling and dangerous as frustrations grew at home and fascism grew on the continent of Europe and elsewhere."[11]

But Grierson's views did not sit well with the British ruling class, which was glad when he eventually decided to leave Britain for Canada. The Ministry of Information in Britain was itself run by conservative bureaucrats who were more interested in cleaning up government departments of what they saw as communists than in fighting fascism.[12] Grierson's interest in tackling issues of social justice and in linking them to the fight against fascism took shape during a period when ideological dichotomies were sharply splitting the views of intellectuals both inside and outside the realm of cultural practice. His own views on the use of film as a social agitator have their roots in an eclectic incorporation of socialist ideas and his personal interest in working-class politics. A student colleague, Charles Dand, describes Grierson's early interest in Marxism and the Russian Revolution:

He was a great admirer of Lenin and Trotsky, more of the latter. He was more interested than most of us in the tremendous social experiment then starting in Russia. None of us, however, ever thought of labelling him as a Communist . . . It was not the methods of organization and government that seemed to draw him, but the hopes the Russian experiment raised of a power-house of reconstruction, a new release and orientation of human energies. It was this conception of revolutionary possibilities that he found in Trotsky, and it was one of the inspirations of his approach to documentary film. Another was his feeling of kinship with the miners and farm-workers among whom he had grown up as a boy and the sailors and fishermen with whom he had lived and worked during his war service and which was also evident in his student days.[13]

Formally, Grierson's interest in the work of early Soviet filmmakers was among the formative elements of cinema's appeal for him. The 1929 film *Drifters*, a film which was the most associated with Grierson's name and which he himself directed and produced, largely reflected the formal experimentations of early Soviet filmmakers. The film itself was chosen to accompany *The Battleship Potemkin* at the premier presentation of the Soviet film in London.[14] Grierson's aesthetic vision that shaped his attention to documentary film practice was also informed by other elements in working-class and socialist culture, including the related theatre movement that grew in Europe in the 1920s:

> [this movement recaptured] the general principles of documentary theatre as it first evolved in Germany in the 1920s, mainly through the work of Irwin Piscator. It was in reference to Piscator's "epic theatre" that Brecht first applied the word "documentary" to the theatre in 1926 – in the same year that John Grierson coined the word in English to describe the films of Robert Flaherty.[15]

Later on, early NFB films produced under the auspices of John Grierson became the first Canadian films to publicly acknowledge and inadvertently make use of the theory and techniques that were laid down both by socialist-oriented filmmakers of the French avant-garde and by the early Soviet montage school.

On the political level, Grierson contributed to the activities of the communist-inspired workers' film movement. This movement sought to provide a theoretical pretext for the creation of a working-class film discourse. Grierson, for example, was among the star participants in the London Workers' Film Society's (LWFS) first summer school. The Marxist press commented on the school's presentations and discussions, and praised their success in "thrashing out the ideological as well as the practical basis for the Workers' film Movement in Britain."[16] Furthermore, Grierson always saw more in film than the commodity profit value imposed in the context of capitalist production relations:

> To some, it is "the film business," which is to say, a business like any other, making profits. Profits depend on the box office and a carefully calculated estimate of what people in the theatre are hungry for: sex and heroism, comedy and adventure, day dreams and romance.[17]

For Grierson, the use of film complemented the work of the social activist in exploring and intervening in social and political struggles. It also provided a forum to encourage public discussion of those issues. Within this framework "Grierson liked to describe his politics as 'one inch to the left' of the government' in office." It was also within this framework that he later began to recruit his NFB colleagues and workers, citing the need to build "a school of progressive (or left-wing, depending upon whose characterizations were involved) young film makers."[18]

I do not, however, suggest that Grierson's early interest in Marxist ideas, the Russian Revolution, the experiments of Soviet filmmakers and his preoccupation with social issues indicated some sort of commitment to Marxism or to Marxist politics. Neither do I suggest that his work fully agreed with the views of the Communist International (related accusations later did surface when Grierson became the subject of an FBI investigation in the mid-1940s). At best, Grierson's commitment to leftist and Marxist politics was eclectic and always considerate of the fine lines that were to be walked in order to remain compatible with his job as a government official. As contemporary filmmaker Joris Ivens attests (Ivens worked with Grierson during the early years of the NFB), what informed Grierson's passion for making films that were conscious of social issues also accommodated a spiritual ideological aspect to it:

> He's a man who was very well read, he read Marx, Lenin, Mao Tse-tung. And sometimes he was a strange man, eh? When he saw a Communist, he quoted the Bible, and when he saw Catholics, he quoted Lenin. I only say that to characterize Grierson, because he was a man who knew a lot, but who, as I said before, went less far in his work.[19]

Grierson's eclectic approach is best exemplified in how he saw the world "entering upon a new and interim society which is neither capitalist nor socialist but in which we can achieve central planning without loss of individual initiative... in which public unity and discipline can be achieved without forgetting the human virtues."[20] However, this seemingly paradoxical view did fit well with the non-sectarian approach of working-class politics as advocated by the Communist Party at the time, but without the latter's conception of this mixture of social systems as an early stage which would pave the way for subsequent socialist transformation. This view that was politically centrist, yet remained at least open to considering socialism as a possible alternative, eventually became the heart of the working-class oriented discourse of a significant number of early NFB films.

Popular Front policies sought to galvanize a heterogeneous social and political movement which went beyond the limitations of class and sectarian party politics and was able to initiate a broad democratic anti-fascist historical bloc. As such, the policies of the front created the basis for an inclusive counter-hegemonic movement. Citing how Grierson himself saw his role in the context of such a movement, Rodrigue Chiasson recalls a conversation with Grierson:

> I asked him, in the course of our conversations, how deliberately he had set out to nurture and develop the documentary-film movement. He replied, "you'd better believe that it was deliberate, and it wasn't just making films, whatever that is. It was social movement."[21]

With this vision, Grierson set out to put together his team to carry out the task of building the NFB.

Several participants in Grierson's NFB team were members of the British documentary film movement, the group that he was active with before he came to Canada. They included the young and well trained team of Stuart Legg, Evelyn Spice, J.D. Davidson, Stanley Hawes, Basil Wright and Raymond Spottiswoode as well as film animator Norman McLaren. In turn this group of experienced filmmakers trained several Canadian apprentices such as James Beveridge, Tom Daly, and Louis Applebaum. The staff of the NFB quickly grew from a five-member team at the initial stage to more than eight hundred people by 1945.[22]

Among the key talents hired by Grierson was Stuart Legg. A pioneer of the British film documentary tradition, Legg became the second in command in Grierson's production unit and came to direct sixteen and produce forty-one films for the Board in the period between 1939 and 1945. Describing the atmosphere within which he undertook the task of producing early NFB films, Legg delineated the shadow of the crisis that was hanging over advanced capitalist countries at the time: "it was a complicated situation moving into possibly revolutionary situation. There was the Depression, there was enormous unemployment, with the whole economy rather undermined, and so on."[23] He then described the political and intellectual climate which influenced his and the views of youth:

> It was a situation where the opinions of young people were formulated to address the possibilities of fundamental economic and political change, and what many of them moved towards was the left of the political spectrum: Young people were left in those days, probably more orthodoxly so than now [1978]. That's all there is to say about it.[24]

Just two years before he joined the Motion Picture Bureau, Legg, in association with the British communist writer F.D. Klingender, contributed to what amounted to be the first comprehensive attempt to write a Marxist interpretation of the economics of the film industry between the wars (the 1937 book, titled *Money Behind the Screen*, is currently out of print and available only through the book collection of the Communist Party of Britain, the New Communist Party of Britain, and private book collections of party members).

Another of Grierson's colleagues in the early years of the NFB was Joris Ivens. The Dutch filmmaker worked at the Board in 1943 directing and producing the film *Action Stations* (the film was also produced in another version titled *Corvette Port Arthur*). Ivens's early work included the late 1920s filming of revolutionary events in cooperation with the workers' newsreel movement in his native Holland. He later went on to work in a variety of projects including documenting issues and problems of socialist construction in the Soviet Union in 1932. Ivens later directed the now infamous documentary on the Spanish Civil War, *Spanish Earth* (1937). The film involved wide artistic and political support from left-wing intellectuals in the United States such as Lillian Hellman.

Ivens's account of his own work as a filmmaker subscribes to an approach which stresses the fusion of cinematic practice with political and social activism. This, he argued, only occurred in the context of revolutionizing the means of film practice:

> I started more from the aesthetic, artistic point of view. I was part of the avant-gardist movement in Europe, with Paris, with Berlin – then into this artistic movement came realism. That was the influence of the Russian film-makers such as Eisenstein, Pudovkin, Dovzhenko. And my work was also influenced by the work of Flaherty. And then with these realisms I started to associate myself with

the social problems of my own country and other countries in Europe, and I made a film about the coal miners' strike in Belgium. I was for the workers and for the strike.[25]

Eventually, many of the activists from the earlier years of the 1930s drifted to the NFB. Among those were Hazen Sise, P.K. Page, Guy Glover, Irene Baird, Mavis Gallant, as well as Lawrence Cherry and Evelyn Spice Cherry, both of whom made numerous films at the NFB during the war years. Earlier films made by the Cherrys before they joined the NFB included material that was already manifesting elements that expressed social and class consciousness and preoccupation. Two important films made for the Saskatchewan Wheat Pool in 1940 come to mind here: *New Horizons* and *By Their Own Strength*.

However, Grierson's own fixation with creating a socially conscious film institution transcended the recruitment of filmmakers. He made a concerted effort to recruit artists and other workers who saw their task at the Board as more than a job. According to Louis Applebaum, a musician who wrote the scores for hundreds of the early NFB films:

> The government looked upon us as not only outsiders, but also as potential rebels. The word "Communist" was associated with all kinds of people at the Film Board, almost from day one. I don't remember whether we ever went through an RCMP check to get the job, but Grierson was grabbing people right and left – people who had a social conscience and had the energy to do something about society . . . The more activist they were, the better film-makers they were going to be. They were going to generate public involvement in what was going on.[26]

The NFB Commissioner sought people who saw filmmaking as means to promote social and economic justice, and did that in spite of the bureaucratic unease about his approach.

On another level, largely among NFB workers and technicians, the Communist Party itself seem to have had some actual organized presence, but this can only be corroborated through second-hand accounts. Marjorie McKay, an employee of the NFB at the time, claims that aside from the fact that the overwhelming majority of the people who worked in the Board were social activists, there were also at least two party cells within the NFB by the early 1940s.[27] Yet, while communists might have indeed become active within the NFB, ideas about the role of film as social agitator were clearly influencing people beyond party circles. The political and ideological framework for how NFB films saw the war against fascism and the building of a society based on collective democratic values and international cooperation and peace was largely being informed by broad discursive formations that were galvanizing numerous artists and intellectuals both inside and outside the NFB.

SCREENING FILM ON THE GRASSROOTS LEVEL

The logistics of bringing a film to its intended audience was for Grierson as critical as the message it put forward. Grierson allotted major efforts to providing an effective base for distributing and screening NFB films. Eventually the Board designed and implemented a networking system that reached a large cross-section of urban and rural communities. The manner in which the NFB films were screened became in itself part of the board's strategy of making film responsive to the needs and concerns of its audience. One important aspect of this strategy was screening films on the grassroots community level and having them discussed and debated by audiences. Working-class, rural, and citizen film circuits created by the NFB by the early 1940s (and later renamed the Volunteer Projection Services) provided forums for hundreds of thousands of Canadians to view and discuss political and social issues raised in the films.

Clearly, Grierson understood that the NFB's success was not simply contingent on producing films. Among the most important challenges for Grierson was to make sure that films reached their targeted audience, and that they eventually made some impact on their understanding of the issues that were being discussed. At a time when television was not yet widely available to households in North America, film was already a major mass communication tool. Film therefore was the only moving picture medium that was widely accessible to the general public, and Grierson realized this very well. The NFB's success in bringing its films to where people could conveniently view and discuss them represented an atypical approach from what Canadians were used to when they watched them in commercial theatrical outlets. John Grierson advocated using film as an information tool and as a means to create a two-way communication connection between the people and the state. This meant inspiring rather than preaching to people.

In an effort to publicize NFB films, Grierson built upon an already growing film exhibition practice in Canada. During the 1920s and 1930s, private companies as well as cooperative movements were already utilizing rural film screening circuits.[28] Local film societies in urban centres such as Toronto, Vancouver and Ottawa, were also beginning to organize their own screening of films that were not successful in reaching commercial theatres.[29]

Grierson instructed Donald Buchanan, the director of the Central Government Distribution Service to help form and expand cross-Canada non-theatrical circuits to screen the material produced by the NFB. Buchanan eventually developed an innovative non-theatrical system of distribution and screening which worked outside of the commercial movie theatre outlets. It involved showing films to groups such as working-class unions, farm workers, and other smaller rural communities and centres. Films were shown indoors, or, weather permitting, outdoors. In many cases, film screenings allowed communities to come together in a picnic-like atmosphere, which involved, in addition to having fun, watching the film and discussing it, and an opportunity to meet each other and discuss their collective concerns. Considering that the films shown were themselves developed with such communities in mind, these films allowed "people to see people like them, rather than the Hollywood never-never land of fantasy."[30] As workers from the Board attended the screenings and led the discussions on the films, meetings virtually became exercises in grassroots democratic participation and in proactive use of cinema. While there were plans to carry these events into the post-war period by way of stimulating discussions on issues of social economic reconstruction, the changing political climate was beginning to shift in another direction. As Whitaker and Marcuse suggest, as "exciting as their ideas were to many Canadians, to others, powerful persons among them, they were subversive and revolutionary notions."[31]

By mid-1942 the number of travelling circuits within rural communities rose to forty-three, with a monthly viewing audience of up to quarter million people.[32] Each circuit was assigned the monthly task of presenting films in twenty rural schools, village halls and other public community sites, and to return the same day of the next month for another screening to the same community.[33] Considering that the majority of the rural population at the time had no access to any kind of theatrical screening, the task undertaken by the NFB represented a monumental leap in bringing film to a substantial number of new Canadian audience. After the films were screened, debates followed, with discussion notes and leaflets provided by NFB employees.[34] While most of the information was "used to develop effective propaganda campaigns," nevertheless,

> The schemes were intrinsically difficult to control from the center because of the geographical distances involved. Open debate often broke out around issues raised in the films shown, and the screenings also functioned as social events, allowing locals, as opposed to national, concerns to be aired.[35]

NFB distributors paid special attention to bringing those films to people of working-class background. The success of such endeavours relied on creating a structured link with the labour movement and its activists on the grassroots level.

The NFB specifically co-sponsored a labour-based National Trade Union film circuit, which involved the Trades and Labour Congress, the Canadian Congress of Labour, and the Workers Education Association.[36] The program was officially inaugurated in January 1943. The labour film circuits functioned in a similar manner to the Board's rural circuits. Leaders and activists from major unions helped prepare and mobilize for the screenings.[37] The films were screened between September and May "as part of the branch activity of the trade union movement," and were conducted in union halls "partly on company time partly on lunch breaks and/or between work shifts."[38] All together, there were more than sixty-six NFB traveling projectionists serving in the industrial and trade union film circuits. Those projectionists covered more than 300 union locals in eighty-four districts across Canada, and a total of 385,000 factory workers every month.[39] This, however, could not have been achieved without a concerted effort and support on the part of activists on the grassroots level.

Organized labour played a critical role in initiating and encouraging the screening of NFB films. By the early 1940s, the most active elements within the trade union movement were in full support of the war effort and the work of the Wartime Information Board. Labour support was expressed "not only through their union membership, but also through other related community agencies."[40]

The screening of NFB films among working-class and rural communities became part of concerted national political efforts. Activists from the labour and left movements made a major effort to mobilize in support of the war in Europe, particularly after 1941 when the Soviet Union entered the war, a war they also saw as one in defence of democracy, labour rights, and in favour of the cooperative reorganization of society.

With Hitler's invasion of the Soviet Union in mid-1941, militant labour leadership in coordination with the Communist-Labour Total War Committees organized a Canada-wide mobilization in support of the war against fascism.[41] The activities by those committees provided a stronger political and organizational base for the working class's direct involvement in the war effort. It also facilitated a wide grassroots buttress for linking the NFB film circuits with a large number of the audience they were aiming to reach.

By 1945, members of three hundred union locals in eighty-four districts were attending regular screenings and discussions of NFB films. The films offered a new outlook on the nature and the importance of unity in the war against fascism and its significance for working-class Canadians. The films also rejuvenated an atmosphere of optimism about the future. They contemplated the possibility of establishing a new cooperative society to replace the chaotic past of war and the Great Depression. Doris Rands, whose husband was fired from the NFB during the Cold War purges, offers a picture of this mood:

> My husband, Stan, worked in adult education in Manitoba and used the films of the NFB as tools for community organizing, farm organizing, and all kinds of grassroots work.... I remember people used to stay up all night talking about what could be done around the Film Board and what good could be done with documentary films. When the purge happened they stopped doing that and the atmosphere around the NFB changed from high creativity and optimism to caution and fear.[42]

Most films stressed the central role of working people in the growth of Canadian industry and in the development of the country's natural resources. They pointed to the impact of manual work in the success of the war effort in Europe and in the preparation for post-war rebuilding. Films' themes included unemployment, recreational programs, rehabilitation, industrial development, labour safety, labour-management coordination, and international relations.

As a result of this concerted effort and even without counting the above-mentioned considerable non-theatrical audience, Canadian weekly attendance for NFB war films is claimed to have reached one-third of the entire Canadian population.[43] This, no doubt, contributed to the organic function of these films, and made a major impact on the way they operated as part of a larger counter-hegemonic movement. This organic role did not simply relate to the themes and views that were presented by these films, but also to their grassroots impact, including the participation of working people in discussions around the social and political issues that were being presented.

Film discussions offered people further opportunities to raise their own views on the social and political issues of the day. As such, the NFB film circuits opened new venues for interactive communication about the films; they became nuclei for political interaction on the grassroots level. Eventually, this process solidified even further the functionary role of these films as organs for political activism and organization.

Many of the films, particularly those aimed at labour groups, included special discussion trailers that proposed ways to follow up on the issues that they dealt with. Those trailers also involved the participation of ordinary trade unionists giving their point of view on the film being discussed and often indulged the audience by posing questions for further discussion. In a way, the films were entwined with union education work and became integral to the political culture of working-class people.

In a 1944 article about the policy of encouraging discussion among the audience, Donald Buchanan, who was in charge of expanding the distribution of NFB film in non-theatrical outlets, stresses that the idea was to move the audience to a higher stage of interaction which itself would make a film live beyond the immediacy of its screening:

> That is how the value of the Canadian documentary movie appears, not as an entity in itself, but as part of a larger entity. Those who direct, photograph, edit, and prepare a film for 16 mm distribution, are only the first participants in its creation as a living object. The men and women who finally bring it to life and useful activity are those who project that particular movie; in some small hall, some factory or club room, and so relate its values to local needs and aspiration.[44]

The ultimate goal, Buchanan points out, was to spur people to group activity and action in their dealing with the issues discussed in the films.

On one occasion, an NFB field representative filed a report describing how six local citizens took the platform with him after the screening of a film. The viewers initiated a half-hour intermission discussion, in which "criticism was not lacking," but was also "quite intelligent and the discussions always took a decidedly positive direction. Very constructive consideration of social issues came to the fore." Similar reports by NFB representatives were regular, and they allowed Grierson and his staff "to keep their fingers on the pulse of public opinion and to measure, in part, the effect of the NFB's propaganda."[45]

By allowing people to provide their own critical viewpoint on the films and their subjects, the films became tools for proactive education. As such, films sought to advance views rather than preach them. They also encouraged ideas about democratic practice within the workplace and in relation to political life in the country. Gary Evans compares this process to Marshall McLuhan's vision of the global village:

> This was a way of making citizens part of the active democratic process. Grierson's idea of totalitarian propaganda, the two-way communication between the governing and the governed, was an application of what Marshall McLuhan would later call the "global village" concept. Film, education, and discussion linked the human-ness and one-ness of the individual human being in his own environment with the world as a whole.[46]

But while comparing McLuhan's vision of the global village to how Grierson saw the function and the role of interactive communication is debatable, what is more certain is that those who advocated Popular Front policies made substantial efforts to champion the use of interactive forms of cultural practice. As we saw earlier, by the late 1930s ideas about using art as a tool for social and political action were already integral to labour and left-wing cultural practices in Canada. Indeed, Popular Front policy supporters conceived of these practices as genuine alternatives to what they viewed as one-sided bourgeois manipulation of media and film.

THE PARADOXICAL ROLE OF THE GOVERNMENT

One of the paradoxes of the counter-hegemonic function of the NFB films during the war years is how they effectively pioneered this remarkable effort, considering that the NFB was, after all, the propaganda agency of a capitalist government that was not even social-democratic in orientation. Therefore, to understand how the discourse of early NFB films on the working-class came to exist, one also needs to account for the way this discourse complemented, yet modified for its own purposes, the fundamentally different political goals of the Canadian government.

As we saw earlier, the government had already recognized the importance of film as a political propaganda tool capable of shaping public opinion. It had also recognized the futility of trying to compete with the American film production giants for any major share or control over the feature film production industry. On another level, the Canadian film industry itself was now content with controlling the lion's share of the film distribution and theatre market. By the time the National Film Board of Canada was officially created in 1939, the idea of launching an educational vehicle to promote the views of the government to Canadians was widely accepted within the Canadian political establishment. For Canadian film producers, and since the Canadian Government Motion Picture Bureau (CGMPB) did not have its own production facilities and the NFB was not yet supposed to be producing films, the idea of getting government contracts to produce educational films represented a viable alternative under the circumstances. Little those producers knew in 1939 about Grierson's intention to have the Board become the main producer of most government films. Grierson's final battle with the (CGMPB) sealed this role for the NFB by 1941.

The government's tolerance of the NFB's advocacy of a proactive role for labour can be partially traced to the interest in mobilizing public support for the war. In addition, the government was conscious of the need to defuse any potential labour and social tensions, both during and after the war (i.e. in the context of reintegrating workers into the post-war social and economic restructuring process). The main framework for the NFB's mission between 1939 and 1945 – at least as far as the government was concerned – was to support the war effort, and later to help ease the process of reintegrating servicemen into civilian life.[47] The films produced by the NFB might have gone further in what they professed politically but they certainly did not contradict or present, as such, any hindrance to the government's overall objective.

As we saw earlier, a level of consensus within the Canadian establishment over the role of government as an educator was already manifest in the pronouncements of Canadian cultural institutions such as the National Council of Education and the National Film Society. In itself, such a role was not necessarily contradictory to the goals set by the Grierson team in the NFB. What differentiated this team's own agenda from that of the establishment was in defining what constituted an educational government role, and what goals the government wanted to stress in an educational film. The definition was eventually left to Grierson to elaborate and to implement. Grierson himself would later pay the price for implanting his own interpretations when it came to educational goals and practices.

In addition to its war preoccupations and its interest in maintaining social peace in the country, the Liberal government's non-confrontational attitude towards labour can be linked also to the fact that labour's role and strength were already part of the new reality in Canadian politics. As I mentioned earlier, a critical factor in the Liberal Party's success in the 1935 elections against the Conservatives directly related to its denunciation of Prime Minister Bennett's belligerent and confrontational attitude towards labour and the unemployed in the early and mid-1930s. Acknowledging the role of labour as part of new Canadian political scene was not only necessary, but also crucial for implementing the government's own war-mobilization strategy.

Another factor that might have influenced the government's tolerance towards the NFB relates to the personal and political agenda of Prime Minister King himself. King's own personal insecurities might have alerted him to the role of the Board as a potential publicity tool. In this regard, the pressures of the war and King's related personal political ambitions might have had an impact on how he eventually decided to give the NFB a relatively free creative hand. As Gary Evans suggests:

> Looking at film propaganda and information in total, (Grierson had become head of the Wartime Information Board in 1943) Prime Minister King and his Government may have been convinced that what Grierson was doing was

worthwhile in the context of the war. Besides, the Prime Minister was benefiting from frequent publicity which disguised his usual awkward manner before the public – Opposition critics had complained that images of King Government propaganda were as numerous as the posterity of Abraham! More likely, the King Government was too busy to devote time or interest to information policy. In fact, it was amazing what the NFB got away with, Stuart Legg admitted years later.[48]

Clearly, the Board did not hurt King politically, and, if anything, helped him sustain a level of support that could only gain from the publicity offered by some NFB films. However, while the parameters of the protracted struggle between the views of the working class and those of the economic and government elite on the political issues of the day assumed a less confrontational appearance, the ideological dichotomies that separated those two views remained well defined.

On the one hand, there was the establishment's perspective, which advocated a nationalist-oriented emphasis on the role of government in educating its citizens. This essentially subscribed to urging these citizens to solve their problems individually and in the spirit of capitalist free will. This vision did not necessarily contradict the parochial (and mostly rhetorical) liberal pronouncements about creating a socially more just society. On the other hand, there was the counter-hegemonic outlook, which claimed and upheld a grassroots cooperative political vision of society. This outlook found its strength and support within a broad working-class-based political, social, and cultural movement. As I will illustrate later, the NFB films' discourse in connection with the two views was anything but neutral.

The concord that characterized the relationship between the NFB's administration and the government during the war was not entirely devoid of sporadic confrontations. While the Board's films appeared not to contradict the government's policy in mobilizing support for the war effort, the social and political messages implicated in those films and the manner in which they practically brought people together on the grassroots level were essentially incompatible with the long-term objectives of the ruling social and political elite. Attacks against Grierson and the NFB during the early years of the Cold War would demonstrate how this establishment implicitly despised the role played by the Board during the war. Within the NFB itself, several filmmakers faced all kinds of institutional pressures. Tom Waugh discusses how filmmaker Joris Ivens, for example, "was not entirely comfortable" with how the NFB handled the editing and the distribution of one of his films.[49] Filmmaker Jane March encountered similar problems in her work on *Women are Warriors*.[50] The difference between the original script prepared by March and the final version of the film was quite vast.

Comparing the two versions illustrates that some NFB filmmakers were insistent on pushing the envelope even further with their class-based analysis, and that by the end they would settle for solutions that accepted the limitations associated with working within a government agency.[51]

Nevertheless, NFB filmmakers were largely successful and effective in forwarding messages that interacted with alternate dynamics within Canadian political culture. A critical element in Popular Front policy stressed the need to support the war against fascism as part of a heterogeneous effort based on a wide class alliance. In other words, this policy measured the success of the working class through its success in forging and leading a mass-based alliance or front; a counter-hegemonic historical bloc. As such, presenting the views of the Popular Front (particularly in support of the war effort) also meant bringing a working-class perspective to the forefront of the struggle around hegemony.

The government and the Popular Front contended over interpreting what fighting fascism and mobilizing people to fight against it meant. They essentially competed to achieve a commonsense consensus around each of their own perspectives towards these issues. The fact that they agreed on the same goals does not change the nature of the struggle between them as one around hegemony. As will be manifested in our reading of the NFB films themselves, these films complemented the broader forms of cultural and political activities that took place during the war but they also built upon earlier working-class actions and struggles that took place in the 1930s and before. The amalgamation of these discursive elements helped establish a certain hegemony (in this case, a counter-hegemony), or cultural dominance of existing institutions and values. As Raymond Williams argued:

> I would say that in any society, in any particular period, there is a central system of practices, meanings and values, which we can properly call dominant and effective ... what I have in mind is the central, effective and dominant system of meanings and values, which are not merely abstract but which are organized and lived. That is why hegemony is not to be understood at the level of mere opinion or mere manipulation. It is a whole body of practices and expectations; our assignments of energy, our ordinary understanding of the nature of man and of his world. It is a set of meanings and values which as they are experienced as practices appear as reciprocally confirming.[52]

As a broad pro-labour and anti-fascist political and cultural movement took form and transcended the boundaries of militant working-class activists and the political left, a significant number of films produced by the NFB became part of a wider course of action which witnessed the labouring of Canadian culture. Eventually the level of activity and the role played by Canadian labour and its supporters on the political left had a vital impact on the ideological paradigm that informed NFB films' depiction of the working class and the manner in which these films were ideologically perceived by this class and other sections of Canadian society. It also helped shape how these films informed and were informed by the politics of fighting fascism, the role of the Soviet Union as a working-class state, and ideas about building a post-war society on the basis of collective utilization and distribution of social and economic resources. In other words, these films became integral to an intellectual stratum associated with a working-class-centred counter-hegemonic historical bloc.

5 OUT OF THE DEPRESSION AND INTO THE WAR: NFB FILMS BETWEEN 1939 AND 1941

In this chapter I discuss the body of NFB films produced between 1939 and 1941. I demonstrate how this body of films engaged counter-hegemonic impulses that complemented Popular Front policies initiated by the Communist Party. This is a transitional period in the history of the National Film Board of Canada, which begins with the establishment of the Board and ends with the disbanding of the Canadian Government Motion Picture Bureau and the transfer of its property and staff to the control of the NFB. This period also coincides with the early phase of World War II just prior to the attack on the Soviet Union and the consequent launching of political and military partnership in the fight against fascism in Europe between the Soviets and western powers.

Linkages between the battle against fascism and forwarding an alternate approximation of democracy in NFB films reflected the view of a significant section of Canadian society. Coming out of the Great Depression, a sizable group of Canadians (specifically those who came from working-class backgrounds) had their own social, economic, and political vision of what constituted a fair, just, and democratic social order, and of why fighting fascism was important for Canada and for working-class Canadians.

By the end of the 1930s and with the full implementation of Popular Front policy, a large number of labour organizations (particularly those with close ties to the Communist Party) and their rank-and-file membership were now stressing a more moderate approach to labour politics. This resulted in a less sectarian view on achieving a socialist transformation that in effect adopted consensus-building concepts such as collective social responsibility, public control of national resources, and a more centralized approach to managing the development/production and distribution of Canadian society's goods and resources. This also involved emphasizing an alternative to the classical capitalist emphasis on the role of the individual, free enterprise, competition, and the separation between the roles of management and labour. In essence, the new Popular Front approach clearly aimed at social and political elements that were outside of socialist and working-class sections of society, and as such had a clear ideological counter-hegemonic relevance. It also had the potential of becoming part of a mass-based sensible philosophy that represented an alternative to hegemonic commonsensical philosophy.

Clearly, all the proposals that were introduced in NFB films were not, as such, socialist proposals. And despite the fact that they were originally and largely promoted by socialists and communists and their supporters, the counter-hegemonic significance of these proposals stemmed from their projection as ideas that made good sense and appealed to significant segments of society. In this regard, NFB films provided a critical venue for the promotion and further popularization of such proposals and views.

UNEMPLOYMENT AND COLLECTIVE SOCIAL RESPONSIBILITY

In March 1939, the Canadian government introduced a legislation to establish the National Film Board of Canada. Earlier in the year, filmmaker Stuart Legg had begun producing two films for the Government's Motion Picture Bureau (CGMPB). When Grierson took charge as the NFB's Film Commissioner in October (shortly after the war broke out in Europe) he hired Legg to organize theatrical documentary production. Ultimately, this prompted a process which eventually led to the 1941 dissolution of the CGMPB and the incorporation of its staff and facilities into the NFB. As a result, some of the films produced between 1939 and 1941 bore the mark of the Motion Picture Bureau, but all of them later became the property of the NFB. The transfer of power between the two agencies had its political significance: it eventually led to a pronounced integration of Popular Front discourse in NFB films. Coinciding with Germany's invasion of the Soviet Union in June 1941, the full transfer of power from the CGMPB to the NFB also ushered in the emergence of the Board's counter-hegemonic approach on the role of labour in the war and to ideas about building an alternative post-war society.

Many films produced between 1939 and 1941 were subcontracted to outside producers. The CGMPB/NFB network produced a total of 66 films, all of which were documentary and mainly dealt with mobilizing support for the war. Many films produced in 1939, however, focused on unemployment and the effects of the Great Depression on working people. Stuart Legg's 1939 films *The Case of Charlie Gordon* and

Youth is Tomorrow marked an important shift in Canadian cinema. Legg did what no other filmmaker had dared to do until then. He walked into the slums of the working-class coal town of Glace Bay and came out with a story about everything that was not talked about before in Canadian films: the hopes and fears of unemployed youth.

In *Youth is Tomorrow*, Legg praises and argues for a more involved role by the government in dealing with the problem of unemployment. After describing how the Great Depression years of the 1930s marked an increase in the unemployment of young people in particular, Legg points out the benefits of programs such as the Youth Training Plan. He reminds us of the positive role played by this program in providing training and apprenticeship for Canadian youth in agriculture, industry and home economics and in combating the problem of unemployment. The film introduces the program as an effective and viable tool in pursuing a socially responsible and organizationally more collective approach to dealing with the issue of youth unemployment.

In *Charlie Gordon*, Legg presents a fictionalized account of a young unemployed worker. As in *Youth is Tomorrow*, the film introduces the issue of unemployment as a social problem and responsibility. It also links success in the task of finding jobs to the level of commitment to social collective planning and the involvement of the government. As it advocates coordinating the effort between unemployed workers, government and local business communities, the film inadvertently links the problem of unemployment to the lack of cooperation between these groups. Shot mostly from the point of view of an unemployed worker, the film takes this worker's own frustrated perspective as he stands in the line to get the local boss's approval to employ him. The film subtly stresses the consequences of business's inability to see beyond its immediate and narrow interests, and urges it to adopt a more socially responsible attitude. The alternative is introduced in the context of the government's initiation and implementation of a program to coordinate between different social groups to meet the needs of the entire community. In essence, both films put forward a substitute to the commonsensical idea of free labour competition and provide new options for dealing with the problem of unemployment. As such, they offer an alternative to forcing surplus unemployed workers to compete with each other over a shrinking job pool, a situation which usually also results in lowering labour wages.

Among the demands put forward by labour unions during the Depression was introducing government programs that provide work and apprenticeship for the unemployed. This demand was at the heart of what the On-to-Ottawa Trek campaign in 1935 advocated. It also represented the essence of how labour contemplated solutions for the unemployment crisis. Clearly, this solution was in total and sharp contradiction to the plan implemented by the R.B. Bennett government. This plan basically forced single unemployed men away from their own communities and into Work Relief Camps that were under military control and located in isolated areas throughout the country.

Both of Legg's films address the problem of unemployment in the context of maintaining a connection between unemployed workers and their communities. They point out the benefits and the feasibility of preserving existing communities as an element of social and moral strength as well as a viable economic alternative to the chaos of dislocation and forced labour. The films stress the need to develop the work skills of the unemployed rather than subjecting them to hard labour. As such they propose that government-sponsored vocational training programs contribute to building a stronger economy and a stronger communities.

Charlie Gordon also advocates coordinating efforts between the government and small business. Finding solutions to unemployment through the partnership between workers, small business and government became one of the features of the Popular Front policy of inter-class cooperation at the time of war. This policy contrasted the all-or-nothing and class-against-class approaches towards capitalism advocated in the 1920s and the early 1930s by communists and their allies within the labour movement. As we will see later, the Front's policy would later expand to include proposing the creation of labour-management committees as an alternative to unilateral control by capitalist management.

The importance of Legg's work, however, goes beyond its interest in the concerns of workers and the unemployed. As Canada was stepping away from the Depression, Legg advocated a consensual interventionist government approach in planning and coordinating the social and economic resources of the country. He also supported finding ways to utilize these resources for the benefit of the entire society. This particular theme would be given more prominence and would be presented with increased urgency in subsequent NFB war films.

The 1940 film *Industrial Workers of Central Canada* (Donald Fraser) describes how the area around the St. Lawrence River and the Great Lakes became the most populated area in the country, and how it came to include the bulk of Canadian industrial labour. As it delineates the operations of large industrial plants, the film demonstrates how the level of skill, organization, and efficiency of the working class contributes to the wealth and development of the entire country.

Other NFB films of this period accentuated the positive role of government in relieving the post-Depression conditions among Canadian farmers and agricultural workers. In light of intense grassroots pressure from farmers and farm workers, the government created the Prairie Farm Rehabilitation Administration that provided government support to farmers. The new government agency provided technical know-how for dealing with problems of conserving moisture, development of new methods of farming, and conversion of sub-marginal land to other uses.

In *Heritage* (1939), J. Booth Scott argues that after years of intensive drought coupled with the disastrous fall in prices during the Depression, many prairie farmers were forced to board up their homes and seek work elsewhere. He describes the conditions of farmers who chose to stay back as they tried to carry on their farm work but were often incapable of securing enough money to make a fresh start. *Heritage* celebrates the government's interventionist approach and points out its success in helping farmers avoid the disastrous effect of unplanned farming. It also offers a glimpse of the benefits of cooperation between federal and regional governments. But as Blaine Allan points out, the film's approach was not totally out of sync with the general direction of Canadian politics during that period:

> *Heritage* was a product of the Liberal era of Prime Minister William Lyon Mackenzie King, but the economic and physical crises that it outlines certainly had a place on the cabinet agenda of his predecessor, R.B. Bennett. Whether Bennett and his Conservatives would have approved the film remains an open question, but in late 1934 his economic and political sentiments were markedly moving in a direction consistent with the government intervention outlined in the film.[1]

The film certainly ignores the more complex questions behind the state of despair suffered by farmers during the Depression. Nevertheless, it effectively and favourably introduces the notion of collective public involvement as a sensible solution to some of the problems faced by agricultural workers. *Heritage* concerns itself not simply with the "anxieties experienced in one part of the country," but also with the potential "beneficent role the Dominion government wished to present itself as playing in addressing those problems."[2] Another film, *Farmers of the Prairies* (1940, no assigned director) similarly explores how the intervention of the government helps farmers deal with their problems. As in the case of *Heritage*, the film argues that there are major benefits to be gained from having the government involved in creating agricultural aid programs and in introducing new scientific research and irrigation strategies.

GENDER AND RACIAL EQUALITY

I pointed out earlier that for the first time in any Canadian labour organization, the Workers Unity League (WUL) implemented in its 1931 constitution the idea of gender and racial equality. The League entrenched a rule which officially accepted all wage workers, "regardless of [their] race, creed, color, sex, craft or political affiliations," as full members of the union.[3] A similar policy was adopted in all WUL's affiliates, including those set up for unemployed workers. The WUL's approach represented one of the earliest attempts to introduce anti-racist and anti-sexist rules as working principles within the Canadian labour movement.

In cinema, and since its early inception, films that advocated working-class views (most of which were produced in the United States before the consolidation of the control of capital in the 1920s and the emergence of the studio system) also tended to promote unity between workers who came from diverse oppressed groups of wage earners. As Steven Ross suggests, American working-class filmmakers of the pre-Hollywood era (i.e., before the early 1920s) saw benefit in using film to bring together workers "whose religion, ethnicity, language, race, and gender differed but whose basic problems were the same."[4]

In Canada, Legg's film *Charlie Gordon* was the first to refer to the reality of gender and racial difference within the labour and working-class movement. Almost subdued by today's standards, and even though it addressed the problem of unemployment mainly as a male problem, the film nevertheless chooses to conclude with a call for solidarity and unity between working men and women. This unity, the film argues, is fundamental to helping move society on the road to future prosperity. The film also includes an indication of solidarity between black and white workers. In one instance, and as the camera pans across the faces of workers in an unemployment line, we catch a glimpse of a black worker surrounded by the predominantly white group of fellow workers. The scene infers a brief but nevertheless important visual message of unity between workers of different racial backgrounds. *Charlie Gordon*'s reference to gender and race equality was, however, the first to be recorded in NFB films, and perhaps in Canadian film history (to my knowledge none of the films that remain in the archives of the NFB and other provincial government agencies contain a similar reference). Trivial as it may appear today – even in comparison to the explicit constitutional clauses adopted seven years earlier by the communist-led labour groups such as the WUL – this filmic citation of gender, race and class unity remains an important indicator of the general ideological direction that the NFB was enhancing at the time.

WORKERS IN THE FISHING INDUSTRY

Another group of NFB films specifically deals with the topic of East Coast fisheries. Legg's *Toilers of the Grand Banks* (1940) depicts the hard work of people in the fishing industry. It shows how "the sunlight, striking through the shallow water stimulates the growth of marine plants in the sea bed, providing food and breeding ground for fish." The film's main theme, however, is the epic of toiling itself "which stands behind the success of Canada's fishing economy." The film draws a detailed picture of the work performed by the fishermen and the shipyard workers on the Canadian east coast. It maintains a thematic dialectic that is similar to the one introduced by Grierson in his British period film *Drifters* (1929), which also depicts fishery workers. Both films capture images of fishermen as they combat and triumph over natural elements. Yet while Grierson relies on editing as his main way of delineating the epic magnitude of toiling, Legg, on the other hand, incorporates a different stylistic approach. He uses strong and uninterrupted camera shots, first showing fishermen building schooners in local shipyards and next as they take them to the fishing grounds where they transfer to dories and haul in the cod as they ride the heavy ocean sweep. Connection between the two aspects of the work performed by fishermen is referred to in the context of a camera work intent on literally connecting the two complex and hard phases of fishing in the Atlantic.

In *People of Blue Rocks* (1941, producers Douglas Sinclair and Edward Buckman), the fishermen of Lunenburg, Nova Scotia are depicted while they make their living from the sea. The film tells the story of a father and son from the village of Blue Rock who both work in the inshore fishery. The village has a close-knit community life; its social centres are the store and church. First, young people gather at the store, and afterwards the whole community congregates in the church hall for a chowder supper and auction for a church fund. The film basically celebrates the work and the community in this rugged region of Nova Scotia, and praises their ability to sustain and enrich the lives of people. Collective work, the film reiterates, is integral to carrying on and enriching the cultural heritage of the community. The themes of work stability (and implicitly rejecting the notion of contingency labour) and the responsibility of the government in maintaining and encouraging community development are presented as crucial for elements for a thriving economic future for Atlantic Canadians. Unlike how later Canadian feature films of the 1970s such as *Goin' Down the Road*, 1980s (*John and the Missus*), and 1990s (*Margaret's Museum* and *The Hanging Garden*), for example, variously portrayed the destruction of traditional east coast industries as an inevitable result of "modernization,"[5] early NFB films offered an alternate understanding of what the notions of progress and economic growth entailed. They focused on sustaining communities as the basis for economic and social enrichment.

THE "PHONY WAR"

The outbreak of war in Europe in September 1939 radically affected the political agenda of the government and consequently altered the NFB's priorities as originally set out by Grierson. With the ascendance of Hitler to power in Germany, the establishment of a fascist government in Italy, and the rise of Japanese militarism in Asia, the world moved steadily towards war. In the first acts of hostility, Hitler remilitarized the Rhineland in violation of the Versailles Treaty, Japan had invaded Manchuria and was extending its war into China, and Mussolini had already occupied Ethiopia. With the *Canada Carries On* series the NFB initiated its first major film program to be solely produced by the NFB in the 1939–41 period when the NFB itself was still considered a non-production agency. The goal of the program was to provide Canadians with information and to encourage their support and participation in the war effort. However, there were some important differences between how NFB films dealt with the subject of war before and after June 1941 (i.e., before and after the Soviet Union was invaded by Germany), particularly in how they characterized the war, and how they conceived of the role of the working class in the battle against fascism. The outbreak of hostilities in Europe created great political anxiety in the country and had a major impact on the politics of labour and socialism in Canada.

Before the outbreak of the war, a major campaign by labour and the left warned of the possible outbreak of a second world war. It also cautioned against the danger of the appeasement policies pursued at the time by the Neville Chamberlain government of Britain. For communists, Chamberlain's policy was seen as an attempt to aid Hitler in his preparation for a major push against the Soviet Union. Accordingly, communists and their allies within the labour movement called for the creation of a system of collective security to stop fascism in Europe and prevent a second world war.[6] During the same period, the Soviet Union introduced several appeals to western powers at the League of Nations to join it in establishing "a system of multilateral alliances for defence against Nazi Germany." Those appeals, however, were rejected.[7]

Subsequent separate political manoeuvres on the part of western powers and the Soviet Union eventually ended in the signing of the Munich agreement between Hitler and Britain's Chamberlain and France's Daladier in September 1938. In response and in August 1939, a non-aggression pact between the Soviet Union and Germany was signed. Hitler invaded Poland in September 1, 1939, two days after which Britain and France declared war on Germany. Canada declared war on September 10.

The unfolding of those events created a major crisis within the labour and communist movements around the world, including in Canada. After years of leading the fight against fascism and building alliances in support of anti-fascists in Spain, these movements found themselves in a dangerously awkward situation. The position taken by leader of the Canadian Communist Party reflected this confusion. As he could not rationalize Stalin's signing of a Friendship Treaty with Germany, Tim Buck simply called for the immediate mobilization of forces to defeat fascism and its "reactionary friends at home:"

> Our immediate tasks are clear. In collaboration with anti-fascist forces everywhere and in the interests of the international working class, we will strive to combine with the military defeat of Hitler in the field of the battle, the political defeat of his reactionary friends at home, turning this war into a just anti-fascist war and the conclusion of an early democratic peace.[8]

Officially, the party considered the war an inter-imperialist struggle between two sections of monopoly capitalism, both of which "made scandalous profits while the burden of the war in terms of lives and livelihood was borne by the workers and farmers."[9] What was clear here is that the party was trying to put the best face on an impossible situation. The government and the right-wing establishment were quick to take advantage of the events and to use the problematic party position as an excuse to launch a fierce campaign against the left and the trade union movement.

For almost two years before the Soviet Union was invaded by Germany, the Communist Party of Canada and its supporters in the labour movement remained politically confused and disillusioned. The bitter reality was that they saw the battle against fascism, a battle that they had mobilized in support of for almost a decade, was now being fought without them on board. The situation also brought factional disputes to the cultural left as well. The situation affected the party on all levels. As Scott Forsyth suggests:[10]

> The unexpected announcement of the Soviet non-aggression pact with Germany and then the beginning of the war disorients many in the Party. It is denounced as yet another Soviet-directed shift in Party strategy by opponents and the Party's liberal sympathizers rapidly disappear with the Party's hard anti-

war, anti-imperialist line; for example, the Toronto Theatre of Action dissolves in political disagreement and confusion. Soon, the Party is declared illegal again and over one hundred Party leaders and members are interned. Even the language associations are attacked and the Ukrainian Farmer Labour Temples all over the country expropriated.[11]

For its part, the Canadian government saw an opportunity to curtail communist activity within the labour movement. A few months after the declaration of war the government decided to ban the party, and several of its labour activists were jailed.[12]

The confusion over the position of the Soviet Union had its negative impact on many Popular Front supporters and gave an excuse to anti-communist groups and politicians to isolate the left within the labour and mass movements. However, militant organizing among workers and the support that had been built since the mid-1930s remained almost intact.[13] While the party suffered the effects of the Stalin-Hitler Treaty fiasco in a major way, the core of the links that it had developed over the years seem to have been sustained.

During the 1940 election the Communist Party was able to get one of its supporters elected to the House of Commons. Dorise Nielsen won a seat in a rural Saskatchewan riding and became the only woman to be elected to the House during these elections.[14] Because of the official ban on the party, however, Nielsen had to run under an independent left coalition ticket. During her tenure as an MP she concentrated on three issues, all of which echoed the political priorities of the Communist Party of Canada at the time. Those included opposing conscription, defending civil liberties and freeing of communists and labour leaders, and finally the advocacy of a "new political organization which would defend the interest of the Canadian people."[15] In Europe, communist parties were already organizing underground resistance to Hitler in the countries occupied by Germany, particularly in France and Yugoslavia, as well as in Hungary, which while not occupied by the Nazis until October 1944 was nevertheless governed by a quasi-fascist regime which was sending its troops to fight alongside the Germans in the Soviet Union.

Moments of political uncertainty, however, usually inform a sense of ideological stagnation and hesitancy. Within the NFB, the clearest sign of the political confusion of the left in dealing with the issue of war was manifest in the tame political tone of the films produced during the early phase of the war. Another element that might have contributed to this restrained tone in early NFB filmic depictions of the war, and particularly in relation to the role of workers within it, can be traced to the fact that most those films were still being officially produced under the auspices of the Motion

Picture Bureau. As we saw earlier, the conservative administration of CGMPB was not particularly keen on promoting a leftist interpretation of the struggle against fascism, nor on discussing what working-class Canadians thought of it, for that matter.

Early NFB war films were mostly subdued in their assessment of the war in Europe. While they clearly supported the war against Germany, the films hardly alluded to the war's significance for workers, its implications for building a new social and political order, or its impact on the battle for democracy. All these ideas would only begin to emerge when the Soviet Union later entered the war. All in all, NFB early war films were largely descriptive in their evaluation of the events. Even as they showed the involvement of working-class people in the fight against Germany, the films' discourse projected a passive tone in regard to the social significance of the war against fascism. They also utilized a largely patriotic and nationalist tone, which emphasized Canada's mobilization for the war but in the context of an ambivalent characterization of Hitler's Germany, which simply pointed out the danger that "stemmed from Nazi designs against the British Empire."

Stuart Legg's first film in the *Canada Carries On* series, *Atlantic Patrol* (1940), described the work of Canadian seamen staffing the war-supply ships as they departed from eastern Canadian ports. The film concentrated on Hitler's military plans and warned Canadians of the goal of these designs and the danger they posed to the welfare of the British Commonwealth. *Fight for Liberty* (1940, producers James Beveridge and Stanley Hawes) depicted Nazi advances in Europe, the invasion of Greece and Egypt, Italy's African defeat, the Syrian campaign, etc. Stanley Hawes's *On Guard for Thee* (1940) presented a historical depiction of Canada's involvement in various war efforts, including the assault on Vimy Ridge in World War I. On one level, all these films stressed the German threat to the territorial and national integrity of Canada as Britain's partner. In one example, and even as it made some reference to the industrialization of Canada in the early twentieth century, Hawes's film was muted as to the role of workers in contributing to this massive economic process.

On another level, and in contrast to the emphasis on the collective role of workers in mobilizing for the war clearly manifest in later board films, the pre-1942 films mainly concentrated on discussing the role of the individual rather than on the social collective action. In *Wings of Youth* (1940, Raymond Spottiswoode) in particular, the war against Germany is portrayed as a struggle led by heroic individuals who are fighting to defend their individual rights and the integrity of the British Commonwealth. The film describes Canada's contribution in building airfields and producing machines and equipment for the Commonwealth's air training scheme. As it renders the role of air force pilots, *Wings* considers individual responsibility as the main ingredient for winning the war. The last scene of the film leaves us with the image of a Royal Air Force pilot and Lorne Greene's voice summing up what the war against Germany is all about. After pointing out that "for every pilot there must be more than 20 men on the ground for maintenance," Green reminds us that this is after all a "battle for individual rights fought by individual skills."

Call for Volunteers (1941, Radford Crawley) tackles the role of women in the war by describing the activity of a volunteer group in Winnipeg. The film suggests that women's participation in jobs such as canning fruit for the troops, raising money for mobile canteens, working in children's clinics, etc., "shows how they could help not only in the war effort but also in laying sound foundation for the peace to follow." But the film has no qualms about presenting the role played by women in the war as being temporary, and as one that is only necessitated by the specific urgency of the war and the need to supplement shortages in manpower. To push its point further the film stresses that the voluntary work done by women does not require skilled training, effectively implying that women are not capable of doing better than this kind of work. Towards the end, the film contrasts the images of men working in factories with those of women working in day care centres, further prescribing the role of women's labour as provisional both to the war effort and to the peace that will follow.

Another feature of early NFB films is their emphasis on the technological advances of modern warfare. In *Battle of Brains* (1941, Stanley Hawes), achieving a higher level of mechanization of the warfare machine is considered as a determining element in winning the war. The film describes the main difference between World War II and World War I as one that relates to the level of technological progress. It also contrasts the new "mobile" tactics and weaponry compared with the "immobile" nature of earlier trench warfare. In the same breadth, *Battle of Brains* accentuates Canadian scientists' contribution to the development of the war machinery.

Similar emphasis on the role of technology is found in films such as the 1940 series *News Round-Up* and the 1940 film *Front of Steel* (John McDougall), both dealing with the development of the Canadian steel industry and the production of Bren guns, ambulances, transport trucks and submarine chasers. *Strategy of Metals* (1941, Raymond Spottiswoode) describes the end result of the manufacturing of crankshafts, tanks and planes.

War machinery and technological progress in all these films is portrayed as the equivalent to and the measure of modernist superiority without which no national integrity can be maintained or defended. The tone of the films and their accent on machinery and on elite scientists echoes views advanced in Nazi and pro-fascist artistic adulations of war machines as high art.[16] All in all, the discourse of the films depicts the war as one concerning national pride, individual bravery, and technological excellence. While subsequent NFB war films would incorporate images and comments about the role of workers in generating quality weapons to fight fascism and end its instigation of war, earlier films seemed to look at war as part of an inevitable and natural exercise in world history and in conduct between nations. One exception to such views, however, is found in Stuart Legg's *Churchill's Island* (1940), the film that won the NFB's first Oscar®.

Legg's film offers a multi-layered political assessment of how the battle of autumn 1940 was won and in the process opens itself to a socially informed approximation of the war. *Island* explores the interrelationship between various forces that contributed to Britain's defence: the Royal Air Force, the Navy, the coastal defences, the mechanized cavalry, the merchant seamen, and Britain's "tough, unbending civilian army." The film makes a brave effort to point out the critical role of workers "who were in the first place the ones who prepared Britain for facing up to the challenge of war." A critical component of the film is its exceptional and innovative sync sound interviews with ordinary soldiers, workers and women, which factors into the film's class orientation. The film shows images of workers in factories and farmers in the fields by way of celebrating the work of the "men and women who in the time of peace made Britain strong." Nevertheless, *Island* remains restrained in its characterization of the war against fascism and the connection between its social and the political dynamics. Legg's cinematic delineation of the war would radically change later and so would other NFB films. Subsequent films would portray events as part of "a peoples' war for democracy and peace," after which workers would be able to harvest the fruits of their effort and the peace that they helped bring about. As militant Canadian labour and the communist left re-forged their anti-fascist Popular Front in 1942, the films produced by the NFB shifted into a new gear. Its films would become more clearly integrated to a discursive formation which was essentially part of the labouring of Canadian culture.

By 1942, the NFB's discourse on the battle against Hitler began to argue that if nations could win the war as a measure of their ability to share and organize their military, economic and social resources, then the same collective and cooperative method could and should be applied to building a peaceful and prosperous future for humanity in the post-war era. Within the same parameters, workers as depicted in NFB films would be portrayed in conjunction with promoting ideas about collective production and sharing of resources and utilizing these resources for the benefit of the majority of society.

6 WORKERS AND THE POLITICS OF FIGHTING FASCISM: NFB FILMS BETWEEN 1942 AND 1945

By July 1941 the dissolution of the Canadian Government Motion Picture Bureau (CGMPB) and the transfer of its operations to the NFB were both concluded. This consolidated Grierson's control over the NFB and allowed him relative autonomy over its operation. The changes also coincided with the Soviet Union's entry into the war against Germany. Consequently, a new political atmosphere was beginning to take shape. The Soviet Union was now a war ally and communists and their supporters were back at the core of political action throughout the country, mobilizing against fascism and praising the role of the Soviet Union and communist-led resistance against it throughout Europe. Within the same context, labour unions and militant working-class organizations, as well as Popular Front supporters, were once again organizing and mobilizing people against fascism.

Clearly, the war was now being perceived differently, particularly when it came to Labour. In a nutshell, the role of workers in the war now assumed a radically different political outlook and goal. At the NFB, films increasingly provided a new point of view, both on the role of labour in the war and on the post-war social and economic opportunities. The films stressed the leading role of workers, not only in relation to participating in the war and supporting the war efforts, but also on the level of achieving a leading political role in building post-war society. This chapter explores how NFB films between 1942 and 1945 linked working-class tasks during this period with the struggle against fascism, support for the Soviet Union and advocating women's equality and political leadership.

Labour and left supporters of Popular Front policy shifted away from their earlier position on the war almost immediately when Hitler's invasion of the Soviet Union began in June 1941. Instead of considering the war in Europe as an inter-imperialist struggle between two capitalist blocs, the communists now characterized it as a war aimed at stopping fascism and defending democracy. In July 1941, the Communist

Party issued a statement calling upon labour organizations and all progressive forces to support the King government in its war mobilization efforts. It also advocated forging a united front of all democratic forces to fight against fascism and to aid the Soviet Union. The party called for the creation of a National Front, cutting across class and party lines in the common struggle against fascism.[1]

The issue of Canadian anti-fascist unity would now become a recurrent theme in the speeches of the lone woman and supporter of the Communist Party in the House of Commons, Dorise Nielsen. For Nielsen the main task now was to ensure that the war against fascism was won:

> In my opinion the greatest need of this nation to-day is for unity to win the war. That should be the overriding consideration of everyone; nothing should come before that. Unity to win the war is our first duty, and then there should be a unity of all forward thinking people after the war to build the good life for Canadians, to give jobs and security on the land and to provide peace. The issue of socialism now splits and divides our people and prevents that national unity which is necessary for the winning of the war and the peace.[2]

Nielsen's approach clearly laid out how communists now identified their political priorities. In this regard, she echoed their return to a less sectarian policy, involving broader segments of the population and wider cross-sections of activists on the left and liberal political spectrums. This would reclaim the political losses suffered by the party earlier due to its confused and extremist left-wing approach, and would broaden the appeal of its policies among Canadians.

Between 1942 and 1945 the NFB produced over 400 titles including trailers and newsreels. The staff of the Board grew from two in 1939, to 751 by the year 1945.[3] Many of the films produced during this time were part of the *Canada Carries On* and *The World In Action* series, both of which focused on the news of the war and on supporting the war mobilization effort. Another large number of films concentrated on labour relations and the role of workers and farmers in economic and social development.

Many of the other films produced at the time covered topics such as tourism and the arts, as well as issues of ethnic diversity and solidarity and some discussions with First Nations' traditions. There were also a good number of animated films addressing various topics and interests. While most NFB films were originally produced in English, French voice-over versions were made for some films, particularly those produced in the *Canada Carries On* series.

While earlier war films avoided making reference to the political significance of the fight against fascism, those that were produced after Hitler's invasion of the Soviet Union provided a cohesive analysis of the nature and significance of this struggle. In most cases views expressed in the film echoed the policies put forward by the Communist Party of Canada (then known as the Labour Progressive Party). The war against fascism was now characterized as one that labour and all classes fought together for the goal of achieving democracy and peace. Solidarity with the Soviet Union and its fight against the Nazi invasion was considered fundamental to the success of the struggle against fascism. NFB films now urged people in Canada and the rest of the western world to learn from the Soviets' experience, particularly their overcoming of the economic and social ills of the "old chaotic and uncoordinated" economy, and in building the social and political infrastructure for the victory against fascism.

The struggle for democracy was professed as interchangeable with political grassroots ideas such as broadening the involvement of people in politics and attaining full economic and political rights for working people. The involvement of labour and the working class and the full participation of working women were now also seen as essential ingredients for victory. In dealing with the social and economic conditions of workers, NFB films underscored the need to guarantee labour a decent and sufficient social safety net and a healthy and safe work environment. In the following section, I focus on the NFB films' association between the role of the working classes and the war, solidarity with the Soviet Union, and building of unity in the fight against fascism.

THE WORKING CLASS, THE SOVIET MODEL, AND UNITY IN FIGHTING FASCISM

As mentioned earlier, the issue of solidarity with the Soviet Union became the subject of fierce discussion within the labour movement during most of the first half of the twentieth century. Opinions for and against characterizing the Soviet Union as a working-class state were of significant importance to debates within working-class and left circles. When Hitler launched his invasion against the Soviet Union, the issue of solidarity with the Soviets became a critical component in the discourse among large sections of militant labour activists and their communist and left allies. Even Trotskyist leftists who continued to oppose Stalin's regime gave military support to Soviet resistance (Trotskyists rationalized this approach as a temporary political engagement in the war not necessarily on the side of Stalin, but against the capitalist attempt to destroy the Soviet Union's 'deformed workers' state'). This high level of solidarity with the Soviet Union was clearly also a central component of the communist-instigated "National Front" and in the mass movement spawned by it.

Most NFB films during this period assumed an aggressive anti-fascist tone. More specifically, the discourse of the NFB films on the war became much closer to the one advocated by the National Front than to that promoted by the government. Their approach also became more explicitly supportive of the Soviet Union, not simply as a war ally but also as a political partner. The films urged respect and support for the Soviet system's socialized planning, and celebrated its ability to mobilize and utilize tremendous social and economic resources for the benefit of its people and in the fight against fascism.

The *World in Action* series began in June 1942 with the goal of reaching out to wider international audience with two specified objectives: relating "local strategies to world ones," and influencing and directing "the political attitudes of North American audiences toward an internationally oriented post-war ethic."[4] With these tasks in mind, several films in the series urged Canadians to look at the experiences as well as the social and political structures of other countries (such as the Soviet Union) by way of learning about the strategies of fighting fascism and to become more effective in the struggle against it. By the last year of the war, the series would specifically promote mutual respect between different social and economic systems as a basis for international relations and as an essential feature for building world peace and saving humanity from poverty, need, and inequality.

Stuart Legg's film *Geopolitik – Hitler's Plan for Empire* (1942) traces historically the ascendance of fascism in Europe. The film implicitly denounces the west's earlier complacency in confronting the rise of fascism and cites western governments' reluctance to support the fight against fascism in Spain. The inability to stop Franco eventually strengthened fascism and helped it achieve an important goal in its larger plan for world domination, the film argues. The commentator reminds us that Hitler's goal of world control, rooted in Karl Haushofer's strategy of Geopolitik, attained its first success after the creation of the "western route to empire" in Spain. Only then, the film suggests, did western nations wake to the danger of fascism.

In the context of earlier political debates about Stalin's treaty with Hitler, and the embarrassing position in which the Communist Party found itself, the film's position was effectively rationalizing earlier communist positions. After all, communists in Canada and around the world always accused the Chamberlain government of Britain of appeasing fascism and of aiding Hitler in his preparation for the push against the Soviet Union. Communists also consistently cited pre-war Soviet appeals to western powers and the League of Nations, which called for creating "a system of multilateral alliances for defence against Nazi Germany" and how these appeals were always rejected.[5] In the same breath, communists considered the September 1938 signing of the Munich agreement between Hitler, Chamberlain and Daladier as the pretext that pushed Stalin to sign the non-aggression treaty with Germany in August 1939, and shortly after, the Friendship Treaty. Hitler invaded Poland on September 1, 1939, two days after which Britain and France declared war on Germany. Canada declared war on September 10. Given this background, *Geopolitik – Hitler's Plan for Empire* assumed an extremely important significance. In hindsight, the film puts the onus squarely on western powers regarding the ensuing events in Europe.

In the 1942 film *Inside Fighting Russia* (also titled *Our Russian Ally*) Legg and scriptwriter James Beveridge describe how "drawing on vast resources of labour and materials, and strengthened by new faith and leadership, the Soviet Union was able to change the course of World War II." The film then pays tribute to the resistance conducted by the Russian people "who withstood enemy attack, fought back, and disrupted Hitler's timetable." It sympathetically refers to how "the Red Star has stopped the Nazis" and contrasts "old starved Russia" with the "new Russia of Lenin." In another segment of the film, there is reference to international workers' solidarity with Russia. The film points out that when the Soviet Union came under attack, "British workers, and Canadian workers in Montreal rushed to send new tanks to our new ally." Lorne Greene's voice reminds us of Russia's secret weapon in the fight against fascism: "they are strong because they have the faith." There can no doubt about what faith Greene was referring to here. The film clearly links Soviet successes on the military front to their socialist economic and political system. *Inside Fighting Russia* suggests that the country's utilization of its collective energies to fight fascism is a direct result of the effectiveness and strong organization of the Soviet system itself. The film favourably discusses the idea of socialized economy and how it improves the workers' stake in society. It suggests that in the new Soviet society "workers work not for a greater share of production but for a greater production in which to share." The film shrewdly offers this argument in conjunction with a new interpretation of the notions of democracy and democratic practice.

With all its expressions of solidarity with the Soviet Union and its sympathy for the role of workers in governing and building the Soviet state, however, the film avoids posing the capitalist and the socialist systems directly against each other. Instead, it allows room for its audience to appreciate the specificity of each system's experience. As *Inside Fighting Russia* concentrates on discussing issues of social cooperation, social justice and democratic values and ideals, it inadvertently suggests that each society has its own dynamics that eventually determine how it upholds and applies these ideals. Subsequently, differences between capitalism and socialism are portrayed as elements that should not constitute an obstacle to their cooperation in fighting fascism. And since fascism is the antithesis of *all* democratic values and ideals shared by humanity, alliance between the west and the Soviet Union becomes a logical and beneficial choice.

To the background of images of women and men at work, the film presents the Soviet socialist experience, not as an antithesis to capitalism but as an alternative which employs a new form of democracy based on the motto: "one for all and all for one." The film describes the Soviet system, and how as a result of the Russian Revolution people were able for the first time in history to embark on planning their future using a grassroots collective control and administration. *Inside Fighting Russia* therefore conceives of the new Soviet system as one that expands the notion of democratic rights by involving its citizens in building their homeland, and by giving them the right to directly administer its resources and share the benefits of its successes. Such allusions to democracy are clearly inspired by a fundamentally counter-hegemonic philosophy, which in many ways expands beyond the traditional and simple interpretation of democracy as free elections. The film's elucidation of democracy is more in sync with a grassroots direct-democracy model (which the Soviet system adopted on paper but departed from by the mid-1920s). Given the broad parameters of how communists and their Popular Front policy inferred the notion of democracy, the film certainly had familiar resonance among the audience of the time. No one could have had any doubt about how the film was essentially endorsing a Marxist viewpoint on the issue. At its first release, the film ran for two weeks in a Washington, D.C. newsreel theatre, the Trans-Lux, and became one of the most popular films to be produced by the NFB at the time.[6]

Similar themes are offered in Tom Daly's *Our Northern Neighbour* (1944). Once again, the emphasis is on the fighting alliance with the Soviet Union, and on solidarity with a Soviet system which symbolizes and enhances the common goals of humanity in progress, social justice and peace. The film discusses the pre-war events leading to the signing of the non-aggression pact between Stalin and Hitler. As Legg did in *Geopolitik*, Daly goes back to the issue of the west's own failure to recognize the danger of fascism. But this time the film more explicitly points out the signing of Munich agreement between Britain, France and Germany in 1938.

Then the film traces the history of the Russian revolution and points out its achievements. It stresses the revolution's success in gaining the support of working people inside Russia and around the world. The new system is described through its accomplishments in modernizing the country to the extent of becoming the "world's second largest industrial power." As we saw in *Inside Fighting Russia*, Daly's film attributes Soviet successes to people's "faith and determination," and their reliance on cooperative and collective methods of governing their country.

Daly's film also assures the west of the peaceful intentions of the Soviet Revolution. To support his point, the film cites Stalin's infamous feud with Trotsky on the idea of building socialism in one country. Stalin's "sensible" approach on the issue of international socialist change is contrasted with Trotsky's "dogmatic" and less realistic one. Gary Evans explains:

> The commentary suggested that Joseph Stalin, a quieter voice than Trotsky, was leading Russia to build a pattern of socialism for all the world to see. The Russian citizen was preparing for the promise of ultimate freedom and good living after all these lean years. The film ended with the internationalist message, "we seek the cooperation of all nations, large and small, to eliminate tyranny and slavery, oppression and intolerance."[7]

Clearly, the film delves into the heart of the debates that were shaking the communist movement around the world since the mid-1920s between the pro-Trotsky and pro-Stalin factions. For its part, *Inside Fighting Russia* does not mince words as to whom it supports and where it stands. This was understandable given that one of the cornerstones of the debate between the two groups concerned the tactics of the Popular Front itself, which the left of the communist movement was vehemently opposed to on principle.[8]

The theme of solidarity with Soviet Russia is reiterated in other NFB films. In Joris Ivens' 1943 *Action Stations*, the story is of a Canadian corvette that goes into convoy duty in the North Atlantic, sights a submarine and sinks it. However, the film uses the story of the battle as a pretext for expressing support for providing concrete military assistance to the Soviet Union. Towards the end of the film Lorne Greene's voice urges: "Weapons for Russia – weapons to fight for freedom."

Other films refer to different aspects of Soviet contribution to the war, particularly its articulation of new war tactics. Once again these films emphasize the need for western governments and societies to learn from the Soviet experience and its success. In *Forward Commandos* (1942) Raymond Spottiswoode draws attention to how the west could benefits from adopting the method of guerrilla warfare in the fight against Nazi Germany. It points out tactics used by the Russians and grassroots communist-led resistance groups throughout Europe as examples that were being used increasingly by armies in Canadian camps and the Libyan deserts. One particular tactic mentioned is training troops to carry the battle onto and behind enemy lines. The same theme is repeated in Legg's *Battle is their Birthright* (1943), which contrasts the methods used by the Soviets to mobilize their forces with those used by the Nazis and their allies. The film refers to the blind military obedience of Japanese and Nazi youth and compare it with the "citizenship education" and grassroots mobilization in the Soviet Union and under the auspices of the United Front resistance forces in China.

Legg's film calls for initiating international efforts to battle food shortages in Nazi-occupied territories. As it alludes to how occupied countries have been forced to hand over their farm produce to Germany, leaving their own populations without food, the film suggests that western countries are obliged not only to feed their own armies overseas, but also to meet the challenge of feeding hundreds of millions in Europe and Asia.

All the films cited above focus on the value of collective heroism, but this theme is even more clearly pronounced in *This Is Blitz* (1942, Stuart Legg), *Forward Commandos* and *Zero Hour* (1944, Stuart Legg). Interest in this theme unmistakably contrasts with how earlier war films from 1939 to 1941 focused on the notion of individual heroism. The three films urge putting into practice the ideals of cooperation and people's unity and consider this a critical ingredient for success in battling fascism. By the end the war, films such as *Behind the Swastika: Nazi Atrocities* (1945, no credited director) would also pay tribute to the utility of and reliance on collective resources and methods as a major contributor to the victory against fascism. Films would also specifically describe how Nazis dreaded and looked down at these practices as ideologically debauched. *Behind the Swastika* illustrates fascism's special hatred for those who fought the war based on the principles of democratic and humanitarian ideals of equality and freedom. It graphically depicts examples of Nazi crimes in concentration camps and prisons and elucidates: "Jews and gentiles who believed in democratic principles were targeted" and "Russian prisoners of war received particularly savage treatment."

In the 1942 film *Inside Fighting China*, Stuart Legg argues that unity between people from different political viewpoints is essential for defeating fascism and other forms of oppression. Such unity is also crucial for building a better and more prosperous future. Sending home a familiar message on the need to overcome political differences, Legg cites the example of the Popular Front in China, where Nationalists and Communists joined together in the resistance against the Japanese invasion in the late 1930s.

The film presents footage shot in political rallies, schools, fields, and factories where Communist and Nationalist sympathizers discuss and address economic and social needs and problems. The commentator argues that even "as the enemy has conquered, people still needed to learn how to conquer poverty, promote the well being of people and labour for the common good." *Inside Fighting China* therefore links resistance against fascism to building a new Chinese society based on freedom from poverty and want. As he argues the case for people's unity, Legg uses images of unemployed people in western countries during the Depression as they stood in line to find jobs and as they fought with the police in demonstrations. He reminds us that earlier western governments' ignoring of economic and social problems eventually also led them to ignoring the growing menace of fascism which fed on social instability and lack of equitable social systems. The film also condemns the inaction of western governments in relation to the pre-war Japanese invasion of China. In a phraseology that echoes those used in statements by leaders of communist and Popular Front movements in Canada and around the world, the film affirms that to counter all kinds of oppression people need to "organize and unite."

Other films from the same period more explicitly elaborate on various historical aspects of the rise of fascism in Europe. In Stuart Legg's *The Gates of Italy* (1943), for example, social and economic injustices are considered as major elements that contributed to the rise of fascism to power. As it traces the history of fascism in Italy, the film argues that Mussolini's manipulation of the Italian working class and the "impoverishment of the Italian people," in addition to his demagogic misrepresentation of socialist ideals in order to get the support of the Italian population, eventually led many Italians in the direction of supporting fascism. As a result, Italy under Mussolini became a major source for labour "overexploitation and enslavement." Legg explains that the goal of fascist governments was to provide the dictatorial political framework for guaranteeing harsher and higher levels of exploitation of the labour force. Nazi Germany, the film argues, was capable of building its war machine relying mostly on the highly exploitative working conditions of its labour force.

A similar analysis is brought forward in films from the series, *The World in Action*. This time, however, the emphasis is on the situation in France prior to the war and on how social instability affected the aptitude of the country to resist the Nazi invasion in the early years of the war. Stuart Legg's *Inside France* (1944) argues that this apathy further helped support for the collaborationist pro-Nazi Vichy government. Legg paints a dark picture of France in the period between the two world wars when the country was struck by riots, strikes, and economic stress. He describes how fascist elements within France attempted to destabilize the situation for the democratically elected Popular Front government in the mid- to late 1930s. He points out later dissension between supporters of the pro-Nazi government and those supporting the resistance. As with other films dealing with the subject of unity, *Inside France* stresses that social factors and the inability of governments in the west to address social concerns and problems led to increased support of fascism. Fascism is therefore conceived not as an idea that attracts people because of an innate human tendency to hate and to seek violence against each other, but rather as a distortion of human nature which grows within atmospheres of instability. The causes of such instability, however, cannot be separated from the realities of social inequality, poverty, exploitation and alienation.

One film in particular raised a major controversy upon its release. Legg's *Balkan Powder Keg* (1944) drew a picture of events in Greece and Yugoslavia, where Popular Front and communist-led resistance movements played a major role in driving out German armies of occupation. As Whitaker and Marcuse explain, as early as 1944 the British government was already in direct conflict with the communist-led resistance in Greece. This conflict eventually led to the Greek civil war and to the creation of the Truman Doctrine of intervention against Communism.[9] In Canada this was a particularly sensitive issue:

> Mackenzie King had recently been burned by an angry response by Winston Churchill to what the British prime minister took to be some slight by the Canadian government on the British position in Greece. Now King was disconcerted to learn that a Canadian-made film about to open to wide circulation in the United States in January 1945 took what his adviser Norman Robertson called a "forthright" and "liberal" editorial attitude, with its plain talk about royalist dictatorships in Greece and Yugoslavia and its sympathetic presentation of the viewpoint of the working-class resistance movements that found themselves in conflict with British troops. This was a red flag to King, who was excessively cautious at all times about foreign relations, especially with his senior allies, Churchill and Roosevelt. Robertson carefully pointed out that the NFB "has done a good deal of excellent work and has shown quite remarkable powers of enterprise and initiative usually lacking in agencies of government." This was because "it has been relatively free from the restrictive controls by the more cautious Departments, such as... External Affairs." King, to the contrary, decided that External Affairs should be consulted by the NFB in making films touching on foreign relations. As for *Balkan Powder Keg*, it was ordered withdrawn from circulation, twice.[10]

The affair with the film was a clear sign of things to come as the war was nearing its end. It indicated that the relationship between the Board and the government was not totally without problems. As such, these problems underlined the boldness and the level to which NFB films ideologically and politically challenged hegemonic politics and values. It is fair to say, however, that the confrontation over *Balkan Powder Keg* was almost unique in its magnitude and outcome. For the most part, NFB films were mostly produced and screened without direct government interventions and hurdles.

THE ROLE OF WORKERS IN THE WAR

An important element in Grierson's and Legg's advocacy of unity in fighting fascism had to do with how they linked it to defending the ideals of democracy and social justice. This was advocated in films that focused on western countries and/or those that focused on the political and social situation in the Soviet Union. In both cases, the welfare of workers and their role in providing a decisive foundation for defending democracy constituted a recurrent topic.

As we saw earlier, many labour militants and union organizers during the days of the confusion around the role of the Soviet Union in the war were reluctant to throw their support behind the government's war mobilization effort. However, after Hitler's invasion of Russia, a different situation emerged within the Canadian labour movement. This situation eventually influenced and reshaped the ideological nature and the level of labour's involvement in supporting the war efforts.

By June 1941 the Communist Party – still operating illegally – began to call for mass mobilization in support of the war. The main political premise for the party's new position was that the defeat of fascism required unity of all social and political forces. The party stressed the paramount importance of full labour participation in mobilization efforts. It argued that unity between workers and other classes and sections of society would be better served through creating a new social and political pact, one that guaranteed a better and more effective setting for building solidarity against fascism. The party used its focus on unity to press the federal government to grant full rights to labour unions, to enshrine and respect principles of collective bargaining, and to ensure the equal participation of workers in the organization of Canada's war effort.[11]

By the summer of 1942 a Canada-wide Communist-Labour Total War Committee (CLTWC) was created with the goal of providing labour support for the war. The Committee launched a campaign to pressure the King government to introduce conscription and step up its contribution to the war in Europe. It also demanded that the government intervene against companies that provoked strike situations, and that a revision of the federal government's labour policies concerning wages, collective bargaining, labour-management relations and participation in the war effort should be undertaken immediately.[12] In return, the Committee pledged labour peace at the workplace for the duration of the war. The Communist Party policy as embodied in the CLTWC pronouncements reflected a new approach on the role of labour in the war. It also complemented Popular Front strategies adopted and variously implemented by communist parties around the world at the time.

Fighting fascism was now considered synonymous with respecting and advocating unity among Canadians. The issue of respecting the rights of labour and its supporters, was echoed in the House of Commons by Communist Party supporter Dorise Nielsen on several occasions. In one particular speech, Nielsen warned that the continuation of government measures against labour activists was jeopardizing the entire cause of fighting fascism:

> The Canadian Seamen's Union [at the time a Communist-Party-led union] is trying to enlist six thousand young seamen to go into the merchant marine – a dangerous and difficult job, for which a young man needs to be well versed in the ways of the sea. The union is not having all the success it would like in obtaining these six thousand men, and I will tell why – because the president of the union is interned in the Hull goal. If he were free, I should like to guarantee to hon. Members that this man Sullivan could recruit six thousand men for the merchant marine. If this is an all-out war effort, you cannot afford to neglect the help of any single man or woman who is ready to do something to enlist the sympathies of the people.[13]

This shift in the positions of the labour movement and the communist left towards the war reinvigorated the enthusiasm for fighting fascism among workers. It also helped improve the organizational skills of communists among workers. All this reshaped how the politics of fighting fascism were construed ideologically among many Canadians. It also meant that Popular Front arguments in this regard were strengthening and sharpening their ideological and organizational influence among broader sections of the Canadian population. As a result, the cultural discourse on the war was also being revamped. While earlier NFB films mainly stressed official government positions on the war and almost entirely ignored the role and input of workers and labour unions, most films that were produced after 1942 offered a different valuation of these issues.

Workers' enthusiasm in joining the fight against fascism and their eagerness to support the war increasingly became a central subject in NFB films. Equally as important, these films would now regularly stress that workers should be appreciated not only for their actual enlistment to go to the front in Europe, but also for their role at home in providing the economic engine for the anti-fascist struggle.

Thank You Joe (1942, no credited director) tells the story of a Canadian soldier recalling his work in building trucks and tanks in Windsor and how this work directly and positively impacted his ability to perform his duties as a soldier. Without the ability of workers to perform on various fronts, the film argues, the country and its allies' capacity to conduct a successful war against fascism would be impossible. In *Bluenose Schooner* (1943, Douglas Sinclair and Edmund Buckman), we are escorted on a cod-fishing trip to the Grand Banks, courtesy of a group of fishermen from Lunenburg, Nova Scotia. The film celebrates the courage of a thirty-man fishing crew as they pursue their work in the midst of the ever-present danger of German submarines. The theme of workers' sacrifice in building a sustained base for fighting fascism and providing Canadians with the economic edge to survive the war is once again reiterated.

Other films, however, would also suggest that the enthusiasm of workers to join the battle in Europe occasionally posed an obstacle to their much-needed presence on the lines of industrial production. This theme is presented for example in Alan Field's *Coal Miners* (1943), which describes how soldier coal miners eventually return home on furlough to help with coal production. The film makes a point of emphasizing the importance of the multifaceted and central role of working-class people. Within this pretext *Coal Miners* discusses the participation of workers in the political process, and enunciates the need to give them a more proactive and role within the country's social and political leadership.

NFB films stressed the need to integrate and release the collective power and energy of society on the widest possible scale. They urged the coordination and mobilization of the country's work force and resources. To achieve this, they argued that the role played by workers in providing the concrete and material ingredients for victory should be rewarded by allowing them a higher level of involvement on the executive and leadership levels, i.e., both within the workplace and in politics. To this effect, films argued for an equal partnership between labour, business and government.

Citing Abraham Lincoln's infamous political pronouncement: "when the common people rise to find their liberty, not the gates of hell will prevail against them," *The War for Men's Minds* (1943, Stuart Legg) argues that unity on the home front is essential for defeating fascism. The film alludes to the creation of the Labour-Management Committees as an example of how such unity is achieved in practice. These Committees, the film suggests, encourage and enhance the eagerness of "the working man" to take part "in the people's war." The film then argues that what would eventually win the war is not "belief in the superman," but "having faith in the unity of people." As it argues the case for supporting people's unity, *The War for Men's Minds* warns of the consequences that might result if western nations were to fail, as they did before the war, the ideals of the French and American revolutions. It reminds its audience that only when we believe in the "supremacy of the common man" in a society that is "founded on cooperation," and that "all men are created equal" will we be able to build a better future for the country and its people. The film marked Grierson's and Legg's "first attempt to predict and discuss the world beyond war."[14]

Another group of NFB film made frequent reference to the relationship between producing weaponry on the factory shop floor and using it on the battlefield. These films emphasized the equal importance of the contributions made by workers and those made by soldiers on the front lines of the battle. By visually coupling clips of images from the warfront in Europe and industrial factories across Canada, these films underscored the variety of and the connection between the ways people can contribute to the defeat of fascism.

Great Guns (1942, producer Graham McInnes) and *Industrial Workers* (1943, no assigned director) describe in detail how the steel and pulp production of the Great Lakes is transformed into actual weaponry. Both films are charged with relentless barrages of shots depicting workers as they "mold steel into fighting weaponry." In *Fighting Ships* (1942, Robert Edmunds and Graham McInnes), Robert Edmonds tells the story of a shipyard worker who feels that he has not been playing a vital role in the war. The worker is taken to watch the launching of a corvette and realizes that each job, however small, plays a major role in the ocean battles. A similar topic is relayed in *Ships and Men* (1944, Leslie McFarlane) where a tribute is made "to the men and women who built Canada's merchant ships during the war and those who sailed in them." Throughout the film images from the Merchant Seamen's School are juxtaposed with shots of workers building a Canadian ship and finally launching it into action from the shipyard. An argument is made in support of an increased government role in providing training to help develop the skills of the Canadian work force.

Keep 'em Flying (1942, producer Graham McInnes) and *Ferry Pilot* (1942, producers Stuart Legg and Ross McLean) both discuss the vital position played by aircraft workers. They also stress the role of women workers in the aircraft construction industries. In the latter, Legg and McLean visually bridge the gap which geographically separates the aircraft factory, the civilian transport pilots, and the battlefront in Europe, to describe how the Allies created the "efficient and diverse systems of the Air Force Ferry Command." A similar theme is echoed in *Target Berlin* (1944, Ernest Borneman), where we are introduced to the details of producing and building a Lancaster airplane, the first large bomber to be produced in Canada. The film describes how the plane's construction relies on the work of an army of "thousands of people." Once again, the emphasis is on the collective contribution made by working people in different stations of work. In *Trees that Reach the Sky* (1945, Beth Zinkan) we follow the process by which labour converts a sitka spruce tree. It follows the tree's transformation from the time it is felled until it is integrated into the edifice of a Mosquito bomber. The thread of images detailing the concreteness and materiality of the production process and the involvement of workers in various stages of construction binds and spurs the energy of the entire film's plot structure.

Trans-Canada Express (1944, Stanley Hawes) introduces yet another facet of the contributions made by workers in support of the war effort. It depicts the chain of events that eventually led to the building of the Canadian railroad system "linking Canada's 25,000 miles of territory." The film discusses how the role of workers of all industries and in supply centres represents the "vein which fuels the Canadian economy throughout the country to sustain the defence capacities of the allied forces in Europe." While the film only briefly deals with the efforts made by workers in building the railroad, it is clearly more concerned with the present day significance of the system and its workers in supporting the fight against fascism. Conspicuously absent from the film's historical approximation of the railroad building epic, however, are the central role and major sacrifices made by Chinese immigrant workers in the construction of this system.

Another film, Ernest Borneman's *Northland* (1942) describes the role of mining industry workers, and looks at the mining towns and camps of the Canadian north. The film travels across different mining locations and draws a vivid picture of the hard and dangerous job of workers as they ensure an uninterrupted flow of Canada's energy resources. *Getting Out the Coal* (1943, no credited director) depicts how British miners big-cut and load coal on conveyors, and how machinery is then moved into battle positions. Both above mentioned films present powerful images and shots that are edited by way of inferring an epical portrayal of the toiling process and the enormous input by workers.

Robert Edmonds' *Coal Face, Canada* (1943) specifically tackles the campaigns initiated by labour unions to mobilize people in support of the war. Co-produced with the United Mineworkers of America and Coal Operators of Canada, the film conveys the story of a young man who, after being discharged from the army, returns to his coal town and finds most things have not changed or improved from when he was there. As he takes a room with a miner who used to know his dead father, and he attends a union meeting and listens to workers speak about the war and their role in it, he realizes the importance of remaining home and contributing to producing coal as a critical task for achieving victory in the war. He eventually joins up to work in the town's mine.

Aside from the idealized and at times simplistic portrayal of harmonious relations between trade union activists, *Coal Face, Canada* nevertheless positively addresses an important subject: the role of labour unions in educating workers about their rights and providing them with an assured sense of pride in their work and their contributions to society. The film affirms the crucial task and responsibility of unions in "defending the rights and improving the lives of workers." Variations on these themes were offered throughout the 1943 industrial newsmagazine series *Workers at War*, but the series also emphasized the benefits of introducing publicly owned and operated economic projects.

Clips from various NFB films were introduced in the newsmagazine, which was screened in workplaces, union halls and other working-class community settings. The series emphasized the socialized character of modern industrial production and the crucial role played by publicly owned industries. It also contemplated the utility of these industries in developing the economic strength of the country, a strength upon which the victory over fascism depended.

In two specific instalments of the newsmagazine we are introduced to a team of 10,000 workers "who over a year's work on the Saguenay River Dam were able to build a facility that would generate enough electricity to light every North American home." This facility, one film affirms, would "produce the gum that provides aluminium for victory and peace thereafter." Another film, *PX for Rubber* (1944, Graham McInnes) depicts the construction of the government-owned Polner Corporation Factory in Sarnia. It dedicates the achievements of this synthetic rubber production facility to the effort of workers from different ethnic origins: "the construction of the plant took the work of a 5,000-strong labour force of several racial origins including Polish, Russian, French Canadian, English, Czechs and Indian men and women." These workers, the film adds, "laboured day and night in 1942 to build the facility." Both films emphasize the importance and efficacy of publicly owned enterprises in creating stronger bases for "fighting fascism and winning the peace." However, not all NFB films depicting workers in this period had the war in Europe as their main thematic backdrop.

Another set of films focused on the role of workers in ensuring economic and social progress and prosperity for the entire nation. For example they delineated the workers' excavation of the country's material resources and wealth, and how this contributed to the development of the economy and to strengthening the welfare of the entire society. In *Coal for Canada* (1944, no credit), we get a glimpse of the tough and dangerous working conditions in an undersea mine in Sydney, Nova Scotia. The film draws a picture of the entire production process. It traces in detail the dynamiting, loading and grading of the coal, and then shows how it is loaded on a freighter that transports it to industrial centres across the country. *Salt from the Earth* (1944, no credit) infers a similar story that looks at the mining and processing of salt. The film takes us on a tour of a salt mine in the Nova Scotia town of Malagash. It describes how the work being performed in this mine is capable of supplying the world with its salt needs "for the next 500 years."

The apparent simplicity of these films' pronouncements involved much more complex propositions that were also at the heart of how Marxists argued the notion of labour value. These pronouncements offered an outlook that affirmed work and the labour value creation process as *the* central element within economic production. As such they inadvertently demonstrated an important component of Marx's economic theory, which placed the onus of creating economic value on the qualitative and quantitative work power put into the production process rather than on capital investment and/or managerial input. NFB films consistently prioritized the value of work in fulfilling the economic and social needs of Canada. They pointed out the prudence of utilizing collective social energy and resources for the benefit of the entire society. Efficient and highly coordinated social and economic planning, and the equitable distribution of wealth, were both introduced as rational alternatives to the inefficiency of the old methods of production that mainly relied on the whims of profit-motivated private economic initiatives. Within this context, these films also prioritized government involvement in organizing and leading the production and distribution of the country's economic wealth.

In addition to discussing issues related to industrial production, NFB films also tackled concerns pertaining to the agriculture sector. Utilizing the society's work force to meet its economic and social needs was the theme of repeated interventions by Dorise Nielsen during the debates of the House of Commons. Agriculture was an important constituent in Nielson's pronouncements. In the following excerpt, she addresses the situation in the agricultural sector and makes some specific proposals:

> [The question of labour] comes up whenever one thinks of agriculture. Perhaps there is a solution of that problem. I know already that high school and university students are again going to help in the fruit-picking areas. I would suggest that in certain areas the boys in the army might also go out and help. After all is said and done, I have heard that in many areas the boys are fed up with being restricted to their routine bit of drill and so on, and at certain times of the year they certainly could and would enjoy helping in some farm operations.[15]

As they dealt with the situation in Canadian farms, NFB films urged organizing labour resources to meet the production priorities of Canada and the world. Films like *Battle of the Harvests* (1942, no credit), *Farm Front* (1943, no credit), *The Farmer's Forum* (1943, no credit), and *Ploughshares into Swords* (1943, no credit) address the challenges facing the agricultural sector of the economy and stress the urgency of creating a rational balance between social food demands and the work resources required to satisfy them. The theme of systematizing social and economic energies was posed as a commonsensical way to approach the question of satisfying the food needs of society. But this issue was of substance not simply because of its relevance for Canadians, but also for the whole world community.

In response to the call to initiate collective international efforts to battle food shortages in Nazi-occupied countries, for example, some films focused on how these countries had been forced to hand over their farm produce to Germany, leaving their populations without food. Important examples are Stuart Legg's *Food: The Secret of the Peace* and Sydney Newman's *Suffer Little Children*, both produced in 1945. These films suggested that western countries were obliged not only to feed their own populations and oversee armies, but also to prepare to meet the challenges of feeding hundreds of millions of people in Europe and Asia after the end of the war.

THE ROLE OF WOMEN WORKERS

The outbreak of the war in Europe resulted in major labour shortages that affected the general performance and output of the Canadian economy. The sudden and substantial increase in demand for war machinery and the mass recruitment of men in the armed forces resulted in an upsurge in demand for a higher level of participation by women in the Canadian work force. These changes took place at a time when the struggle for women's equality was still in its earlier stages.

On the one hand, the increased involvement of women in the work force occurred as the Canadian political establishment maintained a belligerently patriarchal attitude towards women. Arguing against admitting women into the armed forces, for example, the Minster of Defence James Ralston insisted that while he realized "how patriotic these ladies are in their desire to do war work," the fact remains that "everyone who desires to be directly engaged in war work cannot be so engaged."[16] Even working duties outside the battlefields were frowned upon as uncharacteristic of what women were supposed to be doing in real life. Several NFB films saw the increased involvement of women in the industrial work force as a temporary response to the extraordinary specific demands of a war situation. They suggested that after the end of this exceptional situation, women would be expected to return back to their "natural" jobs at home.

As they made a case for the importance of women's contribution to the war industry, the message in NFB films such as *Proudly She Marches* (1943, Jane March) was that this work would be merely temporary. The film even hints that such line of activity (e.g., working in heavy industries or as military personnel) is "unnatural" for women. As it points out the resourceful capacity of women who work as technicians, photographers, photographic developers, aircraft workers and technical experts, the message of the film remains focused on the provisional duration of women's involvement in this line of work.

In *Home Front* (1944, Stanley Hawes), we are introduced to the story of "Canadian women shouldering the tasks of maintaining the home front and providing the support needed by the fighting men." Women's work in ammunition plants, garment industries, aircraft and other heavy machine factories is presented as an example of how women could work "side by side with men." But while it talks about a future where society becomes more dependent on "the skills of women," the film still conceives of women's involvement in the work force as means "to release men for more urgent work." Another film, *Wings on her Shoulders* (1943, Jane March) expresses "appreciation" for the jobs performed by women in the war aviation industry. The primary message, however, is that women are fulfilling those jobs "so that men could fly" their planes in war-torn Europe and contribute to the success of the air-strike campaigns against the Nazis. A similar message is presented in *She Speeds the Victory* (1944, Philip Ragan). The film once again urges women to enlist in the work force so they can "free men for battlefront duty."

Clearly, all the above-mentioned films saw the increased involvement of women within the industrial work force as a transitory response to the demands of extraordinary war circumstances, after which women were expected to return to their natural jobs at home. On the other hand, the relatively well-entrenched leadership-level participation by women within the labour movement, and within various organizations and groups of the Canadian left, made an important impact in forwarding an alternative and ideologically counter-hegemonic discourse on the role of women in society. For their part, other NFB films expressed hope that developments that occurred as a direct result of the war would, and should, plant the seeds for a new attitude towards involving women in the work force. They also argued that the post-war period should witness greater emphasis on guaranteeing gender social and economic equality within Canadian society.

A set of films presented a bold new approach towards the topic of women and work. In *Handle with Care* (1943, George L. George), the discussion is focused on the role of Canada's munitions industries and one factory's reliance on a largely female labour force. A Montreal factory "owned by the people of Canada" is presented as an example to rebuff claims that women are incapable of performing complex work tasks. The film argues that the performance of women in the facility is a testimony to their ability to master "accurate and precarious work." In *Canada Communiqué No. 3* (1943), we are introduced to an "army of women shipbuilders" on the West Coast. These women workers, the film asserts, had proved their capacity to work in an industry that has been traditionally conceived as a "men's domain."

Other films reflected interest in creating a social support system that could help guarantee the future participation of women on a totally equal footing with men. Gudrun Parker's film *Before they are Six* (1943), for example, describes the need, feasibility and benefits of creating day nurseries, where working women can rely on the expertise of a trained staff to supervise the meals, health and play of their children as they get increasingly involved in the country's work force. Furthermore, several NFB films involved an unprecedented participation by women filmmakers.

Film historian Barbara Martineau compiled a list of fifteen films that were irrefutably made by women during this period. In these and other NFB films of the period, women filmmakers played "central roles in the overall output of documentary films."[17] She cites a filmmaker who made a major contribution to offering an alternative discourse on women during this period. While most women filmmakers were subjected to blatant discrimination in their wages and to a concerted effort to suppress their social and political views, one filmmaker in particular was able to become "actively involved in the production of war films at a decision-making level." This filmmaker was Jane March, the director of *Women Are Warriors* (1942) and *Inside Fighting Canada* (1942), among others.[18]

Martineau argues that in contrast to how other films dealt with the theme of women and war, and despite pressures to water down the original screenplay's socioeconomic analysis, Jane March's *Women are Warriors* offered a particularly powerful message about the role of women in society. The film explicitly linked the fight against fascism and the role of labour with the need for an alternate approach to the involvement of women in the work force both during and after the war. The film provides an intricate analytical approximation of how the demand for workers grew during the war, but also points out how women in different countries became involved in all aspects of the fight against fascism even before the war began. In this regard the film describes the contributions made by women in England, Canada and Russia and insists that women were not leisurely idlers before the war, and that in their roles as "domestic workers, secretaries, and whatever work that was available for them at the time," women were always part of the work force. Nevertheless, the film suggests the war itself brought major changes in conception about the role of women in society. In England, for example, "they now transported planes from factories to airfield, and operated antiaircraft guns." In Canada "women have joined active military support service and the work force in tens of war machine and munition factories." In Russia they are fighting "on the front lines and act as parachute nurses, army doctors and technicians."

The film paints a picture of the interactive relationship between issues such as women's equality, liberation from fascism, and the forging of a new society where democratic values would be fulfilled in the context of the "liberation from want." As she discusses the situation in the Soviet Union, March explicitly describes how "over twenty years ago the Soviet Union achieved what only today women are achieving in the West." She is referring here to the constitutional rights achieved by women in the Soviet Union after the Bolshevik Revolution which provided the basis for them to "work equally with men" in all "social and economic sectors including as petroleum engineers and as farmers." This multifaceted participation by women in all areas of work, the films suggests, also strengthened "the formidable ability of Soviet society to mobilize against Nazi Germany." *Women are Warriors* concludes with a note which once again reminds its audience that when the war erupted, and as a direct result of achieving gender equality, women in the Soviet Union were ready to be active "on all the front lines of the battle." Still, as Martineau's article suggests, further progressive aspects of the film were undercut by the studio-dictated narration, particularly when it came to the vigorously feminist live-action cinematography – most of which came from Soviet stock shot selections.

Jane March's other war film *Inside Fighting Canada* describes the transformation of the country into a "fighting machine" with women playing a major role in maximizing the level of war-arsenal manufacture. In the spirit of the democratic cooperation of its people, and as a nation "created by men and women," the film argues that Canada has also become the foremost training-ground for allied airmen and for the recruiting and training of soldiers. The film directly refers to women workers in the lumber, farming and shipyard industries. It also makes a visual tribute to women farmers, truck drivers, those working on construction sites, and those in other industries. As it stresses the importance of women's contribution during the war, *Inside Fighting Canada* emphasizes that this effort should not be conceived as "a temporary war measure," and that instead, it should be considered the start for a new era where women can equally contribute to building a better future for the entire society.

Piers Handling suggests that *Inside Fighting Canada* encountered strong opposition from the Ontario Censor Board; the Board delayed the release of the film, claiming "inaccuracies" in some of its data. He points out that the establishment's hostility towards the film has to be looked at in connection with "some labour strikes and threats of strikes, demands for the resignation of federal cabinet ministers, and a great deal of open criticism of the wartime administration."[19] One among a small number of films that explicitly posed connections between gender, social and economic liberation, it is hardly surprising that the Ontario Censor Board's patience with the film's daring message was so thin.

Stuart Legg's *Inside Fighting Russia* (1942) also pays special tribute to the role of women in the war. In a similar manner to the way March approached the topic, Legg emphasizes the significance of the interactive link between social and economic aspects of the liberation of women in the Soviet Union. This liberation, he argues, strengthened that country's ability to withstand enemy attacks, fight back and ultimately disrupt Hitler's plans and timetable. To the background of images of working men and women, the film alludes to how the Soviet system envisioned a new outlook on the role of women in society. It suggests that women workers were now "represented at all fields and levels of the economy and culture." It also gives examples of how, in the aftermath of the Nazi invasion, "Soviet women had no problem taking over the control and the operation of over 60 per cent of the industry in Russia." This power, the film concludes, "enabled the country to effectively mobilize its resources against Nazi Germany."

Clearly, however, the movement that at one point had been instigated by the Communist Party and the Popular Front did not conceive of the fight for women's equality as part of an independent "women's agenda" per se. Most labour and left wing activists and intellectuals looked at the issue of women's equality as integral to the more encompassing goal of the social and economic liberation of the entire society. The 1992 independent film *Rebel Girls* (T.J. Roberts) presents an elaborate account of the political discourse of left-wing women labour activists of the period and how they looked at their own struggles, both as women and as workers.[20] The struggle for women's equality was seen as an element that supplemented, rather than displaced, the "strategic priority" of liberating the entire society. As such, many NFB films that, on the one hand, promoted values of cooperation, social change, democracy, and labour rights would, on the other, show blatant insensitivity and sometimes total disregard towards the multiple forms of oppression suffered by working-class women.

Nevertheless, the discourse on women workers during the war as presented in many NFB films, in fact represented a watershed in how Canadians traditionally saw women on the screens of their film theatres. For the first time in Canadian history, NFB's films offered images of women performing outside of the traditional private spheres of their homes. These films also presented women playing new roles within the work force beyond nurturing babies and attending to the needs of their husbands and families. In contrast to what was being produced in Hollywood, much of which objectified women sexually or idealized them as mothers, daughters and wives, NFB films presented a different picture that was, at least, more reflective of the reality of women's roles during the war period. In this regard the hegemonic film discourse on women was being challenged not only on the level of how they were represented, but more importantly, in connection with providing an alternative perspective on the nature of patriarchy. Canadians were confronted with the issue of women's liberation not simply as an ethical or moral question, but as an economic, social and political question that concerned the entire society. It is within this context that NFB films effectively bestowed a counter-hegemonic outlook on one of the fundamental cornerstones in patriarchy's ideological pretext: its emphasis on the gender-based division of labour.

7 WORKERS, DEMOCRACY AND SOCIAL WELFARE IN NFB FILMS BETWEEN 1942 AND 1945

Several NFB films from 1942 to 1945 tackled issues with direct impact on management-labour relations, social welfare, housing, and labour safety standards and regulations. As they contemplated the post-war future these films evoked past experiences. They argued that reorganizing society should account for and try to overcome mistakes that hindered progress and led to social and political tensions. The films concluded that there was a need to adopt new methods that specifically addressed economic and social concerns. One important proposal was creating and maintaining a structure for democratic partnership between labour, management and the government. This partnership was seen as beneficial to the entire society.

As I noted earlier, films dealing with labour issues emphasized the link between the general goals of social, political and economic welfare and the implementation of ideas such as collective planning, control and utilization of social and economic resources. In this regard, charting efficient and well-organized methods to address social and economic questions was considered crucial for encouraging stronger participation by workers in the political leadership of the country. This concurrently meant that better living and working conditions for the entire society represented a logical alternative to the old and chaotic methods of past pre-war practices.

This chapter focuses on how the notion of democracy in the workplace was applied through the creation of the Labour-Management Committees. The role of the cooperative movement and the use of film and media as instruments for democratic practice will also be addressed as two major elements in NFB films' propositions. Special attention will be given to a group of discussion films that were specifically produced to encourage workers' and communities' participation in pondering social and political problems. Finally, a separate section will appraise how NFB films tackled the issue of veterans returning to Canada after the end of World War II and how this impacted the notion of post-war economic and social reconstruction.

WORKERS' ECONOMIC AND SOCIAL CONDITIONS

NFB films dealt with the immediate concerns of workers by way of contemplating plans for post-war reconstruction. Social and economic problems facing workers comprised an important topic in NFB films. The war in Europe necessitated taking urgent looks at inflation, job security, health, work safety and housing. In response, many films focused on the benefits of collective economic and social planning and the need to coordinate workers' energies in the post-war reconstruction process.

Films stressed that new approaches should replace old chaotic ways of dealing with problems, which only focused on solutions that could be brought about by relying on private corporate competition and interests.[1] As they dealt with the everyday problems and concerns of average workers and citizens, these films favoured taking a socially responsible attitude, not only as a basis for improving the overall economic performance of the country (i.e., in the context of identifying and allocating resources according to specific economic priorities), but also as a politico-ethical alternative aimed at strengthening the role and position of labour within the political process.

Fighting inflation represented an important topic for labour at the time. With the economy in full swing and with near-full-employment conditions, there was also relative shortage in consumer goods – stemming largely from the shift towards producing war-related goods and machinery – and inflation was becoming a potentially serious problem. To sustain some stability in the level of advances made in labour's living standards during the war, the trade union movement reluctantly accommodated the government's wartime price- and wage-control policy. For their part, NFB films reflected the anxiety about rampant and unchecked inflation. Several films by animator Philip Ragan dealt expressly with this topic.

Prices in Wartime (1942), for example, emphasized the role of government and the Prices and Trade Board in helping sustain the value of wage increases achieved during the war, which resulted in workers' improved living standards. Another short film titled *If* (1942) argued that if wartime controls were to be relaxed, the vicious spiral of inflation would threaten the entire economy. The film underlined the need to deal flexibly and differentially with the conditions created under wartime. It stressed that under a war situation, bidding, for example, raises the prices of goods that are in high demand. As a result, steps should be taken to raise the wages of workers to meet higher prices. This, the film argued, could result in higher cost of production and in inflation spiralling out of control. Several other films by Ragan, including 1942's *Story of Wartime Controls* and *Story of Wartime Shortage*, and the 1944 film *How Prices Could Rise,* offered similar arguments.

Another animated film that tackles the problem of inflation is Jim MacKay's *Bid It Up Sucker* (1944). The film tells the story of an auctioneer who manages to sell a basket of goods worth under $10 for $35. This film, however, pushes further the discussion on inflation by demonstrating how through bidding up of consumer prices, rampant capitalist market forces could trigger economic crises. Equally interesting is the film's depiction of a lone protester who constantly tries to interrupt and warn against the danger of the whole bidding process but is finally thrown out of the auction room! The same theme is relayed in another MacKay film, *Joe Dope Helps Cause Inflation* (1944). This two-minute film (among the first cel-animated films ever to be produced by the Board) once again warns against manipulating prices during wartime.

The issue of inflation, however, was not the only concern raised by NFB films. Job security, and the need to provide social and economic safeguards against future unemployment, comprised another important theme in a number of films. After years of labour protests that advocated creating a national program of economic relief for unemployed workers, the government finally legislated the Unemployment Insurance Act (UI) in 1943. NFB films showed exuberant support for the program, which had been on the list of demands of the Canadian labour movement and the Canadian left since the early twentieth century.

In *A Man and His Job* (1943), Alistair M. Taylor depicts the story of an unemployed Canadian worker. The story spans the man's years of unemployment in the Depression through 1943, the year when UI was implemented. It compares the inefficiency of dealing with the problem of unemployment without the intervention of the government and leaving it to the whims of market forces with the benefits of implementing public policies that socially and economically maximize the utilization of society's labour resources. The film concludes that the Unemployment Act represented a major step towards achieving the second alternative. As a result of the new Act, the film argues, Canadian workers would become the beneficiaries of a national program that for the first time in Canada's history made the problem of unemployment a collective social concern and responsibility.

Other films discuss ways of improving the conditions of workers both inside and outside the workplace. In Gudrun Parker's *Before They Were Six* (1943), we are introduced to a day care program for children of working women. The film demonstrates how for a very small sum of money this program allows a working mother to leave her child at a day nursery where trained staff offer meals and supervise the health and play of children. Parker presents the centre as an example of how communities and governments can and should cooperate to create and maintain programs that are of extreme benefit to society both during and after the war. Another set of films stresses the urgent need to take concrete steps that would ensure workers' well-being at work and at home. Issues of physical and mental health as well the safety of workers in the workplace are considered here fundamental and therefore should become the collective responsibility of the entire society.

In *Thought for Food* (1943, Stanley Jackson), the emphasis is on providing soldiers, industrial workers and other employees with adequate nutrition to keep them in healthy physical condition. Another film, *When Do We Eat?* (1944, no credit), points out that in many cases workers are forced to eat their meals at varied hours and under difficult and stressful conditions. The film warns that numerous industrial accidents resulting from such situations can be prevented, and the illness rate can be substantially reduced, if workers ate "the proper types of food to maintain maximum strength and energy." It then urges the managers and personnel supervisors in factories and other workplace locations to build or improve their employees' eating facilities, and wherever possible provide them with well-run canteens. Stressing the health of workers as a critical element in maintaining a strong society and economy is also the topic of the Discussion Preface and trailers of two films; one American, entitled *When Work is Done*, and another from the Soviet Union, *Sports in the USSR*. Both films focus on the importance of worker's physical and mental fitness and advocate involving workers in recreational programs and activities and providing them with adequate sports facilities.

After Work (1945, producer Stanley Hawes) also illustrates the need to offer recreational facilities to help keep a healthy work force. It argues that a "working partnership between management, civic groups and workers" is essential to provide the support needed for building recreational centres for dancing, singing, handicrafts, swimming, and developing extensive sports facilities. In one episode of the 1943 series *Workers at War* we are introduced to a fitness class in a Vancouver factory designed to help workers keep fit and healthy. The film suggests that implementing such activities into the daily schedules of workers helps them maintain better and more alert job performances.

Another particularly important issue in NFB wartime films is the problem of working-class housing. The urgent need to alleviate shortages in working-class housing was also a critical demand among communist, Popular Front and labour supporters. In a speech in front of the House of Commons, Communist MP Fred Rose alerted his colleagues that the housing shortage in urban centres such as Montreal resulted in an alarmingly hazardous health situation. In the working-class Cartier district, Rose pointed out, "ninety-three out of a hundred thousand die of tuberculosis as compared with twenty in Notre Dame de Grace and forty in Westmount." He then reminded the government that under the War Measures Act it did have the power to effectively deal with the situation:

> We have power to build the five thousand homes which I would say are badly needed in the city of Montreal.... The government must have the power... to undertake a big building scheme, which is very greatly needed. Men are being laid off in factories; materials are available, and such a scheme could be undertaken to-day. In addition to anything done to provide people with houses which they may rent at the rates they are able to pay, we should also make it possible for people to build homes. We have a credit bank for business men, so why not extend credit to people for this purpose. Many aspire to build their homes; this is their dream, so let us help make that dream come true.[2]

Building new housing for working families was clearly deemed by communists and their supporters as a socially and economically feasible alternative to current shortages and degenerating housing conditions.

The NFB film *Wartime Housing* (1943, Graham McInnes) illustrates how rapid wartime industrial expansion pressed the need to build decent housing for workers. It explains that due to the major industrial growth during the war, many workers were moving to major urban centres. Some of these centres had no settlement prior to the new factory construction. To deal with the problem, the film contemplates building small pre-fabricated homes that can be constructed quickly and efficiently. Another film illustrates the possibilities that come with organizing labour resources to efficiently build houses for workers. In *Building a House* (1945, Beth Zinkan) the idea of collective work and using more labour power is considered to be a more efficient way of dealing with the housing crisis. The film poses its argument in the form of a school question: "if nine men can build a house in sixty-four days, how long will it take seventy-two men to build a house?" The question is answered by demonstrating that a prefabricated house can be erected in a single day by using the labour force of a higher number of workers. The workers are then shown laying the groundwork, and doing the carpentry, brick-laying, and painting, and later bringing in the furniture to the house. The film concludes that a collective effort and efficient utilization of the work force not only provide work for people but also supply the grounds for better living conditions for workers, their families and ultimately the entire society. It then reiterates that the efficiency of coordinated socialized work can also be a feasible alternative in other areas of social and economic development: "One man's work depends on another's man work, not only men working directly on a house but also those in factories, mines, etc."

During the period between 1942 and 1945, many NFB films consistently stressed the value of work in producing material goods that are essential to fulfill the needs of people. These films saw economic efficacy in the idea of utilizing collective energy and resources for the benefit of the entire society. Efficient social and economic planning and the equitable and just distribution of wealth and resources were presented as rational alternatives to the inefficiency of the old methods of production and distribution that relied solely on values of individual and private economic profit. In particular, NFB films argued for the need to share and organize society's resources to meet the challenges resulting from the shortage of goods caused by the war.

What Makes Us Grow (1943, no credit) deals with the priority of providing essential nutritional diets for children. It demonstrates how vitamin deficiencies have long-term negative effects on youth. In *Children First* (1944), Evelyn Cherry discusses the value of milk and other dairy products in children's daily diets, particularly in the context of widespread war shortages in other consumer goods. The film focuses on the need to organize the use of milk in a manner that corresponds with the needs of society. It suggests that providing sufficient quantities of milk to children, teenage youngsters and expectant mothers should take precedence in consumption plans. The main message is that sharing is sensible and is a socially and economically more feasible option than selfish or chaotic individualism and over-consumption. The film repeatedly points out that by sharing we ensure that "there will be enough to go around." It also argues that it makes no sense for any society to "waste its selfish luxuries in a world filled with hungry people." *School Lunches* (1944, Evelyn Cherry) presents another appeal to support a publicly sponsored program that provides nutritional school lunches to children in the rural areas of the country.

A similar sentiment is expressed in the 1944 film *Six Slices a Day* (no credit). The film urges Canadians to consume more nutritious cereal products so that other types of foods that take more time and effort to produce will be available for use overseas where war has devastated the agricultural sectors of several countries. In *A Friend for Supper* (1944, producer Graham McInnes), an appeal is made so that children do not waste food. It points out that other children in Russia, China and in occupied Europe are going hungry, and that it is indeed our responsibility to ensure that these allies who have been sacrificing on an even more extensive level as a result of being at the forefront of fighting fascism are supported in their hour of need. Clearly here, social responsibility is considered not simply as a Canadian concern but as a matter of international significance. Expressing solidarity with the needy on a world level is itself regarded as contingent on our ability to more efficiently identify our own production and distribution priorities and our methods of consumption. The above-mentioned films argue that workers and other sections of society would all benefit when a serious effort is made to coordinate the "cultivation" of Canada's social and economic resources, and when society deals cooperatively with both its pressing and long-term problems.

DEMOCRACY AND THE ROLE OF THE LABOUR-MANAGEMENT COMMITTEES

A major set of NFB films during the same period was dedicated to the topic of labour and the decision-making process within the workplace. Films proposed and supported the creation of social and political partnerships, which in addition to involving labour would also include management and government. This partnership, the films suggested, would help improve working and living conditions for workers and, in the process, would meet the urgent demands of wartime industrial production. Films also argued for strengthening democracy in the workplace by expanding consultation and decision-making practices by workers on the grassroots level.

An important aspect of the NFB's discourse on the partnership between workers and business related to the role of the newly created Labour-Management Committees (LMC). As we saw earlier, support for these committees in NFB films has been the subject of criticism by some film critics. In a nutshell, some critics considered the creation of committees an ominous indicator of how business and government were able to force labour into submission to capitalist over-exploitation.[3] The main problem with those criticisms, however, is that they underestimate the specific conditions and the historical moment within which these committees were implemented. Another problem originates in these critics' mystified and largely narrow view of the nature of working-class counter-hegemonic action as consensual revolutionary practice (a 'war of position,' as Gramsci would argue), rather than a "war of manoeuvre" aimed towards overthrowing the capitalist system. With consensual practice the main goal is to broaden the appeal of, and show in practice that implementing alternative approaches to present forms of organizing society and the means of production are indeed possible and feasible and could eventually work better for the subaltern. As such, support for the creation of the LMCs exceeded the working class's own realm of influence and/or the Communist Party's base of political support; in hindsight it incorporated the support of a socially and politically heterogeneous mass movement that included much broader sections of society, and hence allowed the idea of labour's participation in the managing of economic resources to become more plausible among greater number of people.

The creation of the LMCs helped offer a counter-hegemonic perspective vis-à-vis the role of workers in society. Within the framework of the new committees the role of the working class was acknowledged as a central, albeit not necessarily *the* central, element in generating successful economic performance. Hence, the implementation of the LMC structure was an acknowledgment of the need to effectively involve the working class in the management of the production process. The partnership between labour and business essentially became a tool that working people hoped would reverse business's unilateral control over the operational and the decision-making processes in the workplace.

Creating the Labour-Management Committees was partly a result of the efforts by an advocacy policy within the labour movement that stressed unity between various social and political forces in the fight against fascism. This policy echoed how left-wing supporters (particularly supporters of the Communist Party and its Popular Front strategy) identified the political tasks of the working class during the period of fighting fascism. In a speech in the House of Commons, Dorise Nielsen reminded her colleagues of the significance of labour-management partnerships in strengthening the fighting front against fascism:

> To-day labour is asking for partnership with industry in production, not because labour is demanding merely on its own behalf a share of what the pickings might be, far from it, but because the men and women who form our labour forces realized long ago the danger of fascism. They started to fight it long before this government ever took up the case of democracy against fascism. These men and women who work are anxious to have partnership with industry in production.

On the effect of such partnership on improving the level of industrial production, Nielsen stated:

> It is apparent that in their own factories [trade unions] are undertaking to devise ways and means whereby a greater output can be accomplished. If only the labour forces of this country could be granted a little more of the partnership idea with industry in production, I feel convinced that production would go up by leaps and bounds.[4]

Big business's consent to the creation of these committees, however, was not totally voluntary; it was achieved under pressure by an increasingly well-organized labour movement. It was also reached as a result of the government's own preoccupation with maintaining labour peace during the war.

Some NFB films were specifically made to promote the role of the Labour-Management Committees while others were simply part of Discussion Prefaces or trailers to other films. In both cases, films viewed labour-management partnership as an indication of the feasibility of consultative democratic practices within the workplace. The partnership between labour and management was also portrayed as an effective tool for initiating and successfully building projects that would benefit the entire society.

In *The New Pattern* (1944, Stanley Hawes and Fred Lasse), the role of the LMCs in Britain is given as an example of how cooperation results in launching and accomplishing major projects. The film argues that the role played by the committees was behind the successful building of an urgently needed airfield. It also shows the process of electing members of one LMC committee and gives a glimpse into the way in which discussions were conducted and decisions made. The film also demonstrates how suggestions and proposals were incorporated and dealt with, and how this was reflected positively on the level of production efficiency and quality. It also argues that the committees encouraged and maintained a high level of ongoing democratic grassroots participation by workers, which in itself improved the committee's performance and the success of the project.

In *Democracy At Work* (1944), Stanley Hawes discusses the production of weapons in Britain during the war. The film argues that Britain's ability to maintain a high level of industrial production was largely due to the implementation of partnership agreements between the labour movement and the employers' federations. *Partners in Production* (1944, producer Stanley Hawes) discusses how coordination between management and labour helped readjust the priorities of production during the war in a way that increased the volume of industrial output. Two other Discussion Prefaces deal with similar themes and include a presentation by a government official on the issue of labour-management cooperation followed by a related discussion by a group of industrial workers.

The 1945 film *Labour Looks Ahead* (producer Stanley Hawes) surveys workers' achievements during the war in connection with the creation of the Labour-Management Production Committees. It compares these committees to other organs that encouraged and served similar goals such as the Wartime Labour Relations Board, the International Labour Office, and the World Trade Union. The presence and equal participation of workers within these structures is offered as a basis for developing a new kind of relationship between workers, employers and government, as well as among workers of various countries.

In *Work and Wages* (1945, producer Guy Glover) the success of the experiment of labour and management cooperation during the war is rendered as an example for the need to develop this relationship even after the end of the war. *Partners in Production* (1944, producer Stanley Hawes) discusses a similar topic while placing more emphasis on the successful integration of women workers into war factories. The film presents the goal of total democracy within the workplace as an essential ingredient in waging a successful war against fascism. It also refers to the LMCs success and effectiveness within the coal-mining industry. *Partners* points out that this success testifies to the importance of cooperation between all constituent elements of the production process.

The LMCs, however, had limited success in achieving their ambitious goals. As the war neared its end the Committees became a major liability and source of inconvenience to big business. The committees would become among the first casualties of the post-war era when business would regain its full pre-war level of control over the operation of industrial production processes. For workers, the creation of the committees reflected the fruition of their struggle to affirm a new role for themselves. Labour conceived these committees as instruments by which it could at least assume an acknowledged position in the management of the workplace, including the decision-making processes vis-à-vis production priorities, work conditions, personnel problems, etc. For the left, this new labour role was considered a step in the right direction that could eventually help demonstrate the feasibility of its strategic propositions to increase working-class involvement in managing the means of production and, by extension, in setting the agenda for operating the country's economy. As such, the committees offered a counter-hegemonic alternative value system to the commonsensical rationalization of the capitalist division of labour between, on the one hand, management and ownership, and on the other, waged labour. In other words, the committees brought the working class into a sphere, which – in the context of capitalist hegemony – solely belonged to the capitalist class.

THE COOPERATIVE MOVEMENT

The issue of democracy was also discussed in connection with cooperative control and utilization of the country's economic resources. A number of NFB films particularly praised the role of the cooperative movement in advancing a spirit of solidarity among people during hardships, and pointed out its effectiveness in building social and economic prosperity for working people. As with films dealing with the Labour-Management Committees, those dealing with the cooperative movement basically affirmed the values of organizational efficiency, the sharing of resources, and common social goals, and presented them as politico-ethical alternatives for building society and enhancing the economy.

A good number of films focus particularly on the cooperative movement on the Canadian east coast. *Grand Manan* (1943, written by Margaret Perry) illustrates how people of this New Brunswick island earn their living from fishing in the Bay of Fundy. The emphasis is on the collective methods used by the island's fishermen, and the interdependency that involves the people of the community. This mutually supportive method of work and lifestyle is featured as a dynamic that has also helped sustain and enrich the community's cultural heritage.

In another film, *Trappers of the Sea* (1945, Margaret Perry) we learn about the lobster fishing industry in Nova Scotia. A major emphasis here is put on the role of the cooperative movement in improving the economic performance of communities, and in helping them sustain their interactive social and cultural heritage. A keen appreciation of community sharing and collective control over resources is shown in connection with its effect on other aspects of social life on the Canadian east coast. Margaret Perry's 1943 film *Prince Edward Island* offers a glimpse of the Island's history and includes an overview of its social and economic development. The early days of the island's history are described in the context of how wealthy English proprietors owned all the land while Scots, English and Irish immigrants came as tenants and worked without any claim to property. After Confederation, big landowners were forced to sell, and the farmers became owners of their own land. The film stresses that farmers and fishermen of the island later maintained a cooperative and credit union system to help them develop "better processing and marketing" of the island's resources.

The film uses a historical analysis of a specific community that draws a picture of the class dynamics of its economic development. In this regard it points out the historical specificity of the class-based form of economy, and contemplates the possibility of its overhaul. Given contemporary debates around class, capitalism and socialism, in the emphasis on dealing with the social dynamics of the island's history, the film essentially offers a dialectical and thoroughly political approximation of history. Ironically, today's NFB website blurb totally deprives the film of its ideological significance by identifying it simply as one that "offers a look at Canada's smallest province, Prince Edward Island." The blurb continues, "known worldwide for its potatoes, the islanders are expert lobster fishermen as well as world leaders in raising foxes." It then describes how the film also offers a glimpse of the famous Green Gables house as well as the legislature building where Confederation was born.

A similar theme is alluded to in what is probably the only film of the period to deal with a mainly Quebec-related working-class setting and topic, which also involves a filmmaker from Quebec. Jean Palardy's *Gaspé Cod Fishermen* (1944) describes how a collective effort "brings together the people of Grande-Rivière on the Gaspé Peninsula to catch, prepare, and sell the cod upon which they depend for food and income." The work of members of the Grand Rivière Cooperatives is depicted as an example of the efficacy of a socialized organization of production. The film illustrates the joint work made by members of the community from when they set out to fish through to the point when they begin to organize the distribution and sale of their products. It demonstrates how this work constitutes the main element of success in keeping the community united and economically self-reliant. It also depicts further aspects that extend the community's collective practices and control to the town's co-op store, which provides it with most of its daily living needs. Palardy also describes facets of the grassroots political democracy as practised by the community, pointing out its utilization of collective discussion and decision-making practices. As such, the community articulates new forms of "building democracy into their own way of life," the film argues.

Lessons in Living (1944, Bill MacDonald) describes the life in the British Columbia town of Lantzville, where a community composed of people from different ethnic backgrounds works in various economic sectors such as farming, fishing, lumber and railroad building. The community pulls together to improve the town's public school. They transform an adjoining barn to serve simultaneously as a community hall for the parents, a school gymnasium and a workshop for the farm-mechanics class. With the improvements made on the building the whole school program is broadened and the community as a whole has expanded resources; "pulling together can achieve anything," the film commentary suggests.

Philip Ragan's animated film *He Plants for Victory* (1943) tells the story of a man named Plugger who organizes his neighbours to cultivate vegetables in an urban vacant lot. A few weeks later, when his wife looks sadly at the results of her isolated one-person farming, Plugger points out to her how the cooperative garden in the neighbourhood, with its shared tools, seed and experience, produced enough vegetables for all members of the co-op. Collective work is once again presented as means for increasing productivity. Furthermore, organized collective forms of production are perceived as alternatives to individual, and, possibly by extension, capitalist mode of production. Another film, *The People's Bank* (1943, Gudrun Bjerring), delineates a history of the Credit Union movement and suggests ways of organizing these unions. The film praises credit unions as options that offer communities new financial opportunities that, on the one hand, are owned by them, and on the other are capable of addressing their own needs and concerns rather than those of bankers from outside these communities. Once again, what we have here is a potentially bold ideological statement that can only be interpreted as an argument which, at the very least, looks unfavourably at one of capitalism's most sacred institutions, the banking system.

WORKERS, MEDIA AND DEMOCRATIC ACTIVISM

Various NFB films focused on the significance of using media as a tool to advocate grassroots political discussion and interaction. In particular, they perceived film and other new media outlets such as radio as apparatuses that could be employed to encourage workers and other citizens to discuss problems at work, as well as national and international politics and affairs. As such, these films saw the use of media as a tool for discussing labour and other issues as a practice that provides for a stronger basis for a grassroots participatory democracy.

Large numbers of NFB films used a relatively new film forum referred to as Discussion Films. These consisted of three-minute sketches where several people engage in an informal discussion about specific themes. Most of these films were prepared as trailers or prefaces to other film titles. Rather than promoting specific opinions, Discussion Films were intended to provoke grassroots deliberations on various topics including those relating to labour and work. Some of these films incorporated preliminary presentations or interventions by labour activists on other NFB productions or recent British or American movies. Others featured appearances by government officials. Occasionally they would also present shop-floor discussions among workers dealing with issues ranging from workplace problems to international politics.

Unfortunately, most of these discussion trailers have been lost and therefore it is hard to fully evaluate their actual significance. However, some accounts by contemporary filmmakers who took part in making these films allude to facets of their ideological importance. In his book on Grierson, James Beveridge quotes Donald W. Buchanan's 1944 article "The Projection of Canada." The article designates some of the implications associated with producing and utilizing the discussion films:

> A new movie technique, however, is proving effective in encouraging these and other audiences to come forth with their own opinions. This technique consists briefly in the presentation of a three-minute "discussion movie" in which four people appear on the screen in an informal argument centering on some topical theme. The National Film Board has now made "trailers" of this nature to follow the movies *Battle of the Harvests*, *Forward Commandos*, *Inside Fighting Russia*, and *Battle Is Their Birthright*. The last one has been particularly effective and has called forth much debate on the place of youth in modern society.
>
> In such ways the motion picture with its visual impact become a rally to social discussion. It can relate one part of the nation to the other, as in *Coal Face, Canada*; it can make local problems fit into the scheme of work events, as in *Battle of the Harvests*; it can serve as a spur to group activity, as the *People's Bank*.[5]

Such an approach, Buchanan suggests, brings an ongoing living quality to the film as a tool that encourages social and political activism:

> That is how the value of the Canadian documentary movie appears, not as an entity in itself, but as part of a larger entity. Those who direct, photograph, edit, and prepare a film for 16 mm distribution, are only the first participants in its creation as a living object. The men and women who finally bring it to life and useful activity are those who project that particular movie; in some small hall, some factory or club room, and so relate its values to local needs and aspirations.[6]

Discussion Films (the majority of the films in the other discussion series *Getting the Most out of a Film* were produced between 1944 and 1946) incorporated a wide range of topics that in addition to tackling the war-mobilization efforts also dealt with issues facing working-class communities. Issues concerning workers in the agricultural sectors were also introduced as part of discussions that were pertinent to the entire society. All in all the trailers depicted discussions on problems in the workplace, labour and management partnerships, relations between urban and rural workers, and labour union coordination on local, national and international levels.

The topic of economic injustice inherent in capitalist free market, for example, was presented in a trailer to the American short documentary *Story with Two Endings* (Lee

Strasberg, 1945). The film depicts the disastrous result of runaway prices following the First World War and warns Americans against repeating the crisis as the Second World War nears an end. In another trailer, *Tyneside Story* (1944), Stanley Hawes depicts members of a Toronto-based trade union local as they discuss potential problems in post-war employment. The trailer is based on a British film of the same title. Another trailer presents several union members as they discuss the British film *Second Freedom* (1945, Fred Lasse). In the trailer, workers express interest in creating a Canadian social- and health-security system that guarantees the minimum economic and social needs of Canadians. In another, a group of farmers and industrial workers jointly discuss the issues raised in the film *Valley of the Tennessee* (Alexander Hammid, 1945). Among the subjects considered is the co-dependent relationship between rural and industrial workers, rural land rehabilitation, and the improvement of rural living. In *Farm Plan* (1944) agricultural production figures for 1943 are recorded and compared to those of 1944. Farmers are encouraged to discuss and elaborate on plans to meet new essential requisites for wartime agricultural production. Other trailers dealing with labour issues include *Canadian Labour Meets in Annual Conventions* (1944), which features speeches by trade unionists discussing workers' rights and responsibilities.

Discussion films also dealt with the war situation and contemplated the role of workers in the post-war period. They discussed the need to allow workers and the labour movement to become politically more involved in domestic and world affairs. In a trailer for the NFB film *Now the Peace* (1945, producer Stanley Hawes), workers from various Vancouver-based trade unions express their hope that, through economic and political cooperation, the newly established United Nations will be able to reduce the threat of war in the future. They also suggest that international peace and cooperation are topics of vital concern for workers around the world. In a trailer titled *UNRRA – In the Wake of the Armies* (1944, producer Stanley Hawes), trade unionists discuss the work of the UN Relief and Rehabilitation Administration. Discussants stress the importance of joint international cooperation as the basis for the success of humanitarian relief efforts.

The use of media as an interactive discussion tool to deal with issues of social and economic development is also dealt with in a film about the Canadian Broadcasting Corporation (CBC). The film concentrates on the role of the CBC in building links between Canadians from different social backgrounds and from different parts of the country. *Voice of Action* (1942, James Beveridge) emphasizes the role of radio as a democratic mediator which allows people across the country to share their views and contemplate their future. It points out the network's role in offering medical advice and personal news broadcasts to remote northern outposts. Furthermore the film describes how the CBC network provides extensive educational forums on labour and farming. The film's opening scene refers to the central role played by workers in providing the material base for victory against fascism. After depicting some of the forums and discussion circles that the CBC helped organize around the country on several occasions, the film stresses that the network has a responsibility to contribute to the country's fight "to help create a future where the earth and its wealth would become the common heritage of all." The role of media here is clearly seen in the context of its social relevance. It is viewed beyond its entertainment value and as such is mainly regarded as vehicle for building bridges between people. Equally important, the film proposes a new role for the CBC: an instigator of political debates. As such the film boldly advocates that this institution should not simply function as tool for government propaganda. Instead, the film proposes that the CBC contribute to discussions such as how to implement the concept which advocates "sharing the wealth of the earth by all," a finely tuned proposition for the network to facilitate more debate on an ideological concept which directly impacts the discussion on capitalism and socialism.

The significance of the discussion trailers' impact on the political culture of the day is most clearly manifest in their encouragement of debates involving contentions that themselves had major political and ideological connotations. Firstly, these trailers pointed out the prospect of opening media outlets to political debates. In essence, they proposed that public space should also become a space for political action. Secondly, they advocated that workers find their place at the centre of these debates and actions; given their major contributions to the war effort and to creating the country's wealth, workers were reciprocally encouraged to express their opinions about how the workplace *and* the country as whole are managed and run. Thirdly, these trailers addressed a clearly counter-hegemonic outlook on what constituted democratic practice. While the tendency within capitalist democracies is to emphasize elections as the main arena of political democratic practice (or at least the only ones that really count), the weight in the films was given to grassroots political engagement as an ongoing process that surpassed both the temporal and spatial specificity of official election campaigns. Lastly, by encouraging the idea of using government-owned media as an arena for political discussions that reflected more than the views of the government, these trailers projected the possibility of altering the role and nature of media as a political tool. In other words, these trailers contributed to affirming as common sense the idea that since people own these institutions it is therefore normal that they have a stake in how they are run, and what they deal with.

Looking at some of these propositions (particularly the ideas of institutional political 'neutrality' in public debates, and the need for government accountability in publicly owned and administered institutions) from today's vantage point, it is hard to fully appreciate their full ideological significance. Perhaps part of the reason why they are not fully esteemed has to do with the extent to which such propositions have now become integrated and assimilated aspects of our Canadian commonsensical values. Indeed these ideas have now become the standard expectations from government-run public institutions. Today, debates are centred on *how* such ideas are practically implemented rather than on *if* they should be implemented. Looking at the context within which these ideas emerged and the political dynamics behind their materialization helps us understand the dialectics of counter-hegemony and how it affects political and ideological perceptions.

RETURN TO JOBS

As the war neared its end, concern was raised about the future of war veterans who by then were already beginning to return to Canada. Coinciding with the veterans' return, major changes were also taking shape in the Canadian economy; they included shifting the production of war machinery and munitions to a substantially lower gear.[7] This affected the composition of the Canadian work force inherited from the war, and pushed for structural adjustments in the country's economic and industrial priorities. Securing jobs for returning war veterans, many of them victims of unemployment and poverty before the war and during the Depression, represented an urgent and critical task for the government. In contrast to the shortage in labour capacity during the war, the sudden overflow of returning workers was becoming one of the main problems facing the government in the early post-war period.[8]

For their part, left-wing labour unions and the Communist Party advocated maintaining the overall economic production levels achieved during the war. They suggested that Canadian living standards had risen, and that a sudden reversal of this trend would result in dangerously high unemployment and would eventually lead to economic recession. Based on this view, these groups proposed maintaining earlier levels of economic production and creating new government programs to modernize and refashion Canada's economy. They also suggested measures to build and improve infrastructural facilities throughout the country. These proposals were viewed as a means to avoid future social upheavals and to move the Canadian economy in a socially progressive direction. In a speech in the House of Commons, lone Communist MP Fred Rose presented his party's view on the issue:

We should draw up a huge public works plan to include such things as the development of the St. Lawrence waterway, the development of our natural resources, the modernization and reconstruction of our cities, the abolition of slums, the rebuilding of libraries and hospitals, and the development of modern highways to give our people work. Again I may be asked where the money is to be found. Well, during this war we have proved that we can find the money if we look for it and work hard enough to get it.[9]

Rose was referring to the emergency economic measures taken during the war, most of which encouraged the creation and expansion of specific industries such as the military. Rose was hoping for similar approaches to be implemented in relation to peacetime priorities and needs.

The communist left and its allies claimed that if the government adopted the task of modernizing and reconstructing Canada's economy according to social priorities, and if it initiated programs that efficiently reutilized the resources that were put into the war effort into abolishing slums and building homes, hospitals, schools, libraries and recreational facilities, the situation caused by the return of soldiers could be effectively dealt with in a manner that benefited all Canadians by creating full employment. Other funds could be allocated to rebuild and extend Canada's economic infrastructure and develop Canada's natural resources.[10]

A substantial number of NFB films dealt with the veteran's return to Canada and the potential danger of acute job shortages. These films advocated social and economic solutions that would guarantee a smooth shift into the post-war period. The approach put forward in these films reiterated the general framework proposed by the communist left and its labour and left-wing supporters.

In *Veterans in Industry* (1945, Fred Lasse) the emphasis is on coalescing the goal of reinstating veterans in their original jobs with providing these workers with adequate retraining. Developing workers' skills would eventually lead to satisfying the requirements of the post-war period, the film argues. Other films like *Looking for a Job* (1945, producer Nicholas Balla) and *Reinstatement in Former Job* (1945, producer Jeff Hurley) survey government programs to help reassign former members of the armed services to civilian jobs. Both films affirm the need and feasibility of securing the workers' old jobs. They also assert the principle that in the end it is the responsibility of the entire society to ensure that veterans are reintegrated back into the work force and that they become full participants in building post-war peace.

In *Welcome Soldier* (1944, producer Graham McInnes) a discussion featuring a labour leader and several returning servicemen and servicewomen focuses on problems facing veterans as they enlist in former jobs or attempt to find new ones. Once again the accent is on reaffirming belief in public responsibility towards these workers, and on the need to ensure that their welfare and future work contribution to society are not jeopardized. Similar discussion is introduced in *Veterans in Industry*, where the leader and members of the Winnipeg Trades and Labour Council suggest expanding economic growth programs to deal with the problem of reintegrating veterans into the national work force. In *Canadian Screen Magazine* numbers 1 and 7 (1945), we are introduced to programs that train veterans in the areas of building trades, haircutting, mechanics and electronics. These programs are presented as tools that can help Canada face up to the economic and social challenges of the post-war period.

Back to Jobs (1945, producer Nicholas Balla) focuses specifically on the possibilities associated with retraining injured war veterans. The film emphasizes the importance of providing special courses to retrain these veterans and prepare them to resume active roles in Canada's labour force. As it describes the return of workers to farms, fisheries and natural resources industries, the film stresses the need and the feasibility of initiating new programs that could help injured war veterans learn and utilize new work skills. The responsibility to undertake such initiatives, the film highlights, lies in collective cooperation between veterans, communities, government and industry. The theme of direct government involvement in helping veterans adjust to post-war conditions is presented as part of initiating programs that provide low-cost loans to workers and farmers within the agriculture sector. *Home to the Land* (1945, Stanley Jackson) describes the new Veteran Land Act, which was created specifically for the purpose of helping returning soldiers buy town lots and farms as well as farm machinery, fishing boats, building material and livestock.

In general, all NFB films dealing with the war veterans' return echoed themes proposed by the communist left, particularly in the way they stressed the government's responsibility in dealing with the unemployment issue. Clearly, however, these films were short on specifics; to begin, most them were very short (mostly two to three minutes long) and as such were hardly able to do justice to this complex issue. As explained earlier, the communist left proposed creating new jobs on the basis of a programmatic emphasis on modernizing the country's infrastructural facilities, and on identifying new industrial and economic priorities. These films did not offer or deal with such proposals and instead relied on the general affirmation of the principle of government's responsibility in alleviating the potential problem of unemployment.

LABOUR LOOKS AHEAD

With the end of the war looming on the horizon, NFB films looked towards the future and contemplated creating a new international order founded on the ideals of social, political and economic justice and cooperation. They looked at peace as an expression of stability that could only be enhanced by eliminating poverty, social inequality, and national and racial hatreds. Reflecting upon the possibilities of the post-war era was also at the heart of how John Grierson and his executive producer Stuart Legg saw their own mission as the NFB's top executives. For these two major NFB players the post-war phase was to become the highlight of their careers at the Board, and as trend-setting filmmakers. They saw making films about unity and about the war against fascism as a prelude to work in the "more exciting" era of peace. As Gary Evans suggests:

> Unlike the Germans, who believed that war made splendid propaganda, Grierson had long been committed to the Bertrand Russell maxim that peace should be made as exciting as war. As Grierson put it bluntly but privately in 1943, "I confess I can't ever get very excited about the war effort per se and feel that any information regarding it must somehow try to get behind the shot and shell. The surface values – the guns and the campaigns and the braveries and the assembly lines and the sacrifices – are, I think, taken by themselves the greatest bore on earth." Grierson had turned his eyes to peacetime information. He hoped to get relevant government departments behind such concrete themes as conservation, nutrition and people as producers and consumers, so that all the information would be tied to common ends. He foresaw in this organization more a ministry of Education than anything else.[11]

For their part, NFB films constantly expressed their anticipation of the new phase when they would play a part in building the new society. They also looked forward to helping forge a new era in international politics that was based on cooperation, peace and building bridges between peoples and nations. They advocated wider public involvement in discussing, implementing and advocating economic and social projects that would benefit societies and help them curtail future wars and conflicts.

In relation to labour, these films praised the role of workers in the war and promoted increasing their role in constructing the fundamental ingredients for peace: social stability, justice and prosperity. In this regard, they also urged that workers directly benefit from the fruits of peace. The effective utilization of economic and social resources during the war was seen as a demonstrated example of what could be achieved, if emulated, when working towards a better and more equitable prosperity for humanity in the post-war era.

LABOUR, PEACE, AND INTERNATIONAL COOPERATION

On the international level, the Popular Front strategy as promoted by the Canadian Communist Party prioritized continued cooperation between western allies and the Soviet Union. They considered this cooperation as fundamental to the implementation of successful progressive domestic social and economic policies.[12] Continued cooperation between anti-fascist countries during the war was itself seen as a guarantee for world peace and for international prosperity. In this regard, NFB films also urged sustained collaboration among Allied nations and paid special attention to advocating the building of a better relationship with the Soviet Union.

This view concurred with the outlook agreed upon by the Allies (including the Soviet Union) in the late 1943 Tehran Summit. International collaboration at that point seemed possible, and consecutive Allied summits held in Yalta, and then in Potsdam in 1945, confirmed the feasibility of a peaceful coexistence between the west and the Soviet Union. Connection between international peace and national prosperity in the post-war era was itself a recurring theme in Fred Rose's speeches in the House of Commons. In one particular speech, Rose linked international cooperation and Canadian social and economic development:

> [T]here can be no prosperity for Canada in the post-war years unless international cooperation is developed to the fullest possible extent in the world. The issues of peace and prosperity are inseparably linked together. The fight for markets, which in the past has been one of the chief causes of war, can now for the first time be resolved on the basis of a new concept-planned world economic cooperation.[13]

A key to the success of this proposal, Rose argued, would be the joint cooperation between "capitalist democracies and the socialist Soviet Union" and the "resolving of conflict among the capitalist nations."[14] The argument from the left was that international cooperation, particularly between the west and the Soviet Union, would also result in a better political and economic climate for improving working-class conditions in Canada.[15]

Wartime NFB films emphasized the priority of working towards a safe and peaceful future for humanity. In this regard specific focus was maintained on the creation and development of the United Nations with the full participation of all countries, including the Soviet Union. This was seen as fundamental to building better world relations. Mutual respect between different social and economic systems, these films argued, would help maintain peace and international cooperation.

Of particular significance to studying how NFB films conceived of international relations in connection with the Soviet Union is Tom Daly's 1944 *Our Northern Neighbour*. The film presents a historical survey of Soviet foreign policy from 1917 through World War II and argues that it is important to create solid bases for cooperation between the west and its "Northern Neighbour." The film provides an overview of the history of the Soviet Union and describes how Soviet citizens were interested in building an alternative to the state of hunger, despair and economic ruin that characterized their lives prior to the Revolution. It concludes with a message made on behalf of Soviet citizens: "we seek the cooperation of all nations, large and small, to eliminate tyranny and slavery, oppression and intolerance." The theme of post-war cooperation between Canada and the Soviet Union is also discussed in *Global Air Routes* (1944, Stuart Legg). The film tackles the subject of developing air transportation routes during wartime and suggests that considering the success of that experience nations should articulate new approaches to conducting international civil aviation. Critical to such development, the film argues, would be to ensure a higher level of coordination and unity between different nations. The main emphasis in regard to the "new approach to civil aviation" is to create and utilize new air routes connecting the Soviet Union with Canada and the U.S. across the North Pole. These routes, the film suggests, would provide "free access to all and for all" and would become part of a new system "dedicated to the common interest of mankind." In *Gateway to Asia* (1945, Tom Daly), the focus is on developing high-speed planes to create new links between Canada, Russia, China, and India. The film argues that the utilization of these planes could benefit all societies involved, and provide a solid base for economic and social development.

International cooperation was also seen as an essential ingredient for building a world free from poverty, need, and inequality. In this context, the structure of the United Nations was looked at not simply as a tool to keep the peace but also as a vehicle to enhance cooperation on various social and economic issues. In *According to Need* (1944, producer Dallas Jones), the stabilization of consumer prices in Canada is portrayed as an essential step in guaranteeing an effective sharing of Canadian-produced agricultural machinery by all the Allies. The film revolves around the theme that "the needs of one are a problem of all." In *The Peace Builders* (1945, producer Alan

Field) concrete steps are proposed to the Allies and the newly established United Nations to enhance the ideas of peace and international economic cooperation. These policies would be implemented in the context of guaranteeing the internal social stability of each country. A critical aspect of this task would be to avoid "repeating the mistakes of the past." Economic and social development on the domestic level, the film argues, help prevent international tensions and hence provide a better atmosphere for maintaining peace between nations. Dorise Nielsen's speeches in the House of Commons repeated arguments identical to those proposed by several NFB films. Economic and social prosperity in Canada, Nielsen argued, would secure Canada's ability to help create an atmosphere of international cooperation:

> We need cooperation of the Soviet Union. We know that the Soviet Union will be one of the greatest buying nations in the world after the war, and it is imperative for us that we have markets in order that our farmers can continue, and even increase the production of food; so that we can have increased employment on our farms, and better living conditions on them; so that industrial workers and returned men can have employment, and so that our national income can be kept at high levels, or even increase.[16]

The theme of international stability is also presented in the context of addressing the immediate problems stemming from the war.

Suffer Little Children (1945, Sydney Newman) presents the case of over "60 million children in Europe who became part of a major post-war refugee dilemma." The film discusses how clothes and toys from Canadian and American villages and towns helped bring some comfort to these children. It also describes the role of the United Nations' Relief and Rehabilitation Administration in providing food, clothing, shelter, medical care, education and attention to victims of war. But as it argues for finding ways to deal with the situation, the film's main focus is on finding temporary and charitable answers rather than long-term solutions.

In *UNRRA – In the Wake of the Armies* (1944, Guy Glover), trade unionists discuss the work of the UN Relief and Rehabilitation Administration and propose that international cooperation in relieving social suffering is key to world peace. In *Food: Secret of The Peace* (1945) Stuart Legg points to the main problem facing post-war liberated Europe. The film opens with scenes of the food queues and hunger riots in famine-struck areas of Europe. Starvation is a political danger, and Legg reminds us that the ascendance of fascism before the war was directly linked to the west's inability to deal with its own economic and social problems. The film then describes the measures taken by the Allies to deal with the problem of food shortages in Europe.

Communists and their Popular Front policies saw the participation of labour in the process of rebuilding the peace as another crucial element in post-war social and political reorganization. One aspect of labour's contribution to peace was linked to the ability to advance and affirm its own views on international politics. In a speech before the House of Commons, Fred Rose stressed the importance of bringing labour to participate directly in the San Francisco discussions on establishing the United Nations. Rose called for the inclusion of official workers' representatives from the ranks of organized labour as part of the official Canadian delegation. He argued that such a step would reflect Canada's "new spirit and give a lead to other nations to follow." Citing the role it played during the war, Rose reminded his colleagues that labour was

> one of the biggest and most homogeneous groups of the Canadian population. Labour has played a fine role in this war; labour is concerned about the future of Canada's peace and prosperity, and the organized labour movement should therefore have representation at the San Francisco conference.[17]

For their part, and by way of dealing with issues of international cooperation, NFB films showed a similar interest in involving workers in the process of building a new international order. In this regard, they stressed the need to carefully listen to the opinions expressed by workers in connection with international affairs.

In the film trailer *Now the Peace* (1945, producer Stuart Legg) members of various Vancouver unions discuss future world stability and ideas about building peace. Several argue that sustaining a peaceful world largely relies on guaranteeing social and economic prosperity within each society. They also suggest that mutual respect in international relations is another key to stability. The trailer depicts workers as they express hope that through economic cooperation, the newly established United Nations "would be able to reduce the threat of war and in the process increase the security and prosperity of workers everywhere." In one *Canadian Screen Magazine* program (1945) the emphasis is on how workers can directly contribute to international peace and cooperation. As an example, the film delineates how Canadian workers were building railway cars and shipping them to the Soviet Union to help rebuild the Russian transportation system.

WORKERS IN THE POST-WAR ERA

Films also posed an acute vision of the post-war period in relation to social, economic and political development within the country. They asserted that workers needed to feel that their share of social and national wealth had indeed improved in the aftermath of the war. They also urged that working people in the new era be directly involved in a leading capacity in the process of building peace. Communists and their labour and Popular Front supporters presented a similar vision. They advocated raising workers' living standards and saw this as a step towards securing better economic and social conditions for all Canadians, including Canadian businesses. Fred Rose argued this case in the House of Commons:

> ... raising popular purchasing power... would provide Canadian business with an annual market for a half a billion dollars worth of goods. This is practically half of our total pre-war exports. That means that we must have post-war polices which will raise substandard wages, increase farm income and provide a national minimum of social security.[18]

NFB films gave prominence to the theme of providing workers with new means to improve their economic and social lot. They also pointed out the interrelationship between improving working-class living conditions and bettering those of all Canadians.

In *Labour Front* (1943) the argument is that the workers who had been toiling on the assembly lines during the war, and who were able to meet the needs of fighting fascism, have the right to expect new opportunities to share in the benefits of peace. The ability of Canadians to jointly meet the challenges of war is seen as a proof of their aptitude for addressing the challenges of peace. *New Horizons* (1943, Evelyn Cherry) presents a similar view of the positive effects of the industrial development that accompanied the mobilization for war. Such development, the film affirms, has to be rearticulated in conjunction with the longer-term social and economic needs of the entire society.

NFB films also stressed that cooperation between labour, management and government had been instrumental in the success of war efforts. Such cooperation was seen as equally important in peacetime periods. In *Labour Looks Ahead* (1945), Stanley Hawes suggests that achievements made during the war are testaments to the successful impact of equal labour participation in the decision-making process. The film refers to "the successful work of the Labour-Management Production Committees" during the war as an example of how Canadian workers can, in the future, help design, plan and execute the tasks of building peace.

Presenting the story of a young miner who has just been discharged from the armed forces, *Coal Face, Canada* (1943, Robert Edmonds) conveys the hope that with the war nearing its end there are new opportunities for workers to contribute to the political and economic decision-making process. The film emphasizes the role played by the trade union movement in building social and political awareness among workers. As an older worker converses with a young dischargee about the advances in building solidarity among workers, we catch a glimpse of a book in the union hall's library: *The Right to Work*. The miner assures the young worker that "miners today are more aware of their rights and their place in the world." The film concludes that building unity among workers on the local, national and international levels helped open their eyes to the value of their power and to their ability to conduct a mutual struggle to build "a better place for themselves," and "to win and build a better world for all." The tribute to the trade union movement here is clear. But what is more striking is how the film celebrates the political role of this movement. In hindsight, *The Right to Work* not only acknowledges and supports the role of trade unions in advocating workers' rights and addressing their problems in their separate workplaces, but more importantly supports their role as apparatuses within which the working class becomes more politically involved in influencing issues of relevance to it as well as to all Canadians. As such, the film subscribes ideologically to the idea of moving the working class in the direction of, to paraphrase Marx, becoming a class *for* itself instead of being a class *in* itself. Furthermore, it points out ways through which this class can play a leading role within society, the result of which would be to become a gravitating centre for a new Gramscian historical bloc that would lay the ground for a historic transformation away from the capitalist mode of production. The general features of this fundamental transformation can be detected in how NFB films argued the case of utilizing collective energies and sharing the benefits of society's development.

NFB films reiterated the notions of effective economic and social planning, sharing the benefits of economic growth, and the full utilization of labour resources as fundamental features of rebuilding the world in the post-war era. These films also expressed hope that after the war people would learn to avoid tribulations similar to those in the years following World War I, and that they do this by learning how to employ their common and collective resources effectively. They argued that work that was capable of utilizing the energies of people represented an efficient alternative to uncoordinated work and production methods. The ability to plan and maintain a balance between the work of individuals and the larger needs and capacities of society was deemed crucial to maintaining peace and creating future social prosperity. In this regard, social interdependency was presented as a source of strength to the collective as well as to individuals. The value of economic production itself was mainly measured by its ability to satisfy the needs of society, rather than by generating profit. In other words, instead of stressing the value of products as commodities, NFB films tended to emphasize product value in terms of how it satisfied actual social needs and priorities.

Organizing the country's labour resources to meet war needs is the main topic in *Curtailment of Civilian Industries* (1943, Philip Ragan). The success of the nation in shifting its economic priorities towards producing war machinery is conversely seen as an indicator of its ability to shift its post-war future priorities to a new gear which addresses the goal of social prosperity for all Canadians. *A Man and His Job* (1943, Alistair M. Taylor) discusses the economic chaos, waste and overproduction that characterized the years of the pre-Depression. Avoiding the repetition of that situation, the film suggests, would require articulating new programs that streamline social-economic needs with available labour work force. In *Prices in Wartime* (1942, Philip Ragan), we are warned against repeating earlier mistakes that allowed for the wasting of valuable labour and production resources. The film reminds us that during the Depression this waste came at a time when labour was capable of increasing national income by 60 per cent. The film argues for better social and economic coordination and planning to ensure the maximum utilization of the nation's economic resources. Another film, *Subcontracting for Victory* (1942) demonstrates the advantages of reorganizing industrial production operations to take full advantage of the productive capacity of large and small industries. It argues that this redeployment would allow industries to satisfy the needs of war machinery production.

A similar theme is discussed in Raymond Spottiswoode's *Tomorrow's World* (1943). Once again, the film begins with a warning against repeating post-WWI mistakes, "when countries went into overproduction, and when chaotic and reckless production failed to meet the needs of people." The world has to learn the benefits of using its energies and resources in an efficient manner, the film argues. Since society has now acquired the skills needed to utilize its collective resources, to conserve its needs and identify its priorities, and since the production capacity of the nation during the war has reached new heights, Canadians and people around the world can now look for new opportunities. With the devastating experience of the war behind them, people realize that the human energies and resources that were summoned for war can also be "released for the service of common men." They would now have more conscious appreciation of the feasibility of the idea of building a "better tomorrow" which would be more prosperous and better planned than ever before, one in which the earth would be rid of "fear and want." In *Workers at War* (1943), the building of the Saguenay River Dam in Quebec in less than one year using the labour of ten thousand workers is offered as an example of the effective utilization of resources for peacetime goals. *Training Industry's Army* (1945, Vincent Paquette and Ronald Dick) delineates that during the war, Canadian industry adopted more efficient methods to develop labour skills. Similar application of vocational training, the film suggests, can be used to develop, adapt and expand war-based skills and industries to meet peacetime priorities.

Other NFB films discussed the possibilities and benefits of utilizing the available work force on a nationwide level to address the issue of labour shortages in specific regions or certain economic sectors. *Land for Pioneers* (1944, Margaret Perry and James Beveridge), for example, visits Canada's north and reminds us that this is a major area of untapped resources that are still waiting to be explored and developed. The film encourages Canadians to invest some of their energies and labour to help develop this area of the country.

While films like *When the Work's All Done this Fall* (1944) appealed to farmers and farm workers to give temporary help to wartime industries after they finished their yearly harvest, most other films addressed problems within the agricultural sector by way of emphasizing the need to relieve shortages in farm labour. Similar arguments in support of utilizing planned farming resources as means of meeting the needs of the Allies were raised in the House of Commons. Dorise Nielsen argued the case:

> We need the planned production of food.... I would say to [Minister of Agriculture] that the time has come when we should have a gathering of all the farm bodies in Canada. Let them plan. Let them know what the requirements of Britain are going to be. Let us correlate our plans for food production with the plans of the United States. Let us see that in this western hemisphere we build up huge stocks of food which will be a weapon for victory in our hands and help us to bring the peace we so much desire.[19]

A similar theme is reiterated in several NFB films. *The Farmer's Forum* (1943) stresses the importance of discussing and implementing strategies that ensure adequate agricultural production quality and quantity. The goal is to provide enough food for every human need, and the message is that too much is at stake and the world is counting on the success of farmers.

In *Hands for the Harvests* (1944), Stanley Jackson illustrates that coordination between various levels of government combined with the full utilization of Canada's work force resources can help meet the challenge facing the agriculture sector during and after the war. The film suggests encouraging high-school students and workers from other parts of the country to help alleviate shortages in agricultural labour during the peak farming seasons. It also argues that the traditional underestimation of women's capacity to contribute in this area of economic activity hampers the efforts to better utilize Canada's labour force. The film also suggests adopting cooperative methods to share the use of machinery and other resources by the farmers.

Among earlier NFB films dealing with the issue of agricultural planning is Stuart Legg's *Food, Weapon of Conquest* (1941). The film's main topic is the Nazi attack against the Soviet Union and its destruction of the Ukraine's agricultural sector, resulting in disastrous effects on the Soviet Union's entire food supplies. The film urges Canadians to learn from the Soviet experience in building "well-organized collective farms." It argues that before the Nazis destroyed these farms, they were "the bread-basket which helped feed the entire Soviet population." It then draws attention to the success of the Soviet Union in parting ways with older forms of "production anarchy," and recommends that as we Canadians adopt similar alternate farming methods. These methods include helping farmers finally free themselves from the "glutted markets and surpluses of former days" and allowing them to devote the use of their land to meet the "real food needs of fellow men."

Clearly, all these films were conceived as tools of instruction; they talked about a specific social problem, delineated its sources, and suggested curative solutions. It is within these parameters that the counter-hegemonic relevance of these films is found. While each film presented ideas about specific problems in the context of different locations and circumstances they all, on the other hand, shared common views on the possibilities for their solution. An important element in this regard is how these films pondered the role of workers in the process of reshaping history.

NFB films explored how workers were instrumental in developing and expanding social wealth, and promoted values of equitable social and political control and distribution of resources. By challenging the commonsensical view of history as fate, or as a vehicle within a predetermined evolutionary process, NFB films inscribed working people as agents in reshaping the historical moment of which they were part. They advocated a leading role for workers where they, as part of a class, would deliberately contribute to remoulding and reshaping the course of history to satisfy both their own class objectives and the needs of society in general.

But these films also envisioned a society that would be reorganized on the basis of its shared goals. In this society people's involvement in the work force is informed by their genuine interest in producing and sharing what is needed to overcome the devastation of war and in laying down a strong basis for future social prosperity.

When it comes to the notion of democracy, NFB films stressed the importance of applying grassroots democratic practices both inside and outside of the workplace. In this regard these films promoted ideas about the direct participation of workers in discussing and making decisions in all areas of political and economic endeavours, both within the workplace and on the national and the international levels. As such they envisaged grassroots democratic practice as fundamental to ensuring the participation of all classes and sections of society in the process of building the country's future.

8 STYLISTIC TRENDS WITHIN THE DISCOURSE OF NFB WAR FILMS

Various stylistic approaches complemented, informed or developed in parallel to NFB films. In conjunction with John Grierson's vigorous search for a new articulation of the role of cinema and documentary in particular, these approaches enhanced the unique contribution made by early NFB films to the evolvement of working-class cultural practices in the early twentieth century. This chapter supplements the discussion on the NFB films' utilization of multiple institutional, political, cultural, and stylistic elements that were also part of the left and working-class discourses. This chapter, however, does not offer a comprehensive stylistic analyses of the films referred to in earlier chapters; such a task is well beyond the general framework and scope of this book. The goal here is to demonstrate and more specifically map out yet another dimension in how NFB films informed and were informed (this time stylistically) by left-oriented discourse of the time.

The interactive link between the stylistic approaches and the ideological workings of NFB war films has been largely missing from Canadian film studies. Without going into detail about the reasons behind this failure (I have dealt with some of the reasons in the first chapter of this book), suffice it to say that it originates within the tendency to marginalize contextual, historical and empirical considerations within various cinema and film studies research circles. In fact, critics from Evans to Nelson almost never acknowledged the importance or the significance of such issues to understanding and analyzing NFB war films. Ignoring these components led to dismissing – and/or to considerable misreading – of the stylistic and ideological confluences manifested in NFB films. Ironically, the only historically and ideologically contextualized evaluations of the stylistic dynamics of these films originate from outside the Canadian film studies disciplinary canons. Such discussions, for example, are found in the work of labour historians Gary Whitaker and Reginald Marcuse. The writers offer this assessment of the films:

There was also the question of style. The documentary style of Grierson and his collaborator, Stuart Legg, was very much that of the 1930s and 1940s. Vivid, forceful images of people and things in motion flooded his films: soldiers, workers, the great engines of warfare and production. Staccato musical scores raced from crescendo to crescendo. Narration was stentorian. The deep voice of Lorne Greene boomed out authoritatively on the soundtracks of the *World in Action* and the *Canada Carries on Series*. The narration summed up what the images and sounds together were designed to convey: a didactic message of the travail and triumph of ordinary people the world over in mastering their own destinies."[1]

By way of expanding the discussion on the nature of the NFB films' stylistic links and background, this section of the book provides an overview of various stylistic origins and underpinnings that complemented these films' function on the ideological level.

GRIERSON AND THE BRITISH DOCUMENTARY FILM MOVEMENT

There is no doubt that the style of NFB films during the war was influenced by the British documentary film movement, led by Grierson himself in the early 1930s. Eventually, this movement held considerable sway on British film culture in the 1930s and 1940s. What is today referred to as the documentary film movement in Britain involved a group of filmmakers, films and writings from the period between 1927 and 1939. Much of the work of this movement was conducted within two British government film units, the Empire Marketing Board Film Unit, and the General Post Office Film Unit. Films were made as part of government service campaigns promoting political and cultural reforms (it is imperative to note here that the British government grudgingly accepted the sympathetic depiction of working-class people within its films; the main concern of the government at that time seemed to be to encourage grassroots support for the international project of the British colonialist empire). Grierson's influence and leadership within the British documentary movement had a monumental impact on the development of the movement.

British films made by proponents of this movement, however, also bore the signature of film practices associated at the time with various left-oriented filmmakers in Europe, the United States and the Soviet Union. In this regard, Jack C. Ellis specifically refers to a group of films out of which "the aesthetic origins of British documentary grew," such as Robert Flaherty's *Nanook of the North* (1922) and *Moana* (1926), Alberto Cavalcanti's *Rien que les heures* (1926), and Walter Ruttmann's *Berlin: Symphony of a Great City* (1927). Ellis also cites a group of Soviet films such as Sergei Eisenstein's *Battleship Potemkin* (1925), V. I. Pudovkin's *The End of St. Petersburg* (1927) and *Storm Over Asia* (1928), Victor Turin's *Turksib* (1929), and Alexander Dovzhenco's *Earth* (1930).[2] Ellis also refers to a book titled *Projection of England* (first published in 1932) by Stephen Tallent. An early participant in the work of the British documentary movement, Tallent explicitly describes the major stylistic impact of Soviet films on the British group:

> Through these films we came to appreciate the need for concentrated work in the editing of the raw material. Their "massing of detail," one of our programmes of that time noted, "the distribution of detail and sequences of rising or falling tempo, the enthusiasm of dramatising working types and working gestures, combine to make their films of work as exciting as any in the world."[3]

This clear appreciation of the techniques introduced by Soviet filmmakers transcended mere aesthetic interest, and eventually contributed to the creation of a genuine interest in the subject matter and the iconography of these films. Of significant importance to British filmmakers was Soviet cinema's introduction of a different kind of depiction of people of working-class backgrounds. This interest resulted in the British movement's incorporation of a similar approach to depicting workers in their own films and publicity material, something that did go well with the British establishment, for which members of the movement were making some of their industrial films. Grierson subsequently recalled:

> When the posters of the Buy British Campaign carried for the first time the figure of a working-man as a national symbol, we were astonished at the Empire Marketing Board to hear from half a hundred Blimps that we were "going Bolshevik." The thought of making work an honoured theme, and a workman, of whatever kind, an honourable figure, is still liable to the charge of subversion. The documentary group has learned freely from Russian film techniques; the nature of the material has forced it to what, from an inexpert point of view, may seem violent technical developments. These factors have encouraged this reactionary criticism; but fundamentally, the sin has been to make cinema face life; and this must invariably be unwelcome to the complacent elements in society.[4]

Grierson's critical writings during at the time also attest to his early interest in looking at the film camera as a unique instrument for exploring various levels and depths within and without the immediacy of the "realities" that it intends to depict:

> The camera-eye is in effect a magical instrument... [its magic] lies... in the manner of its observation, in the strange innocence with which, in a mindtangled world, it sees things for what they are. This is not simply to say that the camera, on its single observations, is free from the trammels of the subjective, for it will not follow the director in his enthusiasms any more than it will follow him in the wide-angled vision of his eyes. The magical fact of the camera is that it picks out what the director does not see at all, that it gives emphasis where he did not think emphasis existed.
>
> The Camera is in a measure both the discoverer of an unknown world and the re-discoverer of a lost one. There are, as everyone knows, strange moments of beauty that leap out of most ordinary news reels. It may be some accidental pose of character or some spontaneous gesture which radiates simply because it is spontaneous.[5]

Grierson's early articulation of the significance of the British movement in the context of its simultaneous incorporation of alternative stylistic and social values would eventually lead to more concrete theorization of the role and aesthetics of documentary filmmaking. Ultimately, Grierson's authority would extend beyond this movement's short-lived existence and would be transformed into a gravitating centre for most of the debates around understanding and defining what constituted a documentary, and how and if film can and should seek to reflect reality.[6] Grierson's stylistic approach would be developed further in the context of his later work outside of Britain, including in the context of his work with filmmakers and artists of the National Film Board of Canada.

GRIERSON'S THEORY OF DOCUMENTARY AND THE NFB'S INCORPORATION OF SYMBOLIC EXPRESSIONISM

Grierson's elaboration of his documentary approach has its critical roots in early writings within local British film journals. In an article titled "First Principles of Documentary" published in *Cinema Quarterly*, Grierson makes one of his early attempts to define his outlook on the subject:

> (1) We believe that the cinema's capacity for getting around, for observing and selecting from life itself, can be exploited in a new and vital art form... the living scene and the living story.
> (2) We believe that the original (or native) actor, and the original (or native) scene, are better guides to a screen interpretation of the modern world.
> (3) We believe that the materials and the stories thus taken from the raw can be finer (more real in the philosophic sense) than the acted article... the movement which tradition has formed or time worn smooth.[7]

In essence, Grierson's theory on documentary primarily favoured using film as an emblematic illustration: it subordinated naturalistic representation to symbolic expression by way of reflecting upon underlying and subtle realities.

Grierson always stressed what he liked about the term symbolic expressionism, which basically chose the allegorical, rather than the unembroidered images. In the context of his previously noted interest in the iconographic significance of presenting working-class images, Grierson's NFB work reflected similar interest in the symbolic significance of cinematic approximation of work's and worker's iconographic images as being at the centre of world events. This is seen, for example, in his encouragement of visually coupling clips depicting the war front in Europe with those of industrial factories across Canada in many NFB war films. In their portrayal of the variety of ways in which people could contribute to the defeat of fascism, films like *Great Guns* (1942) and *Industrial Workers* (1943) described in detail how the production of steel and pulp in the Great Lakes is transformed into actual weaponry. Both films are charged with a relentless barrage of shots depicting workers as they "mould steel into fighting weaponry" in conjunction with images of war in Europe. In *Churchill's Island* fast-paced footage depicting workers in their factories and farmers in their field, delineates the work of the "men and women who in the time of peace made Britain strong."

The 1940 film *Industrial Workers of Central Canada* uses a similar technique to describe how the area around the St. Lawrence River and the Great Lakes became the most populated area in the country, and how it came to include the bulk of Canadian industrial labour. As it delineates the operations of large industrial plants, the film uses heavily edited shots of images that demonstrate the dexterity, skill, organization, and the efficacy of workers as they operate huge machinery and transform raw metal into industrial products.

Building on montage techniques, Jane March's films such as *Women are Warriors* (1942) similarly rely on dynamic editing to present symbolic aspects in the history of the gender division of labour and the epic struggles of women to achieve full equality. For its part, Stuart Legg's *Toilers of the Grand Banks* (1940) depicts the hard work of people in the fishing industry. The film first describes how the sunlight, as it strikes through shallow water, stimulates the growth of marine plants in the seabed, providing food and breeding grounds for fish. The film's main theme, however, is the process of labouring, "which stands behind the success of Canada's fishing economy." The film draws a detailed picture of the work performed by the fishermen and shipyard workers on the Canadian east coast. It maintains a thematic dialectic similar to the one advanced in Grierson's earlier film *Drifters*, which also tackled the topic of fishery workers. Both films capture the images of fishermen as they combat and triumph over natural obstacles.

Yet while Grierson relied on montage editing as his main source for delineating the epic magnitude of toiling, Legg, on the other hand, incorporated a different technique. Using long takes to depict workers building schooners to be used later by cod fishermen, Legg mainly relied on long and medium camera shots to give a feel of the epic dimension of the workers' labour and the fishermen's struggle as they ride the heavy seas of the Atlantic. Such optical effects were used efficiently to link between the dialectical interaction of elements within the same frame such as those of the fishing boats, the roaring ocean, and the fishermen on top of the boats. Descriptive information about the fishing work process seemed to be dominated by symbolic camera techniques whose function was to express the struggle of workers as they battle the elements to achieve their goal. Legg reserved cuts to indicate adjoining spaces and to build spatially coherent cinematic progression. The result was another dramatized symbolic depiction of the fishermen's life and labour that was as dialectically charged as any montage-based portrayal.

In their re-contextualization of archival footage many NFB films also offered unabashedly editorial comments on the issues of the day that in some ways challenged epistemological assumptions normally embedded in documentaries. This stemmed from Grierson's emphasis on documentary film as a propagandist tool with explicit social and political goals and functions. In this context, aesthetic considerations were meant to be secondary:

> In our world, it is necessary these days to guard against the aesthetic argument.... Documentary was from the beginning – when we first separated our public purpose theories from those of Flaherty – an anti-aesthetic movement.

What confuses history is that we had always the good sense to use the aesthetes. We did so because we liked them and because we needed them. It was, paradoxically, with the first-rate aesthetic help of people like Flaherty and Cavalcanti that we mastered the techniques necessary for our quite unaesthetic purposes.[8]

Nevertheless, if NFB films tapped the well of authenticity inherent in the newsreel tradition, they also retained a necessary distance from it through the assimilation of avant-garde impulses pioneered by Cavalcanti, Ruttmann, and especially by Soviet cinema, as we will see later in this chapter.

What seemed like a utilitarian approach in NFB filmmaking was largely moderated by collective and individual contributions made by the artistic talent that worked within the NFB. In this regard NFB films under Grierson's guidance did not entirely dismiss, for example, the struggle for "objectivity" associated with documentary filmmaking practices in comparison to the more self-proclaimed illusionary realism of fiction films. As Aitken suggests:

Grierson's naturalist ideology consisted of a belief that the world, as it was perceived through the human sensory apparatus or through the camera lens, must constitute the basis of aesthetic representation, because it (the perceived world) was the empirical manifestation of underlying determining forces. Because of this, the film-maker, though at liberty to restructure actuality footage to some extent, must retain a commitment to naturalist representation.[9]

Most NFB films during the war reflected interest in depicting genuine settings of working people in Canada: their communities, their workplaces, their union halls, their houses, the products of their labour etc. Nevertheless, these films, both those that were compiled out of existing film footage from Canada and around the world and those produced and shot by NFB talent, seemed consistently bent on using the immediacy of cinematic representation as a basis for symbolic allusion to broader and more abstract social, political and ideological concerns. To this effect, the cinematic camera as well as montage editing approaches were utilized by NFB filmmakers as interventionist rudiments into "raw realities," providing in the process additional modules to their stories: the hidden reality of people's lives that, as in the case of looking at a subject under a microscope – or for that matter through a telescope – allows us to discover elements that we would not have been able to see without the intrusion of a supporting mechanical apparatus.

Film as used in NFB documentaries clearly sought to fill a major gap in how working people saw themselves and each other, and how the rest of society saw them. One can argue that the impact of many of these films was hampered by their heavy-handed editorial voice-overs – partly forced by the war-related urgency of mobilizing people into supporting the Allied campaign in Europe. Progressive filmmakers around the world at the time indeed correctly acknowledged that the voice-over, also used by the NFB, inadvertently contributed to disenfranchising the voices of marginalized social segments of society, including workers and farmers. This does not change the fact that these documentaries endeavoured to provide what they perceived to be a more realistic depiction of workers: this time not as inferior social and economic outcasts (a portrayal which variously continues to dominate even today's cinematic depiction of working-class subjects), but rather as key forces at the core of the country's economic engine.

The significance of the role played by filmmakers such as Legg, Hawes, March, Ivens, Glover, and the Cherrys, among numerous others (in addition to immense contributions made by hundreds of other artists, technicians, and administrators) were of major significance to the creation of this singular body of film work during the war. In this regard, Grierson's model of the compilation film represented an additional element which enhanced both collective and individual initiatives as part of NFB filmmaking practices.

THE COMPILATION FILM MODEL

On the one hand, Grierson's relationship with fellow filmmakers has been frequently described as authoritarian and quite lacking in allowing for mutual creative input. After all, Grierson's near-full control over the NFB transformed it into a "tightly regulated regime, based upon the mass production of standardized, formulaic propaganda films."[10] In the words of Louis Applebaum, one of NFB's young musician recruits, "the object of film-making at the NFB was to make films which contained 'realistic war-time propaganda messages' with 'no room for improvisation.'"[11] Irrespective of exaggeration or of their validity, such claims at least indicate the amount of influence that Grierson mustered within the NFB, and the level to which the films' stylistic (let alone the political) approach has had his signature on it. On the other hand, the compilation film model which was extensively utilized by the NFB during this period indicates the basis formation of a more collective approach to documentary filmmaking.

The compilation model drew on practices that were occasionally used by the British documentary film movement in the 1930s. This technique, along with dynamic editing and editorial voice-over, became typical of many films produced by the Board at the time. The NFB's utilization of this model involved incorporating film footage from various sources. Dozens of films from the series *World in Action*, for example, regularly integrated Allied and Axis footage into their forms, sometimes with virtually no NFB live-action footage. In other cases NFB films assembled old film footage with newly shot material while in others older footage was usually taken from the Board's own films.

Jane March's *Women Are Warriors* (1942) represents an excellent example of the creative application of the compilation model in NFB films. The film brings together huge pre-edited chunks of British and Soviet footage with practically no NFB-produced material. March's editing approach and her ability to incorporate a multitude of distinct newsreel footage was instinctual with a powerful artistic and political force. The film interweaves a dynamic depiction of the relationship between the fight for women's equality, and for a new more equitable society, with the struggle against fascism. Robust images of Soviet women at work and on the battle front are constructed with superior fluidity of dramatic movement to show how women in the Soviet Union became world pioneers in achieving "work equally with men" within all "social and economic sectors including as petroleum engineers and as farmers." Still, March was able to achieve this despite being undercut by the studio-dictated narration, particularly when it came to preventing her from adding even more enthusiastically feminist live-action Soviet stock cinematography.

Another major example of the successful incorporation of the compilation model is seen in the 1942 film *Inside Fighting Russia* (also titled *Our Russian Ally*). Director Stuart Legg and scriptwriter James Beveridge bring together extensive footage from Soviet newsreel as well as Canadian and other world film-footage to describe the Soviet resistance to the Nazi invasion and the worldwide solidarity with Russia. Heroic images of Soviet soldiers are juxtaposed with images of workers from Britain and Canada demonstrating their support on the streets of London and Montreal. The film also brings together chunks of fast-paced edited Soviet footage of workers at their factories, farmers in their fields, educators and students in their schools, doctors in their hospitals, all symbolizing the country's utilization of its cooperative energy to fight fascism. The editing style of these images clearly reminds us of the dynamic use of montage in earlier Soviet cinema.

Grierson's application of the compilation model only became a dominant practice after he became the head of the NFB. A significant aspect of the compilation model as far as this study is concerned, is how Grierson rationalized its use as a format that complemented his collective approach to film training and filmmaking:

> Grierson combined this approach [compilation film] to film-making with a labour model based on threshold specialization. Inexperienced apprentices would be trained to master aspects of film-making to a satisfactory level, then moved on the other areas. Although the film-makers became familiar with different areas of film-making, none developed specialist skills or expertise.[12]

Several filmmakers from inside and outside the NFB such as Basil Wright, James Beverdige, Paul Rotha, and Stuart Legg "took a dim view" of that model and considered it "unsuitable model for the future development of documentary."[13] Yet, we should not underestimate the level to which such practice allowed for the major development of Canadian filmmaking skills. In this regard, the NFB no doubt became an excellent workplace for those interested in pursuing the creative application of new editing techniques and utility.

Here we should underscore that Eisenstein's and Soviet experimentations with montage were only just being discovered and applied in the west, that is, despite full earlier familiarity with those techniques by people like Grierson, Legg and many others. This means that the NFB's employment of the compilation model has probably had a major stylistic impact on the work of many filmmaking apprentices at the Board. Similarly, this practice also probably enhanced the Board's and the films' own emphasis on encouraging collective debates and generating ideas through discussion and exchange. On another level, we should not underestimate the extent to which this model also facilitated an efficient and less expensive system of film production within the NFB.

FINDING THE DRAMA IN THE NEWSREEL

NFB films mostly appeared preoccupied with presenting a new way of looking at events and peoples. They sought to disentangle "reality" and discover the dialectics that were at work within it and behind it. With this goal in mind they echoed Grierson's accent on finding the drama that can be excavated out of the camera's ability to observe the world: "in the actual world of our observation there [is] always a dramatic form to be found."[14] In other words, what was to make a documentary film different, and what was to help it move beyond its prescribed observational or neutral function, was to be found in the organization of the observed material around what Grierson identified as "treatment," a term he used as a synonym with dramatization: "'Treatment' or dramatization (also sometimes referenced as 'interpretation') reflects the documentarist's desire and willingness to use actuality material to create a dramatic narrative."[15]

As early as his mid-1920s articles on modern art, Grierson began to sketch his views about reproducing the real. He argued that paintings did not reproduce the real, but articulated it, through a manipulation of the intrinsic properties of the medium in order to convey an illusory impression of mimesis:

> Visual storytelling... involves a manipulation of character and acting and stage as in legitimate drama, it involves a manipulation of visual composition as in painting... it involves a manipulation of tempo as in music... it involves visual suggestion and visual metaphor as in poetry. Beyond all that it involves a manipulation of such effects as are peculiar to itself. This includes (under camera) the manipulation of dissolves, double exposures, trick shots etc.; (under continuity) the manipulation of long shots, close ups, medium shots, truck shots and so on, and of recurring visual themes as in music.[16]

The dramatic, as conceived by Grierson, was a fundamental characteristic of reality, which itself advanced constantly in "a world on the move, a world going places, within an endless process of growth and decay which revealed the 'dramatic nature of the actual.'"[17] Therefore, it was through the patterns of drama that documentary film was to be able to represent "the dramatic processes which generated change and development within society."[18]

In contrast to how the cinema-direct movement (which became an important feature in Quebec NFB productions of the late 1950s) sought to advance a socially committed cinema through reliance on film's own neutral ability to reflect its subject, NFB war films appeared at ease with their use of editorial and narrative dramatization interventions as a means of advancing their political views. Equally as important they seemed more appreciative of how the clarity of political vision gave cinematic form an anchor that allowed it to assume specific social and political relevancy.

On one level, a critical aspect of the NFB's attempt to deal with the social and political realities of the day can be found in the dramatized tropes of live-action re-enactments in numerous films. Good examples are found in the talking head monologues appearing in *Churchill's Island*, the discussions and the narrative involving issues of unemployment in *Youth is Tomorrow* and *Charlie Gordon*, the dramatized building of a home by the collective effort of group workers in *Building a House*.

Robert Edmonds' *Coal Face, Canada* (1943) is an important example of how several NFB films of the period ventured towards feature-film narrative construction, *mise-en-scene*, characterization, and synchronized recorded dialogue – all standard attributes of the fiction film. The film presents a dramatized story of a young worker returning from the war. The worker is disappointed by the economic and social stagnation of his hometown. After he takes a room with a miner who used to know his father and who recalls the tragedy of his death in the mines, the two men begin to discuss the important role played by workers, particularly miners, and their unions on the home front. The young man eventually joins up to work in the town's mine. The film's re-enactment of events and its attention to composing an authentic-looking working-class setting presented a genuine attempt in revamping closed expectations of documentary films. As such, this along with many other NFB war films provided new dramatized tropes to documentary filmmaking practices.

As Jack Ellis suggests, despite the fact "the semi-documentary represented a reaction against Grierson's first principles, it nonetheless stemmed from the movement he had founded and the people he had trained." Films such as *Coal Face, Canada*, along with *Charlie Gordon, Youth is Tomorrow* and others gave a glimpse of what would carry over into the post-war era and beyond. Such films would earn a much wider audience than the more sombre documentaries linked with compilation as well as with live-action NFB films of the time. In the meantime, "though he may have resisted the impulse during the war years on grounds of too much aestheticism and artistic self-indulgence, [Grierson] would be closely associated with the semi-documentary form and even the fiction film in post-war Britain."[19]

On another level, the creative use of the newsreel by NFB filmmakers reached its peak in the context of their attempt to reconstruct stories that gave specific political perspective of and background to major contemporary events. To this effect, compilation films of the period played a major role as harbinger of a new collective memory. Stuart Legg's *The Gates of Italy* (1943), for example, traces the history of fascism in Italy and follows the trails of Mussolini's manipulation of the Italian working class and the "impoverishment of the Italian people," and his demagogic rhetoric which eventually led many Italians to support fascism. Legg explores the topic formally through splicing newsreel footage of official events, speeches, demonstrations, political discussions and rallies, together with symbolic shots of "Il Duce," monuments, statues, and museums, editing them carefully to provide the viewer with a chronologically linear narrative about the rise of fascism in Italy. Hundreds of metres of standard newsreel film footage, apparently from multiple sources and vaults, are reconstructed into a cohesive and informative narrative about class, political populism, and resistance.

Direct Cinema's stipulation of transparency and non-control as a paradigm of authenticity was later challenged as futile and disingenuous. If anything, as Euvrard and Véronneau suggest, *cinéma direct* inadvertently allowed some filmmakers to hide their politics and eventually brought more ideological confusion to the messages they sought to bring forward; they confused "the means with the end... by turning the direct into an ideology itself."[20] Seth Feldman raises a similar concern in his appraisal of the 1970s NFB's program *Challenge for Change*.[21] He cautions against relying on alternative techniques (i.e. direct cinema) to forward social and political messages, and questions the legitimacy of the program's celebrated emphasis on giving direct voice to those who are incapable of articulating their own concerns. He argues that thinking along those lines by way of discussing issues of interest to Canadians of working-class backgrounds is based on erroneous assumptions and could lead to wrong conclusions.[22]

In hindsight, NFB films diametrically contrasted assertions raised later by the *cinéma verité* proponents who claimed that film could attain an unmediated representation of the real.[23] In some ways these films were more capable than their *verité* counterparts of acknowledging the contradictory dynamics inherent in the use of any formal strategy. As such NFB filmmakers seemed more in tune with understanding the limitations embedded within the medium itself, and in that context they appeared more reflective on how audiences, political and social moments, and grassroots organizational skills and connections provided major input into how films functioned. In the case of the NFB's Discussion Films, for example, using an observant camera that simply recorded workers as they discussed issues of relevance to them was not sufficient on its own. What made a difference was how these films assumed their organic function in the context of the highly politicized climate within which activists from the left and the labour movement were key and effective contributors. In other words, the ability of the NFB's cinematic practice to acquire a counter-hegemonic bearing on the worker/subject and its audiences in general had to do with the presence of a programmatically clear, broadly based, and well organized and led counter-hegemonic movement. The situation in the late 1950s and even in the 1960s, when *cinéma verité* emerged, was clearly different, at least in connection to the less cohesive and organized and more spontaneous nature of the radical movements of the time.

OTHER PARALLELS AND CONNECTIONS

This section will deal with various other parallels and connections that emerged within the same general timeframe as the NFB. Those include Soviet and American influences, as well as parallels with some progressive film practices in Europe.

In his evaluation of Soviet cinema, Grierson found an artistic force capable of "reading into all fields of inquiry and imagination." He appreciated the dramatic fluidity of its movement, the strength of its approach, and the social emphasis of its themes.[24] Grierson's interest in the work of early Soviet filmmakers was among the formative elements of his interest in cinema. The 1929 film *Drifters*, the film most associated with Grierson's name and which he himself directed and produced, largely reflected the formal experimentations of early Soviet filmmakers. The film itself was chosen to accompany *The Battleship Potemkin* at the premier presentation of the Soviet film in London.[25] Later in United States, in the mid-1930s, Grierson took on the responsibility of setting up the titles for *Potemkin*, which enabled him to come to know the film "foot by foot and cut by cut."[26] Grierson concluded that the film's use of intrinsically cinematic techniques was able to advance "knowledge of tempo, montage, and composition in the cinema."[27] He also stressed that *Potemkin* impressed him with the amount of naturalistic representation that involved research into press and documentary records of events, shooting the entire film on location, and the use of non-professional actors.[28] All these elements would later constitute the hallmark of Grierson's as well as the NFB's documentary stylistic approach.

Another figure in the early years of the NFB was Joris Ivens. Ivens was hired to make one film at the NFB, but was already well-established internationally. The role played by this filmmaker within the Board reflected his international stature. Ivens's account of his own work as a filmmaker subscribes to the fusion of cinematic practice with political and social activism. This, he argued, only occurred in the context of revolutionizing means of film practice:

> I started more from the aesthetic, artistic point of view. I was part of the avant-gardist movement in Europe, with Paris, with Berlin – then into this artistic movement came realism. That was the influence of the Russian film-makers such as Eisenstein, Pudovkin, Dovzhenko. And my work was also influenced by the work of Flaherty.[29]

The one Soviet filmmaker who did not seem to stylistically hit a chord with earlier British documentary movement filmmakers was Dziga Vertov. In spite of its critical influence among intellectuals and within progressive circles, the work of the man behind *Man with a Movie Camera* was largely marginalized by the documentary film movement in the west.[30] In the words Paul Rotha, one of the "Griersonians" of the British documentary movement: "Vertov we regarded really as rather a joke you know. All this cutting, and one camera photographing another camera photographing another camera – it was all trickery, and we didn't take it serious, quite frankly."[31] In his review of *Man with a Movie Camera* Grierson wrote: "Vertov has pushed the argument to a point at which it becomes ridiculous." In a review of another Vertov film, *Enthusiasm* (1930) he argued that the film was botched "because he was like any bourgeois highbrow, too clever by half."[32] The reflexive approach emphasized by Vertov was clearly considered a distraction from the main goals associated with Griersonian documentary filmmaking, which emphasized clarity in communicating messages to the audience. Stylistically, Vertov's approach seemed to contrast, at least on the surface, with the unobtrusively editorialized and structurally linear and "cohesive" Griersonian documentary.

Years later, the NFB's approach to the role of film echoed in many ways the theoretical premises by Soviet filmmakers of the 1920s, including Dziga Vertov's approximation of the interventionist role of the movie camera in revealing the reality behind reality. As Grierson himself would suggest, the emphasis on the "creative treatment" of reality essentially functions by way of blunting the charge of propaganda.[33]

While NFB films never shared in practice Vertov's interest in exploring the camera's full cinematic potential, they did nevertheless appear to be in sync (at least philosophically) with his fascination with the camera's superior sensory capacity to that of the human eye. In hindsight, NFB films of the period inadvertently complemented Vertov's programmatic objective in utilizing the cinematic eye (or the Kino-eye as he called it) to help people see the world in a different manner than they were used to.

As they discussed the critical role of workers in fighting the war against fascism and building a more equitable society after the war, NFB filmmakers incorporated similar stylistic techniques to those used in earlier Soviet films. Their films depicted countless images of spinning industrial machinery operated by men and women workers and farmers in a way that went beyond any claim of "objective" realism.

NFB films such as *Salt from the Earth* (1944) and *Coal for Canada* (1944) used visual techniques that were utilized earlier in the British documentaries of the 1930s, only this time those techniques were reintroduced with a higher level of urgency and stronger vigour. Streams of fast-paced film clips depicting workers in factories, shipyards, mines, and prairie farms were used to show that working on the home front is no less intense, spirited or vital than fighting fascism on the battle fronts of Europe.

The dynamics of Soviet montage made a major impact on filmmaking all over the world. For their part, NFB films captured elements of Soviet editing style that also adhered to its general ideological parameters, particularly in relation to its emphasis on workers and its epic depiction of political and social dynamics in general. Between 1939 and 1946 the NFB developed two major film series. The first series was *Canada Carries On*, which included sixty-two films that were primarily concerned with Canada's role in the war, and the second was the *The World in Action* series that included thirty films dealing with current international events. Stanley Hawes was in charge of *Canada Carries On* and Stuart Legg produced *The World in Action*. Grierson in particular pressed his own stylistic and political outlooks for the two series: "This isn't a documentary war, it's a newsreel war," Grierson declared.[34] Keeping pace with the daily events and developments on the war front, as well as with the changes impacting the role of workers and working-class unions in Canada, major changes affected even the roles traditionally played by various film artists. Jim Ellis describes the nature and scope of these changes:

> [I]t was necessary to use more and more newsreel footage shot by anonymous cameramen scattered around the globe; less and less of the material could be specially shot. The director, or director-cameraman, hitherto dominant in documentary, gave way to the writer and editor as controlling figures. In addition to the work of the Canadian combat cameraman, footage was drawn from Britain and the other Commonwealth countries, from the United States, the Soviet Union, and China. The style was hard-hitting, the diverse images briskly edited to a preconceived commentary.[35]

What we alluded to earlier as the compilation film practice dominated the NFB's work during this period and involved the use of old footage in conjunction with newly shot material, allowing the production of larger number of films to be made more quickly and inexpensively. A huge number of films were made this way and were eventually used under numerous titles. The selection of, and editing strategies for, the archival materials also impacted the filmic discourse both in concert and in tension with the voice-over commentary. Most of the corpus of films produced during this period was the fruit of the NFB's interactive use of both live-action and compilation film practices. For its part, the use of Soviet montage theory and techniques contributed to the Board's effective and complex utility of both components of its film corpus outcome.

The question of Soviet montage influence on the NFB film practice, however, needs to be qualified. It is imperative to point out that the NFB itself consistently acknowledged indebtedness to the American *March of Time* series (where Legg himself did an internship). In general, the stylistic approach that was developing within the NFB paralleled a contemporaneous documentary development in the United States, where Popular Front policies were equally influential on much of the documentary activity during the war, though with cultural specificity that transcended film into other areas of cultural practices. Stylistic and political parallels between NFB and American films from the same period can be easily drawn, such as in the case of *Heart of Spain* (1937) by Herbert Kline and Charles Korvin, which featured Canadian communist Dr. Norman Bethune as he worked in Spain in support of the republicans. Another example is the American film *Our Russian Front* (1942), which was directed by none other than Joris Ivens, and produced by the Russian War Relief Inc. (an American Popular Front social and cultural organization). Similar to its Canadian counterpart *Inside Fighting Russia*, the film mainly utilizes footage taken from Soviet battlefront cameramen.

Since the 1930s, progressive cultural circles in the United States, as expressed in the aesthetic manifestos of groups associated with the Popular Front, demonstrated time and again an interest in what they called a revolutionary symbolism. This included a media-encompassing interest in documentary journalism:

> By focusing on the voracious appetite for documentary journalism, particularly the documentary book, that hybrid of photographs and text epitomized by Erskine Caldwell and Margaret Bourke-White's *You Have Seen Their Faces*, [William] Scott persuasively documented the documentary impulse as it infiltrated radio news, film newsreels, novels, sociology, reportage, and even the American Guide books of the Federal Writers' project.[36]

Nevertheless, this kind of documentary journalism was also conscious of the need to involve the document itself in a process of transformation into a broader project, rather than sanctifying and celebrating a presumed aura of authenticity and/or objectivity. In this regard, American filmmakers from the Popular Front tradition were unabashed in their emphasis on using the document (in our case, film footage, clips, voice-over) in a larger and politically coherent project. In the words of American filmmaker Leo Hurwitz, "Tiny documents in the form of shots and sounds bore the same relation to the film as the small pieces of coloured stone and glass to the mosaic mural, the brush-strokes to the painting, the individual words and phrases to the novel. The stuff was document, but the construction was invented, time-collage."[37] In essence, many American artists of the Popular Front provided the basis for a fusion between modernist tendencies with "a recognition of the social and political crisis," as Michael

Denning affirms. He goes on to argue that one might even "accurately call the work of the cultural [popular] front a 'social modernism,' a third wave of the modernist movement."[38]

On another level, there is no doubt that films both from the *Canada Carries On* and *The World in Action* series, with their emphasis on edited stock footage and dramatization of war events and labour issues, were in most ways closely modeled on the American series *March of Time*. But as Edgar Anstey suggests, Legg's technical approach in producing *The World in Action*, for example, was conducted with much more literary grace than its American counterpart: "maximum commentary impact [of the films] depended on a very precise relationship between picture and, not word, but sometimes even syllable."[39] The same thing can be argued in connection with the *Canada Carries On* series.

Soon, both NFB series were competing with, and in most cases surpassing, the American *March of Times* not only in Canada (where *World in Action*, for example, was being shown in some eight hundred theatres) but also in the world market. Eventually the series "reached a combined United States-Canadian monthly audience of 30 to 40 million."[40] Commenting on the film *Food – Weapon of Conquest* (1942), *Time* magazine in June 15, 1942 enthusiastically said: "This cinematic editorial is almost a blueprint of how to make an involved, dull, major aspect of World War II understandable and acceptable to moviegoers."

When it comes to its European connections, the NFB's emphasis on a self-described edited or a dramatized version for depicting the realities and views of working-class Canadians paralleled in certain ways aspects of 1930s French cinema. Of particular importance were the films that came to prominence during the period of the Popular Front, when a left-wing alliance of socialists, communists and the centre-left won the 1936 elections and a government under socialist Leon Blum took office for a brief period. Among the most famous examples from that period is Jean Renoir's feature documentary (partially acted) *La Vie est à nous* (1936), produced by the communist-backed collective Ciné-Liberté. Other films were made by members of a group calling itself L'Equipe. The group was attached to the Socialist Party, and directed by Francois Moch, brother of Jules Mock (Prime Minister Leon Blum's assistant) and by Marceau Pivert, a prominent left-wing socialist.[41] Some NFB filmmakers even saw elements in left-wing French fiction filmmaking that were of particular interest to their attempts to present a dramatized depiction of reality. Discussing how he and other filmmakers were impressed by the techniques used by Rene Clair in his film *A Nous la Liberté* (1931), Stanley Hawes, the man who was in charge of the NFB's *Canada Carries On* series, praised the use of sound in the film: "You don't realise, until you a see a film like this, how stereotyped and dull the majority of films have become. Our critical faculties have become deadened by the regular diet of uninspired productions made to formula."[42] This by no means indicates direct influence by certain French work on the NFB's films at the time, but rather the presence of some parallel interests between the two filmmaking practices.

While NFB films concentrated on the war effort, the role of workers within it, and on the image of the worker as a consensus builder, the French films seemed more preoccupied with the heated social and political struggles and debates that were taking place in France and Europe in the 1930s; they mainly featured political strikes and demonstrations as well as events taking place in connection with the Spanish Civil War. In both cases, however, the philosophy behind using film as a social commentator was similar in its broad parameters; they both saw and used film as a medium that intervened in the process of depicting reality. Whether within the framework of its "dialectical" outlook (this term was used by self-described Marxist French filmmakers), or within the context of dramatized interpretation of "reality" (as Grierson preferred to label his own version of cinematic "intervention"), both Popular Front filmmakers in France and NFB filmmakers in Canada sought to expose the drama of social and political veracity and the epic role played by the working class within it. As such, both groups were clearly influenced by the Marxist critique of formalism, and by theories of critical social realism (before Stalin's inscription of his own version of "Socialist Realism"). These theories argued that, besides the truth of detail, it was important to represent typical characters under typical circumstances, in order to give as full an account as possible of individual and social relationships. This was close to Grierson's model of an epic-naturalist cinema, which sought to explore interactivity between social and individual forces.

Earlier still, Grierson's stylistic vision that enhanced his interest in documentary film practice was informed by other elements in working-class and socialist culture, including the related theatre movement that grew in Europe in the 1920s.

[This movement recaptured] the general principles of documentary theatre as it first evolved in Germany in the 1920s, mainly through the work of Irwin Piscator. It was in reference to Piscator's "epic theatre" that Brecht first applied the word "documentary" to the theatre in 1926 – in the same year that John Grierson coined the word in English to describe the films of Robert Flaherty.[43]

But Grierson's and the NFB films' stylistic philosophy of interfering in the depiction of reality was even more deeply informed by Soviet cinema of the two first decades of the twentieth century.

While NFB films did not subscribe to the rhetoric of the more explicitly political and class-partisan work of Soviet cinema, or to some extent French documentaries during the Popular Front period, they nevertheless fully appreciated and sought to use cinema as a political medium. As such they consciously avoided tendencies towards formalist self-indulgence, while their unambiguous goal revolved around reaching out to the public, to inform it, and to mobilize it for battles that were seen as crucial to humanity's future. There is therefore a considerable continuity and consistency in how the stylistic motto of the NFB during the World War II period, with Grierson at the helm, gravitated around bringing the "affairs of our time" to screen "in a fashion which strikes the imagination and makes observation a little richer than it was."[44]

In the words of Stanley Hawes:

> Grierson was a communications man with a social conscience and he believed that painters, poets, writers and musicians should use their skills in the service of the community and project social problems into the national consciousness… (documentary) is film in the service of humanity.[45]

As a result, NFB films were indeed effectively utilized to reach out to broad audiences where they sought to instigate discussions about matters that meant a lot to the country and to its working class. In the end these films were able to present accessible ideas with accessible film forms that were politically challenging to the status quo, ones that were also ideologically forceful, particularly in their depiction of the working-class subject.

9 THE NFB IN A MOMENT OF TRANSITION: WORKERS IN THE NFB FILMS BETWEEN 1945 AND 1946

This chapter discusses shifts that affected the discourse of NFB films between 1945 and 1946. This was a transitional period where the NFB's discourse on workers and labour began to reflect new social and political influences that ushered Canada's transition into the post-war era. Tensions on the labour front were on the increase, and manifestations of early Cold War strains were ignited by the defection of a cipher clerk in the Soviet embassy in Ottawa. This period also saw the departure of NFB founder John Grierson. In August 1945 and in light of increased criticism and accusations from conservative political circles, Grierson finally resigned from the NFB. Grierson's resignation occurred just one month before Soviet embassy functionary Igor Gouzenko's defection signalled the first shot in the Cold War between the west and the Soviet Union.

NFB films' portrayal of labour-related issues between 1945 and 1946 would signal major changes that subsequently transformed the NFB's discourse on the working class. On the labour front, the trade union movement was reaching a peak in its organizational strength and political activities. While the NFB continued to produce films that showed an interest in labour issues, these films began to reflect aspects of anti-labour and anti-communist rhetoric. These views would later dominate the political discourse of the Cold War period.

CHANGING LABOUR AND POLITICAL CLIMATE

As we saw earlier, the war period itself had witnessed rapid growth in the membership and in the political and organizational strength of the trade union movement. On the political level, as the Allies proclaimed victory in Europe in May 1945, the relationship between labour and the political forces of the Communist left reached an all-time high. By the time the war ended, a new political climate was taking root in Canada. In conjunction with the growth of the labour movement and its leftist allies, tensions on the labour front were also on the increase. Labour's uneasy truce with business initiated during the war was being hampered by businesses' attempts to retract from the agreements made by the two sides earlier.

The increase in labour's political power and the rise of militant influence within it clearly strengthened the hand of labour in its partnership arrangements with management. By February 1944, the King government introduced a Wartime Labour Relations Regulation that basically recognized labour's status as a bargaining agent on behalf of workers. In addition to allowing all employees to join unions on principle, the regulation created fundamental rules that legally entrenched labour's bargaining power. Those rules also

> called for the certification of bargaining agents in appropriate units; introduced compulsory collective bargaining which mandated the obligation to bargain in good faith and to attempt to reach an agreement; maintained a combination of conciliation officer and conciliation board mechanism; introduced the demand that all collective agreements contain a clause creating mechanisms for the handling of disputes during the life of contract.[1]

The trade union movement and the working class as a whole were clearly assuming a new status as one of Canada's major economic, political and social players. The achievements made by the Canadian labour movement before and during the war placed the working class in a position where it had the potential to play a qualitatively new and unprecedented role in shaping the political and economic future of the country in the post-war era.

This strength, however, was also becoming a major source of tension. By late 1944, in response to attempts by employers to retract from their wartime concessions to the labour movement, a working-class strike movement was rapidly developing. Over that particular year around 500,000 working days were lost through labour strikes. This figure tripled less than one year later, due largely to strikes occurring in the second half of the year.[2] In September 1945, the Ford Motor Company reneged on its wartime commitment to recognize the Union of Auto Workers (UAW) as the bargaining agent for Local 200 in Windsor. Despite attempts by the federal and provincial governments to intimidate them, workers staged a major successful strike that represented a watershed moment in the history of the Canadian labour movement.[3] But the strike also reflected labour's anxieties with the new post-war situation, particularly in reaction to consistent attempts by business to reclaim some of the political losses it incurred during the war.

The labour movement and its militant leadership saw these attempts as a signal to them to become more vigilant in defending the gains achieved during the war:

> The Canadian UAW and indeed the entire Canadian Labour Movement did not see the end of World War II as a time to surrender. Important gains had been made with high employment, and this was not the moment to back down. But corporate Canada was preparing to move in an entirely different direction, looking back to the control of the pre-war years as its goal.[4]

Another major labour action that took place during the same period was the 1946 Stelco strike. Workers' demands centred on wages, union recognition, and the forty-hour work week. The strike ended by defeating the wartime freeze on wages. Subsequently, the success of the strike guaranteed an even stronger position for workers. This was manifested in the company's recognition of the principle of collective bargaining.

All these new labour gains, however, were implemented in the context of several legal and political uncertainties and as such were open to reversals and manipulations by business and by the government. As Kealey argues,

> Aside from the uncertainty for labour of the rule of law in itself, the complex labour relations system finds its rationale in two pervasive myths; first, that the two parties involved – capital and labour – meet as equals in so-called "free" collective bargaining (what liberal theory terms "industrial pluralism"); and second, that the role of the state is simply that of a neutral umpire, aiding the two hostile leviathans to make peace and thus protecting the interests of the unprotected public.[5]

Nevertheless, concessions by employers resulted in the further growth and influence of the trade union movement. By now this movement has become a decisive force in Canada's economic, political and social life. The protracted strike movement around various labour demands, particularly the institution and implementation of collective bargaining, continued until 1947. This movement basically sought to ensure that "rights won in wartime would not be lost during reconstruction [post-war period]."[6]

Within labour there was a major increase in the influence of the forces of the communist left in all the major trade unions. Supporters and friends of the Communist Party of Canada (CPC) had been elected to posts within almost all the larger labour unions, including the International Woodworkers of America, the Longshoremen, the Seamen's Union, the Fishermen's Union, the aircraft union, the Boilermakers and Marine Workers' Union as well as other marine-workers' groups.[7]

On the political level, the support for Communist Party Popular Front strategy was greater than ever among mainstream sections of Canadian society. The influence of the left in Canadian politics was translated in relatively important increases in their support on various electoral levels. A few days after winning two Toronto seats in the Ontario Legislative Assembly in 1943, Communists won another seat in the House of Commons during a by-election in a working-class Montreal federal riding (the other pro-communist seat was occupied since 1940 by independent Dorise Nielsen). Fred Rose became the first (and until today, the only) openly Communist Canadian to be elected to the House of Commons. Rose was elected under the banner of the Labour-Progressive Party, which was formed in 1943 in light of the continued official government ban on the Communist Party as such. These successes on the federal and provincial electoral levels accompanied similar accomplishments in municipal elections across the country.[8]

Already influential within the labour movement and among workers, communists were becoming a force to be reckoned within Canada's mainstream political institutions themselves, a phenomenon that was unprecedented in the CPC's history since its founding in 1921. For many Canadians, socialism was now an acceptable and viable political alternative. This counter-hegemonic climate transcended the Communist Party's own fortunes to benefit the other labour-based Canadian socialist party, the Co-operative Commonwealth Federation.

As Ian McKay suggests, the new political atmosphere in the country reflected a "certain convergence within a common formation" between the CCF and the communists on the question of the socialist state.[9] Basing his argument on a major CCF propaganda document authored in 1943 by two of the party leaders, David Lewis and Frank Scott, McKay suggests that despite its paramount importance for understanding the dynamics of this crucial moment in Canadian history, the mere presence of this formation, and its influence, remains largely muzzled or ignored by most CCF/NDP historians. Irrespective of various other differences between the revolutionary nature of the Communist Party with its disciplined organization and mobilization, and the mass party and coalition-oriented CCF, McKay argues, both parties still shared at the time a common vision of Canada. They both advocated a country "in which capitalist ownership has been replaced by social ownership, and 'the rapacious system of monopoly capitalism' replaced by a 'democratic socialist society.'"[10] Furthermore, McKay points to the fact that the CCF adopted a similar position towards the Soviet Union to that of the CPC. McKay describes how the CCF looked at the Soviet Union:

It is in the Soviet Union that "we" find proof of a post-capitalist society's ability to mobilize its population to meet a great purpose. "The Soviet Union is an example of a whole economy being run successfully on new lines." It is the "Russian" people that we can see a vast population embarked "upon a colossal plan of organized social revolution," which has already given them' a powerful new system capable of withstanding the onslaught of the world's mightiest armies.[11]

The 1944 election of Tommy Douglas in the province of Saskatchewan as the leader of North America's first socialist government was in itself a major indication of the level to which socialist politics in general had become more or less institutionalized within Canadian political culture and discourse.

The combination of increased labour strength, and the growing influence of socialist ideas among mainstream sections of Canadian society, raised fears within economic and political establishment circles. With its history of sympathetic discourse on labour and on working-class views now becoming more alarming to the establishment, political pressures on the NFB would result in changes to how its films would depict those issues.

PRELUDE TO THE COLD WAR IN THE NFB

As labour and political tensions loomed on the horizon, the role played by the NFB was itself coming under increased scrutiny. As we saw earlier, the NFB's discourse on labour and workers during the war emphasized ethico-political values that encouraged working-class involvement in politics, collective decision-making in the workplace, and cooperative social and economic development. It also promoted government involvement in social and economic planning and supported the creation of public social systems and institutions. While NFB films never expressed positions in support of labour strikes and actions, they nevertheless encouraged a proactive approach to the role of labour and workers in Canadian politics. Such an approach was incompatible, to say the least, with how the political and economic establishment saw the function of labour in the post-war era.

Inside the House of Commons, the clamour against the NFB was already being voiced even before the war came to its end. In 1944, conservative MP Agar Adamson accused the NFB of being a propaganda machine "for a type of socialist and foreign philosophy." Adamson accused the NFB of attacking the "adolescent mind." The

Board, he argued, was manipulating the "receptive mood" of young people and their vulnerability in their "comfortable surroundings" to "spray [them] with an anaesthesia of propaganda which in most cases [they are] not capable of resisting."[12]

Even as early as 1942, fear of John Grierson's views and displeasure with the discourse of NFB films was being raised in the United States. According to Kirwan Cox, the FBI was concerned that the *World in Action* series, which at the time was being screened in most American mainstream movie theatres, was too leftist in its analysis, and that Grierson himself was a "communistic sympathizer."[13] Cox quotes a 1942 inquiry about Grierson sent by FBI director Edgar Hoover to the American Embassy in London:

> From information appearing in Bureau files, it is indicated that John Grierson is Communistically inclined and that several of the films he has produced in Canada appear to be written and directed from a pro-Soviet viewpoint.[14]

Having Grierson at the helm of the NFB clearly did not sit well with some prominent political forces on both sides of the border. Furthermore, Grierson's plans for the NFB in the post-war era did not do much to reassure these forces about his political motivations and intentions.

For his part, Grierson was contemplating the future role of the Board even before the war had ended. In essence, his peacetime social and political values did not seem different from those he talked about before and during the war:

> In keeping with his firm opinions on the social importance of filmmaking, Grierson wanted the Board to turn its attention to the education and development of a more socially aware and responsible citizenship. Specifically, it seems that Grierson wanted the Board to endorse the concept of an advanced social-welfare state, such as the one proposed in Britain by Lord Beverdige. The Board was also to continue to discuss themes of international importance and, if Grierson had his way, it would be aligned with External Affairs in an effort to promote a new spirit of international cooperation. Education, internationalism, citizenship: these were the Griersonian watch words.[15]

Grierson's vision, however, would not be allowed to materialize, at least not in the manner that Grierson intended to. Grierson resigned from the Board in August 1945. The NFB's first production supervisor, Stuart Legg, left the Board a few months later.

The resignation of Grierson occurred just one month before the defection of a cipher clerk in the Soviet embassy in Ottawa.

In February 1946, just five months after he defected, Gouzenko's case became the pretext for an official campaign against the Canadian left, particularly against the CPC and the militant leadership of the trade union movement. By the time the campaign officially ended in the early 1970s, it had affected the lives of hundreds of thousands of Canadians.[16] For their part, NFB films between 1945 and 1946 featured remnants of the earlier progressive-oriented discourse as well as elements that reflected the rising Cold War climate and anxieties.

REMNANTS FROM THE OLD DISCOURSE

Commonsensical counter-hegemonic ideas inform and are informed by subaltern consensus. This means that the ideological impact of such ideas in a specific moment in history at once depends on their ability to build upon *and* to contest other philosophies that constitute the mainstream ideological dispositions. By 1945, ideas about social solidarity, grassroots democracy and collective responsibility had become integral to the ethico-political values of a wide cross-section of Canadian society. Such values largely remained integral to the discourse of NFB films during the transition period between the end of the war and the full-fledged outbreak of the Cold War. As the ideological significance and impact of the films was being reshaped by an emerging Cold War climate, new NFB films were increasingly inscribing a new emphasis on the role of government officials and bureaucrats, the function of technology and technological innovations, and on the notion of a free-willed individual. Counter-hegemonic ideas that had left their imprint on earlier films, nevertheless, continued to inform, albeit temporarily, the discourse of several early post-war films.

For its part, the 1945 series *Canadian Screen Magazine* kept on depicting aspects in the everyday life of workers, their families and their communities. The series also continued to present glimpses of workers at their picnics, union meetings, and during their discussions of issues of world peace and food shortages in Europe. Occasionally, films also maintained interest in new social programs and how they helped alleviate poverty among working-class Canadians. *Who is My Neighbour* (1946), for example, describes the goals and the growth of welfare organizations and the community chest movement in Canada. The film argues in support of centralizing the administration of revenues and expenditures from overlapping programs to increase the effectiveness of the Canadian Welfare Council's work. In *Small Fry* (1946, Jack Olsen), workers discuss the positive impact of the newly created Canadian Family Allowance system. The film demonstrates how public aid to needy children enhanced their chances of growing up healthy and "physically and educationally prepared to make their way in the world."

The Third Freedom (1946) discusses a report to employers and other community members concerned with reintroducing amputee veterans into civilian jobs. The film argues that "no job requires all skills such as strength, intellect and manual dexterity in both hands and constant use of both legs." It goes on to suggest that with proper utilization of effective planning and a survey of employment needs and human resources, people and jobs can be matched individually to aptitude.

The 1945 series *Getting the Most out of A Film* upheld the tradition of offering discussion films for use at workers' meetings. Films in the series perceived democracy as an ongoing process involving steady reassessment of labour-related concerns and problems. The series as a whole continued to instigate discussions among workers. As such it also represented continuity in advocating grassroots interpretations of democratic practice among workers in the workplace. Democratic practice in the workplace was presented in conjunction with contemplating the level to which workers, as producers of the nation's wealth, felt part of the actual decision-making process. Three films were produced in the series in 1946. These trailers dealt with issues of work and wages, housing, and the role of trade unions in political elections. One particular film produced by Stanley Hawes (*A Racial Unity Discussion Preface and Trailer*) tackled racial concerns and the need to battle prejudice inside and outside the workplace.

While NFB films continued to tackle themes of labour and public social programs, they simultaneously or conversely accentuated a new discourse. This discourse incorporated several features affecting the depiction of labour. First, an increasing number of films stressed a clearly nationalist slant on Canadian unity. This approach represented a clear departure from earlier emphasis on social (e.g. class) identity. Second, films began to reflect a shift in focus away from issues such as the participation of workers in implementing social and political strategies. Instead, new films gradually highlighted the role of authority, and in particular the role of government, politicians and bureaucrats in articulating and implementing specific economic and social programs. The third feature of this transitory discourse related to its emphasis on science and technology as emblems of human progress. In this regard, films focused more and more on technology as an alternative to labour inefficiency. The fourth feature of the new discourse stressed the case of maintaining labour wage controls in the post-war era period as a means of keeping down the inflation rate. The fifth feature reflected an increased focus on the role of the individual. An important example in this regard is a group of films that dealt with issues of job safety. All these films advised workers about their personal responsibility in regards to performance on the job. The sixth feature related to the depiction of women workers. Now that "the boys were back from the war front," films encouraged the return of women to their "natural" place at home. This retrograde move away from earlier filmic celebration of the new role of women workers became increasingly noticeable in subsequent post-war NFB films.

NEW EMPHASIS ON NATIONALIST UNITY

A new feature in early post-war NFB films had to do with renewed interest in the issue of nationalist identity. Films were shifting back in the direction of presenting a homogenous image of Canadian society in a manner that subsumed its social diversity and heterogeneity into one ubiquitous national character. This represented a clear departure from the previous emphasis on the specificity and the roles of different social components of Canadian society, such as those based in class and gender.

In and of itself, the notion of national identity is not synonymous with a specific hegemony. For example, the NFB's earlier depiction of national unity was used by way of ushering values of collective sharing and control of social and economic resources. As cultural signs, notions such as national identity acquire their ideological significance within specific historical moments, and are therefore informed by ascending social and political views and perspectives. The ideological significance of cultural signs is largely influenced by the shifts that take place within social and political formations and structures. In the words of Dick Hebdige,

> The struggle between different discourses, different definitions and meanings within ideology is therefore always, at the same time, a struggle within signification: a struggle for possession of the sign which extends to even the most mundane areas of everyday life. "Humble objects" can be magically appropriated; "stolen" by subordinate groups and made to carry "secret" meanings: meanings which express, in code, a form of resistance to the order which guarantees their continued subordination.[17]

To the background of increased labour tensions and class antagonisms, and as the ruling class began a process of reaffirming its social and political hegemony within Canadian society, the notion of national unity in the period directly after World

War II became increasingly synonymous with loyalty to an essentially socially homogeneous (read: classless) society. Implicitly this meant that attempts to instigate class disharmony would be in effect counterproductive to the interest of the entire nation. Such interpretation of the nation and its interests fundamentally complements advocating the abandonment of the specificity of a working-class social perspective, especially if it is seen hindering or contradicting the interests of the capitalist class.

Stanley Jackson's *This is Our Canada* (1945) discusses how Canada succeeded in developing its resources and industries during the war. The emphasis throughout the film is on a patriotic vision of what it means to be a Canadian. The film begins with a journey across the country's geographic landscape. After it presents a literally bird's eye view of the vast and diverse spaces of the country, the film zooms in to show people playing hockey, in the stampedes, in parades and on the streets. The film delineates the multicultural "English, French, Irish, Scandinavian, Scots, German, and Ukrainian background" of Canada then describes the major industrial production strides made during the war as attributes to "national unity and loyalty." In *Salute to a Victory* (1945) the narrator repeatedly affirms Canada's victory in the war as "a virtue of its unity as a nation." In an attestation to the benefits of national accord and harmony, the film symbolically compares achieving victory through unity to achieving harmony in a musical symphony performance!

LABOUR, AUTHORITY AND THE ROLE OF GOVERNMENT

NFB films also began to prominently feature government officials and bureaucrats. Dealing with social and economic issues was increasingly being juxtaposed with praising the role of authority. A close examination of the films produced in and after 1945 indicates clear and increased presence of government officials and/or politicians introducing or arguing the case of specific social or economic plans and programs.

In one segment dealing with problems affecting returning war veterans, the commentator in the 1945 film *The Road to Civvy Street* (Vincent Paquette) authoritatively reminds workers that the government "knows better what is good for veterans." In sharp contrast to the earlier emphasis on the responsibility of government towards the collective will of society, and in an obvious departure from the previous accent on participatory grassroots democratic discussion, films such as *The Road to Civvy Street* are characterized by the domineering presence of government officials and bureaucrats intent on getting credit for initiating and implementing specific programs.

Another film, *Back to Work* (1945, Vincent Paquette), deals with how government, with the help of the military, "re-equips ex-servicemen and women to return to civilian jobs." An army rehabilitation officer conducts a final interview with a dischargee. Then, a placement officer assists the veteran in securing new suitable employment. The film gives several examples depicting the process of training veterans in areas such as electrical maintenance, typing, repair work, bricklaying, woodwork, garage work, hairdressing, and secretarial work. The central point in all these examples is to show how government officials estimate, evaluate and determine how veterans could be reintegrated into the work force. The depiction of the military as the administrator of the entire recruiting process further affirms the film's paternalistic celebration of the role of authority.

Along with an increased focus on officials and other authority figures, the discourse on democracy and democratic practice was increasingly becoming synonymous with participating in general elections and with the notion of free speech. Pluralism, diversity of opinion and the free will of Canadians were increasingly submerged into the unitary national scheme of the act of electing a government. *Everyman's World* (1946, producer Sidney Newman), for example, gives a summery of how Canada's political system works. As the film opens, the phrase "you are free, and therefore responsible" sets the stage Prime Minister Mackenzie King to deliver a speech on Canada's policy on international treaties and agreements in front of the United Nations' General Assembly. King affirms that a fundamental component of Canada's policy lies in its belief that "peace affects the well-being of the world's peoples and as such is a concern for Canadian citizens." The commentary affirms the theme of free speech as the essence of Canada's political system. It describes how Canadians enjoy the freedom of belonging to "any political party" and how they practice the "freedom of determining their own political views." Footage depicting election rallies and activities by different political parties (including a glimpse from a communist Labour Progressive Party rally) are introduced as examples of Canada's democratic traditions. "National consciousness," the film argues, is the embodiment of the individual freedom that binds millions of Canadians and allows them to speak in "one voice."

LABOUR AND WAGE CONTROLS

Appearance by government officials not only became a regular feature in NFB films, but it also became the core of a specific argument that would imprint these films at least until the late 1950s. Towards the end of the war, labour was fighting to lift the freeze on wages. This freeze was part of the price and wage controls that were agreed to earlier by labour, business and government as precautionary war measures.

Naturally, business had no problem with lifting government control on prices but was on the other hand adamant on maintaining the freeze on wages. In light of the tensions on the labour front, and considering that price controls were, to begin with, less likely to be effectively maintained, advocating the continuation of the controls was becoming synonymous with retaining the freeze on labour wages. NFB films between 1945 and 1946 increasingly reflected the views of the business community on this issue.

In *Price Controls and Rationing* (1945, produced by Philip Ragan) the focus is on supporting the renewal of the controls during the post-war period. Reminding us that our government has "learned from the experience of history," the film argues that overcoming potential problems after the end of the war requires the continuation of economic control measures. *Main Street, Canada* (1945, Alistair Taylor) tells the story of small towns living through the prosperity of the 1920s, the Depression of the 1930s and the stress of wartime economy. The film points out that people during these periods worked together using measures such as rationing, and salvaging drives and victory gardens to alleviate the problems of shortages and inflation. The main argument of the film, however, focuses on maintaining wage controls. As a result of this measure, the film argues, and as an outcome of the contributions made by the government to help workers by providing them with "cost of living expenses" support measures, the lives of communities have changed and "youth, men, and women are working and making more than ever before." As in all films with similar themes, *Main Street Canada* uses the situation that prompted imposing wage and price controls during the war to rationalize its continuation in the post-war period.

TECHNOLOGY AND PROGRESS

An increasing number of NFB films accented advances in technology and scientific research, and the role of people who worked in these areas. In this regard, films gave special attention to technology and scientific ventures, and tackled them as potential remedies for social and economic problems. They also perceived scientific and technological advances as prospective contributors to improving work efficiency.

In *Wasp Wings* (1945), images depicting workers and celebrating their role in producing the "tools of victory" as presented during the films of the 1941–44 period are noticeably replaced by a newly found fascination with technology and with the operators of war machines. The film describes the research by aeronautical engineers and the skill of the pilots who helped "keep the Spitfire plane in the air during the war." For its part, *Soil for Tomorrow* (1945, Lawrence Cherry) presents an account of the depletion and erosion of soil on the Canadian prairies. It discusses the restoration measures taken under the Prairie Farm Rehabilitation Act of 1935. The film opens with a telling dedication:

> To the national leaders, the scientists, the agronomists, and far-seeing farm people who struggle during good years and bad to make the best use of available waters and to preserve the soil.

Summarizing the history of the Depression, the film focuses on problems related to soil depletion, the use of outdated machinery and the effects of drought. It also stresses how the "mistakes by farmers" in planning and economizing their work and their lack of technical and scientific skill contributed to the Depression. In clear contrast to earlier war films, no mention is made here of the role of "chaotic" market production methods that were conceived of as the major instigators of the Great Depression. Consequently, the film makes no mention of cooperative production, marketing and/or distribution practices as possible tools for improving agricultural performance. Instead, it weighs on the role of technology, the government and the need to improve the technical and managerial skills of individual farmers.

A similar theme is presented in *Farm Electrification* (1946, Evelyn Cherry) when it depicts a farming community in Manitoba campaigning to obtain hydropower under Manitoba's Rural Electrification Plan. The film opens with Manitoba's agriculture minister making a presentation on the benefits of the project. It then follows a campaign aimed at convincing hesitant farmers to contribute to covering the initial expenses of the project. Farmers finally recognize the importance of the proposal and the benefits they will get in return in terms of comfort, convenience, efficiency, and financial advantage. The film concludes by a statement which stresses that the implementation of the project will result in "decreased labour, and improved output."

In *Fishing Partners* (1945, Jean Palardy), scientists are conducting research to increase cod fishing productivity. Sea life is studied and possibilities for marketing and processing liver oil are evaluated. Scientists discover that fishing can start in May as opposed to June. As fishermen watch from the sidelines or occasionally lend a helping hand, scientists carry on with their experiments to help them "perform better in the future."

Tom Daly's *The Challenge of Housing* (1946) surveys ways of dealing with the problem of the slum housing conditions in working-class districts. Daly discusses the causes and effects of such conditions and points out to the progress made by other countries in their attempts to provide adequate working-class housing. While it acknowledges the need to coordinate efforts between industry and labour, and as it describes the menacing social consequences of housing shortages, the film argues that finding efficient technical alternatives in construction methods represents the crux of the solution to the problem. Developing and utilizing technical innovations is the only feasible answer to the problem, the film suggests. In sharp contrast to the earlier 1945 film *Building a House*, where the focus was on the cooperative social organization of work power as one way of dealing with housing shortages, *Challenge of Housing* deals with the issue solely on the basis of finding technical solutions to the problem.

THE ROLE OF WOMEN IN THE LABOUR FORCE

As we saw in earlier chapters, during the war women played a major role as part of the industrial working class. The participation of women in the work force helped alleviate labour shortages resulting, on the one hand, from sending large numbers of recruits to the war in Europe, and on the other, from the drastic increase in demand for war machinery. As the war neared its end, however, voices began to demand that women return to "their natural work and role at home." In the words of Beckie Buhay, labour leader and communist activist at the time,

> The war had no sooner ended than efforts were made to drive women back to the kitchen. Married women were driven out of the civil service. Women in higher paid specialized jobs at pay almost equal with that of men, were forced into the less skilled industries and into sweat-shop occupations.[18]

Attacks against gains achieved by women workers during the war years, however, were accompanied by attacks on women's political rights even before the war ended. In 1943, and the midst of the war, the right of women to be part of the political process was itself being undermined by none other than the Prime Minister himself. Inside the House of Commons, Dorise Nielsen expressed her indignation with the Prime Minister's failure to acknowledge the role played by Canadian women in support of the war effort. Nielsen criticized remarks made by the PM in which he ignored any reference to women during his call to involve returning men in the political process. Nielsen reminded King of the major contributions made by women during the war:

> Women have gone into practically every one of the industries which are vital to war production. They have undertaken heavy physical labour. They have also taken on types of work requiring executive ability and the kind of ability which is of the brain and not so much physical... when we realize what women have done, are doing and will continue to do to fight for the preservation of democracy and for Canada, all must agree that they have a place among legislators to decide on the issues of peace and war, to see to it that this country in post-war years has those things which the people need.[19]

As signs of economic and political discrimination against women became more evident, there were also some shifts back to emphasizing patriarchal perceptions of women's roles in society. The NFB filmic discourse between 1945 and 1946 reflected such shifts.

In a film which makes a point of considering itself a "a tribute to the women of Canada and their part in World War II efforts," the emphasis is in fact on sending a "thank you message" to women for their role in "releasing men to do other jobs or to fight the war." The 1946 film *To the Ladies* (producer Nicholas Balla) makes no qualms about the way it envisions the role of women in the post-war era. After presenting examples of the wide range of jobs that were taken up by women throughout the war, the film revels in the fact that, now that the war is over, a Canadian woman can "look back to do her job: a wife. A better wife."

INDIVIDUAL RESPONSIBILITY AND JOB SAFETY

Within a capitalist ideological perspective on change and progress, to be able to pass through the ordeals of social, economic and technological change, one has to articulate one's own survival strategy: one needs to negotiate one's own way of coping with the benefits as well as with the problems associated with inevitable progress. In the end, social and political passivity is conceived of as the only sensible way to ride the tide of this inevitability. In this context, ideas such as individual self-determination and "free will" represent fundamental features of a bourgeois hegemonic discourse. Within such a pretext, if uninterrupted evolutionary change represented the main trait of the history of humanity, then individuals need to recognize that their survival and success depends on how they privately adjust their own fate to accommodate unavoidable progress.

An important shift in the NFB's discourse on labour occurred in connection with accentuating the role of the individual and personal responsibility in dealing with social and workplace problems. In addition to what I alluded to earlier in relation to NFB films' increased emphasis on technological progress as a remedy for work-related problems, these films for their part virtually put the onus of work safety squarely on the workers themselves.

Vocational Training (1945) presents the story of former Canadian servicemen as they adapt to life after the war. After it describes their training in government-sponsored programs, the film stresses that it is now "up to these veterans to deliver the goods," and that this will now depend on "their desire to help themselves." Along similar lines a large group of films produced in 1946 tackled the issue of safety in the workplace.

Focus in connection with safety issues in the workplace is determinedly put on the individual's role in preventing accidents such as tripping, operating machinery, and handling of heavy loads. Ronald Weyman's (1946) film *The Safety Supervisor* deals with problems confronting the safety manager in his relationship with other management and with labour, and illustrates typical accident hazards. David Bairstow's *Safe Clothing* (1946) conveys the story of a worker who is baffled by the decision of his foreman to send him to the emergency clinic although he was feeling perfectly well. As the nurse begins to operate on his dragging necktie, baggy sleeved sweater, cuffed pants and worn-out shoes, he begins to realize the dangers associated with wearing improper clothing at work. The essence of the argument, however, is on the responsibility of individual workers in avoiding hazardous work practices. *Workers on the Land* (Ernest Reid, 1946) offers suggestions to improve the lifestyle, skills and the working conditions of farm labour. It points out ways to reorganize and plan farm work to guarantee profitable employment during the winter season. The film argues that careful training of farm workers and more efficient planning by individual farmers constitute the main ingredients of successful farming.

The strength of these films is that they do make sense: no one can argue about the need for personal vigilance on the part of workers when it comes to applying better safety and productivity standards. But when these films and their arguments are looked at as the background to the shift that was taking shape in the general discourse of NFB films (particularly the shift away from previous emphasis on collective responsibility), they begin to reveal an altered ideological slant. Consequently, these films begin to make sense as complementary to a broader hegemonic outlook (and consensus) which in this case reintroduces previous commonsensical values vis-à-vis work, workers, and responsibilities.

But while most films during this period deal with issues of work safety and improving work conditions on the basis of seeking personal remedies (or as we saw earlier on the basis of finding technological solutions), a 1946 film titled *Organization* by Don Mulholland argues in support of creating workers' safety committees to lower the rate of industrial accidents. As an example, the film demonstrates how one such committee investigates dangerous work areas and reports on bad lighting and the hazards of crooked floors. In the end, the prudent training and supervision of newly hired workers is seen as the responsibility of the safety committee. The film then proposes that safety committees should be created as part of a collective strategy that involves labour and management. Another film titled *Silicosis* (1946) by Vincent Pacquette demonstrates how lung disease is caused by exposure to silicate and quartz dust. The film emphasizes improving health conditions through developing better collective supervision methods of mine ventilation techniques.

THE NFB UNDER ATTACK

Accusations by Soviet defector Igor Gouzenko about a Canadian spy ring working for the Soviet Union were publicly disclosed five months after Gouzenko's defection to the RCMP. Just one month later, with the arrest of the lone communist member of the House of Commons Fred Rose in March 1946, a full-fledged political offensive against the Canadian communist left was now in full gear. Eventually the campaign would target a wide range of labour and social activists of different leftist and liberal-oriented stripes.

Among those referred to in Gouzenko's allegations were various NFB personnel, including Frida Linton, Grierson's secretary for six months in 1944.[20] Grierson himself was named as a potential conspirator but was eventually cleared of the charges. On the level of internal bureaucratic politics, Grierson had "too few trustworthy allies and too many detractors." According to Ted Magder, specific films produced by the NFB during the war only added to the political isolation of Grierson:

Some of the NFB's wartime films, most notably *Inside Fighting Russia* and *Balkan Powder Keg*, had unnerved government officials: the former for its seemingly wholehearted endorsement of the Russian Revolution, and the latter for its criticism of British policy in the Balkans.[21]

Problems faced by leftist intellectuals and filmmakers inside and outside the NFB in the mid-1940s, however, were not simply related to the government's attempt to "curtail a dangerous subversive spy network," as Magder suggests. As we saw earlier, the relationship between the labour movement and the Communist Party of Canada was at an all time high during and shortly after the war ended. The influence of the CPC both inside and outside of the labour movement was also on the increase. At the same time, tensions resulting from labour's concerted push to lift the wartime freeze on wages were also on the rise. In the end, and as Len Scher suggests, the government's anti-Communist campaign was connected with practical labour-related motives:

> Communism was influential in certain parts of the labour movement, and consequently the Mounties increased their surveillance on left-wing unions. Communists had organized unions throughout Canada, fought bitter strikes, and were intensely dedicated to workers. Bill Walsh, a long-time union activist and Communist, told me he believed the real reason for the red-hunting during the cold war wasn't ideological but practical. "There was concern largely because business felt threatened by the ability of Communists to get better wages for their workers," says Walsh.[22]

The practical threat that Walsh was talking about was real. The labour strike movement between 1945 and 1947 was picking up steam on unprecedented levels.

According to the *Canada Year Book* of 1952–53, after the number of strike days tripled from 500,000 in 1944 to 1,500,000 in 1945 (largely as a consequence of the major Ford Strike in the second half of the year), this number tripled yet again to over 4,500,000 in 1946.[23] Strikes spread across Canada to include almost all major industrial production sectors, including lumber, textile, fisheries, steel, rubber, auto, mining and electrical industries.[24]

All these battles on the labour front had major ramifications on social and political stability. At the heart of tensions was what labour and left-wing activists saw as an attempt by big business to retract from earlier commitments on labour-management cooperation. Coinciding with the anti-Communist campaign was a "post-war putsch" against left-wing labour unions. Even before his arrest on spying charges, Fred Rose described the atmosphere that was brewing in the aftermath of the war:

> Workers in various plants and industries have felt for the past year a change in the attitude of employers. Before V-E day, when war materials were necessary, employers were willing to collaborate, but once they felt that the war was coming to an end they started to provoke trouble in the shops. They laid off active unionists and fired certain workers and rehired at lower wages. All these methods were resorted to in order to prepare for the post-war period.[25]

Merrily Weisbord confirms that the push against communists occurred in conjunction with a wider campaign by employers to lay off workers and reduce wages in an attempt to "get back to pre-war conditions."[26] Within five years after the start of this campaign, thousands of communists and their supporters were purged from labour unions. As a direct result of this campaign, and in spite of their ability to sustain some level of authority within a shrinking number of unions, the influence of communists and their allies within the labour movement was radically reduced. The CPC's strategic role within organized labour was to eventually become part of history.

With Cold War hysteria taking hold, the Canadian government calmly continued its witch-hunt – of leftists, internationalists, pacifists, and of other "subversives" in the civil services, in the NFB, as well as in the Canadian Broadcasting Corporation.[27] In 1986 Rick Salutin would open up aspects of this largely forgotten period in Canadian history in the CBC's television drama *Grierson and Gouzenko*. The film depicts events relating to the NFB during World War II and the Cold War.[28]

Attacks against the left intensified into a fear campaign. In 1947 the Canadian Chamber of Commerce (CCC), one of the main voices of business in Canada, published a pamphlet for mass distribution which accused communists of being revolutionary agents of a foreign power and whose loyalty was to an "imported ideology." It alleged that communists were attempting to destroy Canada's way of life with lies, strife and bloodshed.[29] No sooner had the CCC published its article than business circles began to target the NFB itself.

In a 1949 article titled "Film Board Monopoly Facing Major Test," the *Financial Post* accused the NFB of becoming a leftist propaganda machine. It also revealed that the Board had been labelled a "vulnerable agency" and that the Department of National Defence was no longer using its services.[30] Another campaign by private film production companies compounded the ferocious nature of the attacks against the NFB. Quoted by Len Scher, Margorie McKay, a National Film Board employee at the time, suggests that an effective lobby by private film producers was pushing to gain access to government money, which at the time was exclusively set for the NFB production unit:

> All government departments were supposed to have all their films made by the National Film Board. Private film producers wanted to cut in and make films for such departments as Health and Welfare, National Defence, the Post Office, and Justice. There was more money for private producers from government than from any where else.[31]

This view is echoed in an article in the *Ottawa Citizen* from the period. The article states that "the National Film Board has its defenders as well as detractors. Its critics appear to be chiefly persons connected with the private film industry... the board's supporters appear to be the public."[32] No further corroboration of how private companies specifically encouraged left blacklisting or any specific evidence that can identify these companies. What is certain however, as Whitaker and Marcuse stress, is that much of the anti-NFB campaign was directly connected to the Canadian "political, bureaucratic and economic elites," and clearly had no support among the general Canadian public. The two writers take the case even further and suggest that, if anything, the NFB enjoyed good public support manifested in strong protests in support of it that were initiated by various grassroots organizations:

> Labour unions, farmers' groups, cooperatives, universities, public libraries, local film councils and movie appreciation societies, women's groups, and small-town service clubs wrote to Ottawa in bewilderment, anger, and concern about the future of an organization that they cherished.[33]

Eventually, in November 1949 fierce accusations against the "leftist bias" of the National Film Board came to a head with direct accusations of "communist infiltration" of NFB employees. Thirty Board employees were presumed security risks. When the NFB's director Ross McLean refused to fire any employee he was himself let go. Consequently, his deputy assistant resigned. McLean was later replaced by *Maclean's* editor W. Arthur Irwin.[34]

The atmosphere of fear created within the NFB as a result of the anti-communist campaign had a major political and personal impact on all NFB employees. Len Scher describes how James Beverdige, an NFB manager and filmmaker during the war and post-war periods, regretted not interfering in support of the employees who were under fire at the time: "in an emotional moment, he confided to me that 'every fibre in his body' regrets not standing up and fighting for those who were fired at the Film Board. But the overall political climate suppressed acts of individual heroism."[35] Rick Salutin provides a similar account:

> They [the RCMP] asked some employees to inform on others. Some private film makers were asked to provide incriminating information, and at least one happily drew up his own list of possible subversives. People began leaving the board, sometimes for political reasons, sometimes with an ambiguous reference to "budget cuts." New people moved in. Some were assumed to be informers, others enforcers of the new political line.[36]

Even some CCF members of the House of Commons joined in the attacks on the NFB and its employees. Pleading guilty for his party's earlier defence of the NFB, and now calling for complete security screening of all its employees to ensure that they all are "working for us," the CCF's representative from Cape Breton South strongly attacked the Board and its alleged communist connections:

> It was not yesterday that this Film Board became suspect. We remember the espionage trials. We remember Freda Linton and the position she occupied on the Board [Grierson's secretary who was accused of being a Russian spy in the aftermath of the Gouzenko affair]. We remember... [Grierson], who is no longer in this country.[37]

Many filmmakers and employees from the Board were fired and some others, seeing the writing on the wall, simply chose to resign on their own. In reference to the effect this atmosphere had on the entire work culture of the NFB at the time, Salutin recounts moving recollections by one of the Board's most talented filmmakers:

> Evelyn and Lawrence Cherry had been driving forces at the board. "One day we were invited up to Mr. Irwin's office," says Evelyn. "He asked us some innocuous questions, then he said, 'Would your assistant be able to carry on the agricultural section if you were gone?' We said, 'Yes, our assistant has been well trained.' That was that was said. Some time later I resigned. I suppose I should have refused to quit, made them fire me. But I was physically exhausted. There had been all that incredible energy expended during the war. Then with peacetime, the pressures,

the uneasiness, the opportunism. And always less and less work. I guess at that period we spoke less than at any time in our lives."[38]

The new NFB management tried to bring the Board closer to the government line on communism, and by extension to its position on labour issues. By the early 1950s, the new director of the NFB announced the creation of a series entitled *Freedom Speaks Programme*. The series proclaimed as its main goal "counter[ing] communist propaganda with a positive statement in effective dramatic form of the values which we as a free people believe to be basic to democratic society."[39]

The years of producing films that championed the contribution of workers to society and extolled working people as builders of a "new tomorrow" were coming to an end. Canadian film historian Peter Morris contends that the NFB later concentrated on making films about "ordinary Canadians" that tended to include "middle or lower middle classes" such as "professionals (teachers, bank clerks, editors), skilled workers, or rural workers (who are associated with the prestige of the land)." "Unskilled industrial workers or the chronically unemployed," he continues, "had no place in the NFB."[40]

Morris attributes these changes to the middle-class background of the filmmakers. He suggests that their social background, combined with Canada's "comfortable slippage... into an era of modest social reform under the paternal guidance of Mackenzie King's Liberal government" might have resulted in the Board's shift towards depicting "ordinary Canadians"[41] instead of industrial workers. Morris's proposals are clearly problematic. To begin, when he characterizes the shift which resulted in the NFB's retraction from depicting industrial workers and the unemployed as a shift towards depicting "middle or lower middle classes" Morris is clearly basing his argument on the assumption that clerical wage-earners and other workers from outside of the industrial and blue-collar sectors of the economy do not belong to the working class. The real and important difference between industrial and non-industrial labour has a major bearing on the problems of working-class consciousness and struggle; but it is not the yardstick for setting boundaries to the structure of the working class itself. Changes in the make-up of Canadian labour, which in the post-war period began to move in the direction of an increase in white collar workers as compared with industrial workers, does not as such represent an expansion of a middle class.

The change in labour composition in the post-war period reflected a gradual movement towards less reliance on manual labour. This change partly occurred due to advances that affected the technological structure of the means of production. Furthermore, changes in the working class's demographics also reflected an expansion of the services sectors of the economy and the amplification of government bureaucracy which was beginning to take shape in the late 1940s. This occurred in conjunction with the major expansion and implementation of government-sponsored social and public programs.

NFB films during the post-war period did indeed reflect a shift towards depicting professionals and skilled workers, as Morris correctly suggests. This shift, however, was indicative of a change of emphasis from one labour sector to another rather from one class to another. It was a shift directly connected to the attacks against communist influence within the labour movement that existed mainly among industrial workers. It also aimed at uprooting the NFB's counter-hegemonic filmic discourse on labour issues in general and, as such, hardly reflected a "comfortable slippage into a period of modest social reforms" as Morris claims. What took place within the NFB amounted to a virtual shutdown of films about militant sections of the Canadian working class at the time (i.e. industrial labour). This shutdown complemented and enhanced the overall campaign against militant labour and coincided with the campaign against the communist left. This shutdown also directly complemented the interests of big business. Under the banner of fighting communism, big business felt the urgency of putting a stop to a discourse that encouraged and sustained a class-conscious orientation in its analysis. As Whitaker and Marcuse attest, big business's indignation towards this discourse even went back to the war years when business leaders lobbied against what they saw as dangerous threat to their interests:

> Even during the war years, private-sector critics were fastening on Grierson's alleged "Communist" tendencies. In the spring of 1942, H.E. Kidd of Cockfield, Brown Advertising wrote to Brooke Claxton, MP, to complain about Grierson on behalf of many of his business clients. Kidd was an invaluable supporter of Claxton in his Montreal riding and was later to become a cabinet minister and one of the most important political figures in the Liberal Party organization. Kidd's complaint to Claxton was to the point: "I have heard from some of our clients that Mr. Grierson is getting a reputation as one of the most dangerous characters in Canada. Somebody had seen the documentary film [*Inside Fighting Russia*].... This film deals with Russia. It glorifies, in the opinion of my informant, the Communist faith and is a very bad insidious piece of propaganda for Communism."[42]

Even the Canadian private film industry (at that point largely connected with Hollywood business interests) was not far from the campaign against the NFB. What is of particular interest in this regard is the possible role played by the pro-Hollywood lobby during this post-war period in jeopardizing not only the development of the

NFB itself with its documentary form (i.e. in contrast with fiction film) but also the development of a Canadian independent film industry altogether. Whitaker and Marcuse insinuate such a scenario:

> Opposition to Grierson's NFB from the private sector was, in the Canadian context, a two-headed beast. One head, much the smaller, was that of the private Canadian film industry which did not, in truth, amount to much. It could, and sometimes did, act as a Canadian lobby against any expansion of the publicly owned NFB. The dynamo of American cultural industries, was well represented in Canada by the U.S. Embassy and by the American-owned theatre and distribution chains. The core of Hollywood production was, of course, feature films, which the NFB did not produce, and which the Canadian government had no intention of sponsoring. Yet the NFB did represent at least a marginal rival, especially in the pre-television age when people still depended on the cinema for images of news and events in the world. Above all, the NFB represented a breeding ground for Canadian talent under public auspices that had the potential of forming nucleus of an indigenous Canadian film industry after the war. Hollywood was (and is) quite intolerant of any rivalry in its market on the northern half of the continent.[43]

This argument bears important consequences for understanding the dynamics of the development of the Canadian film industry and the marginalizing of the documentary form as a whole. There is no doubt that Hollywood and the private sector of the Canadian film industry (irrespective of how insignificant it was), had a joint and vested interest in eliminating any possible growth of a public-sector-supported Canadian cinema. Despite his attempts to lessen the American domination over the Canadian film industry by proposing the creation of a quota system "to ensure at least minimal opportunity for Canadian films to be seen in theatres in Canada," Ross McLean, Grierson's successor at the NFB was clearly no match for a Canadian government increasingly under the sway of C.D. Howe, "economic czar, 'minister of everything,' and forceful exponent of continentalist economic development, who had no interest in subsidizing a local film industry."[44] This episode alludes to some of the politics that accompanied the campaign against the NFB. It also indicates the political significance of what was being achieved in the NFB and the level to which the Board was becoming a source of agitation for big business circles.

The main distinguishing feature of Canadian cinema (and the NFB in particular) during its early years of existence was indeed its near exclusive documentary focus. In contrast, both European and American cinemas gravitated toward fiction narrative.

The start of World War II provided an impetus for Canadian documentary production to thrive. NFB's documentaries brought editorially enhanced presentations of events and labour politics to hundreds of thousands of Canadian spectators. This documentary practice was enhanced by various factors that went beyond the subject matter that they focused upon, and involved the nature of the documentary medium itself. NFB films were cheap to make and economical to market – as we saw earlier they were essentially produced and moved through to circuits almost entirely in-house. As such NFB filmmakers had a ready-made market niche, and as a result their films achieved a level of popularity that remains rare in documentary film history. Therefore the argument as to the possible impact that the attack against the NFB at the end of the war might have had on the development of documentary form in general and on shaping Canadian cinema in particular is certainly of major relevance and begs further research.

By the late 1940s, NFB films dealing with labour issues were reduced considerably. Between 1942 (the year in which Canadian labour and the Communist Party became fully involved in supporting the war effort) and 1946 (the year when the anti-Communist campaign officially began with the arrest of Communist MP Fred Rose), NFB titles that were categorized under "work and labour relations" were produced on an average of 14.8 films per year. The annual production of such titles consecutively dropped to: four in 1947, none in 1948, and two in 1949 (i.e. an annual average of two films between 1947 and 1950). This drop massively exceeded the less than one third drop in the NFB's overall annual average film production output in the two periods (from 97.4 films per year between 1942 and 1945, to 62.7 films per year between 1947 and 1949).

To reiterate my earlier argument vis-à-vis Peter Morris's de-politicization (particularly in connection with the Cold War) of the changes that occurred in the NFB after the end of the war, the atmosphere during this period was anything but "a comfortable" social or political transformation. Canada's entry into the post-war era was brimming with fierce struggles that eventually resulted in a decisive victory for monopoly capital and the "slippage" (to use Morris's term) into a rather uncomfortable reaffirmation of capitalist hegemony. But Morris's account of the transitional years in the NFB after the end of the war is characteristic of how many in Canada tend to look at McCarthyism as something that Canada was immune to or as a phenomenon that never affected Canadians. Unlike in the United States, when we write the history of Canadian cinema we don't even acknowledge the victims of our own McCarthyism:

All this constitutes a standing rebuke to the bland liberal myth that McCarthyism was something that happened in America but not in Canada. Yet the lesson of this story is worse yet. As Rick Salutin has written, the Americans have actually celebrated the Hollywood witch-hunt by the House Un-American Activities Committee that took place in the late 1940s. The victims eventually became martyrs, even heroes. The victims in Canada have been ignored, relegated to silence. "In the U.S., the film witch hunt all happened under Klieg lights and TV cameras. It was impossible to miss. Here it was done in a more Canadian way: secretive, subtle, even polite. And yet our version was, if anything, more pervasive than the red scare in Hollywood. It began earlier, lasted most of a decade, and the aftermath is with us still in the form of the film industry we have – or do not have."[45]

What took place in Canada in the aftermath of World War II reflected a wider and more in-depth shift in the social and political balance of forces in the country. This shift affected the struggle around capitalist hegemony. Events of the early Cold War period signalled the beginning of a hegemonic reclamation by the capitalist class of whatever retreats it was forced to take during the earlier counter-hegemonic working class's charge as exemplified in the success and the increased influence of Popular Front policies. This charge occurred in the context of a protracted *war of position*, to use Gramsci's famous term, which is characteristically symptomatic of heightened moments of contention between the working class and the capitalist class in advanced civil societies.

In light of earlier successes achieved by the political and ideological forces that constituted the National/Popular Front, the Canadian capitalist class launched a major offensive to reclaim full control of the social and political situation in the country. As the war ended, there was no more need for full labour support to meet earlier increases in industrial production demands; the capitalist class had no urgent reason to maintain its wartime partnership commitments with labour. On the contrary, such a partnership now represented an imposition of some sort on the right of capital to fully control the decision-making process within the private sphere of its economic enterprise. Veteran filmmaker Evelyn Cherry described aspects of this battle as they became evident in the campaign against the NFB and the attempts to silence it:

The basic thing was an attack on the *kind* of film – of social meaning – we were doing. We felt deeply involved in the country and we were filming it. Canadians were seeing themselves and their country for the first time, and they liked it. We were a threat to the way things were and the way some people wanted them to continue. In the U.S. there were a few people doing it, but up here it was a movement – the National Film Board![46]

CONCLUSION

Grierson's original project at the NFB envisioned film as a tool to expand the role of government in improving the lives of its citizens. Based on how he saw the need for the intervention of the government, Grierson clearly advocated expanding the participatory role of citizens in discussing public concerns and issues:

> By stressing social purpose, Grierson wanted film to become a buttress of modern democracy, helping to buttress an informed citizenry as the foundation of progressive political development, in an age when communications technology encouraged social interdependence and collective enterprise. The appropriate instrument for such film-making was the State – not simply the government of the day, but a progressive public organized according to the principle of the "general sanction," that is, the limits of tolerable social change across the range of dominant partisan interests.[47]

In itself, Grierson's vision was far from being counter-hegemonic. While his outlook did not necessarily contradict those of the Communist Party and its Popular Front policy and the labour movement at the time, it did not endorse it either, at least not explicitly.

Ideologically, Grierson consistently projected himself at the centre of the political spectrum. Clearly, his pronounced ideas seemed more in sync with the centrist politics of the social democratic movement than with those of the Marxist and communist left. Like the British documentary movement within which he apprenticed his film and political careers in the 1930s, Grierson's ideas were positioned "to the left of dominant conservatism, to the right of Marxist and socialist opinion, and within a constellation of centrist ideologies associated with currents of social democratic reform."[48] In this respect many promoters of these ideas (including Grierson) insisted on projecting an image of themselves as rejecting both Communism and Fascism. But while social reformist ideas were indeed "diverse and heterogeneous... they [nevertheless] shared a common core of agreement on the value of established social institutions, the need for public regulation of market forces."[49] Such values inadvertently complemented the thrust of the Popular Front policy strategy of the Communist Party of Canada during the war, which by that time had already parted from the earlier class-against-class approach of the 1920s and early 1930s.

Additional influence exercised by prominent NFB artists and intellectuals, many of whom might indeed have been informed by Communist Party ideas and policies, also probably played a role in how Popular Front ideas came to be integral to NFB films. Future research might bring more substantive evaluation and evidence of the practical dynamics that might have motivated specific prominent NFB filmmakers at the time, such as Stuart Legg, Jane March, Stanley Hawes, Evelyn Spice, Norman McLaren, James Beveridge, Tom Daly, Raymond Spottiswoode, and Basil Wright, along with many others. This kind of research could eventually identify some of these figures as major examples of the sort of organic intellectuals that Canada never fully acknowledged or paid due homage to. However, as I emphasized throughout this study, the counter-hegemonic significance of NFB films took shape within much broader social and political contexts that pertained to the political moment within which they were made.

The counter-hegemonic discourse on the working class that underscored NFB films during the early years of the Board's existence was an extension of a specific historical moment, where many practices, forces and players amalgamated. As we examine areas of influence that contributed to the development of the NFB's discourse on the working class, we begin to discover that it was informed by elements that were not necessarily or exclusively related to Canadian cinematic practices, or to the NFB's internal institutional dynamics, John Grierson, or specific filmmakers at the Board. To be sure, this discourse was primarily a materialization of multiple discursive emergences originating within working-class and socialist oriented political and cultural practices that were occurring in Canada and around the world. As such, it was informed by social, political and cultural formations whose dynamic strength existed outside of the Canadian political and social establishment's own discursive ideological domain.

Over the span of seven years between 1939 and 1946, NFB films functioned within a politically and ideologically polarized atmosphere. The vigour of this divergence was not restricted to the war front in Europe, however. Increasing social and political divisions within Canada set the stage for a major showdown between two major class-based forces whose war was temporarily put on hold. The function of NFB films grew and acquired its counter-hegemonic ideological workings in the context of how these films interacted with, enhanced, and/or contradicted the views and values of the two main forces that dominated the political and social arena at the time, namely a militant-led working class and the capitalist establishment.

Today, the films that we have examined have lost most of their original impact and power. They mostly look and sound crude and overbearing. Tom Daly, a contemporary NFB filmmaker commented recently: "Many of those wartime films don't stand up now. They are too time-locked."[50] Nevertheless, among the unique features of these films was their artistic and dramatic use of a disembodied voice to add historical and ethico-political nuance to their visual images. Rather than presenting bureaucratic reports to Canadians, these films offered fervent editorials. In some respect, these editorials and their filmmakers played a role similar to the one suggested by Gramsci for organic intellectuals who were to respond to and stand for the interests of working-class social groupings struggling to maintain or attain their own hegemonic status. This role was to be achieved through claiming a clear stand, in ideological terms, in relation to the struggle for a new social system which reorganizes the hierarchies of producing and distributing economic and cultural resources and power.

Now customarily decried as manipulation of the audience by what amounts to a Voice of God, the NFB films' voice-over was that of the filmmaker, unabashedly explicating the newsreel footage, re-recreating historic moments, maps, and original footage devised to build his/her arguments. What is missing in some of the critiques against NFB films of the period is their disregard for the political culture of the day, which (relatively speaking), was largely cognizant of the debate around objectivity in politics and in media. The popular influence of Marxist analysis and politics in part encouraged the affirmation of the inherently political, and for that matter, the class natured, and as such acknowledged ultimately the inadvertent bias of all cultural practices. In this regard communist critics were forthright in claiming and even celebrating their class and political impartiality. This stood in contrast to traditional claims of objectivity that were largely associated with mainstream media as well as with the political establishment's pronouncements, particularly when it came to admitting their own class affiliations and biases. This is why the idea of discussing films after they were shown became a popular modifying aspect of the process of watching films during this period. This practice was encouraged, as we have seen earlier, both by the Board and by supporters of the Popular Front.

To claim that the voice-over in NFB films attempted to dupe audiences to consent to government policies (as Nelson and Morris tend to maintain) is, for one, dismissive of the possible impact that the particularly politicized culture of the day might have had on these audiences. One can argue that, in the context of audience's general familiarity and involvement with contemporary political players, the use of an editorialized voice-over in these films might have even worked reflexively, and in a way that may have enhanced rather than subdued the proactive reading of these films.

Numerous NFB war films subtly celebrated the period's fascination with socialist-oriented programs as an effort to end unemployment, share the wealth, develop the economy, and build a new world of peace and cooperation by sponsoring new communities and attitudes built on cooperative rather than capitalistic principles. These films' arguments, however, were indeed largely muted, suggesting this may be only a short-term solution for larger and more fundamental social and economic problems.

Ideas that became part of the NFB's film discourse (e.g., collective work, sharing of resources, labour solidarity, democratic and equal participation of workers in the affairs of society, and solidarity with the Soviet working-class state), were put forward during a time that witnessed a major development of a militant working class, labour movements, and their supporters on the political left. Those ideas promoted a vision within which the working class assumed a prominent position within the Canadian political and social decision-making process.

By projecting values that complemented a working-class perspective, many NFB films inadvertently stressed the leadership role of workers within a widely based counter-hegemonic historical bloc. The success of several NFB filmmakers in presenting a vision that placed the working class and its role in Canadian society at the centre of their film discourse also placed the Board itself at the middle of struggle around class hegemony in Canada.

A significant characteristic of NFB films between 1939 and 1946 is how they inferred the role and position of the working class within the process of continuity and change in Canadian society. Under capitalism, change is equated with natural and inevitable evolution. Individual self-determination is also a fundamental feature of capitalist ideological values, one that needs to be acknowledged and adhered to if change is to occur without major social upheavals. In other words, in order to be part of late capitalist evolutionary change, one needs to articulate his/her own way of surviving through the ordeals that accompany technological and economical adjustments and readjustments. Therefore, individuals have to negotiate ways of accepting, or at least coping, with the benefits as well as with the negative repercussions of progress.

NFB films provided a challenge to how the working class and working-class individuals were traditionally portrayed and how they functioned within Canadian political and film discourse. As such, these films' discourse on labour and the working class was neither a continuation of preceding Canadian cinematic culture nor a simple reflection of the policies of the Canadian government. Indeed, this discourse constituted a major (albeit brief) break from what dominated Canada's film culture since the development of cinema in the late nineteenth century. It ushered in the emergence of a new perspective on the issue of social class, which specifically presented a counter-hegemonic outlook on the role of the working people in society.

For the first time in Canadian cinema, working people were not presented as passive observers of a history that links the past, the present and the future in a chain of incessant evolutionary change, or as victims of its inevitability. For the first time, working people were not portrayed as lone heroes, each fighting his/her own way out of the curse of labouring. Instead, and through challenging the commonsensical view of history as fate or as an uninterrupted evolutionary process, these films explored how the conscious intervention of working people moulded and re-shaped history. To this end, these films also urged and celebrated the possibility of expanding democratic practice by making it more reflective of the direct and grassroots involvement of working people, hence they provided concrete demonstrations of the commonsensical feasibility of democratizing democracy.

Intellectual formations were, and remain, especially integral to the modern era (and I deliberately use this term in distinction from the loaded and mostly mystified term of postmodern). Sociological studies of culture remain crucial to understanding the ideological significance of such formations to specific moments in history. But these formations are ephemeral, developing eventually into individual careers or offshoot movements; equally as important, they sometime disseminate their ideas widely, leaving more or less permanent traces on the general culture of their societies. As Raymond Williams contends, such formations are typically centred in a metropolis, at points of "transition and intersection" within a complex social history; and the individuals who both compose and are composed by them always have a "range of diverse positions, interests and influences, some of which resolved (if at times only temporarily)… others of which remain as internal differences."[51]

The specificity of the institutionalized and discursive formations and the ideological workings of the ideas that came out of the specific films dealt with in this book are long gone and are part of history. Aspects of these ideas themselves, however, have indeed spun off "into individual careers or breakaway movements" and more importantly disseminated "widely, leaving more or less permanent traces" (to reuse Williams' words) on Canadian political and cultural discourse. One only needs to look at how Canadians love to define their identity in terms of its compassion and its sense of collective social responsibility, and how we tend to express pride in our collective health and social programs, although we tend to de-historicize these ideas by looking at them as aspects of the Canadian way of life that has been with us from eternity!

Eventual disintegration of the left's historical bloc can be traced to complex economic, political, and social circumstances that can only be addressed in the context of the ensuing dynamics that dominated the period of the Cold War. Nevertheless, what remains clear is that the post-war period heralded the celebration of the Canadian national myth proclaimed in the name of triumphant monopoly capitalism. Under these new conditions the NFB was forced to face a major political offensive that eventually changed the composition of its leadership as well as the ideological crux of its political discourse. In the words of Thom Waugh, the post-war situation in the NFB was a "dramatic reflection of the play of cultural, political, and ideological factors, the confrontation of ideals and realities, in an era that both saw the dissipation of the cultural left of the Popular Front and the baptism under fire of the young Canadian cinema."[52]

APPENDIX
ANNOTATED FILMOGRAPHY

This appendix includes two lists of films with direct relevance to the topic of workers in the NFB's war film period. The first list includes NFB films of the period itself, and the second includes important films from various periods and by different producers (including the NFB) with topics of direct connection with the World War II era and the role of the working class and the left within this war.

The NFB films produced between 1939 and 1946 contain material useful to the study of the depiction of the working class and labour. Considering that this book presents an analysis of the political and ideological significance of the films' depiction of the working class, I have included films that directly refer to the workers and labour as well as those that indirectly impact the topic. Among these films are those dealing with general social and economic issues, a selection of films that depict the fight against fascism in Europe during World War II, and films that deal with and assess the role of the Soviet Union and related issues of peace and international cooperation.

The films are classified chronologically under the year of production. Films within each year are then listed in alphabetical order. The name of each film's director, producer or editor is listed in brackets (some films, however, originally do not list specific names), followed by its duration (in minutes and seconds), and finally a brief annotation. Some series titles are accompanied by a brief description of specific subtitles that contain material relevant to topics listed above. The second list includes selected NFB and non-NFB films also relevant to the study of the working class and the NFB in the period between 1939 and 1946.

1939

The Case of Charlie Gordon (Stuart Legg) 16:00. Within a Maritime setting the film provides a discussion on the issues of unemployment, the Great Depression, and government social programs.

Youth is Tomorrow (Stuart Legg) 15:00. Training and apprenticeship of youth and the unemployed.

Heritage (J. Booth Scott) 17:00. Prairie farmers and the Parry Farm Rehabilitation Administration program.

1940

Atlantic Patrol (Stuart Legg) 10:00. The role of Canadian seamen in supplying ships departing from Canada's eastern ports during the early stage of the war.

Controls for Victory (Philip Ragan) 4:00. An animated film dealing with the shortages of civilian goods during World War II; the film also discusses how uncontrolled buying leads to inflation.

Farmers of the Prairies 16:00. Prairie farmers and the use of government research and irrigation programs.

Front of Steel (John McDougall) 18:00. Steel workers in modern warfare.

Industrial Workers of Central Canada (Donald Fraser) 16:00. Industrial labour and the economic prosperity in central Canada.

News Round-Up Series. Includes footage on the role of industrial workers and farmers in the war.

On Guard for Thee (Stanley Hawes) 27:00. An impressionistic kaleidoscope of the effect of World War I on the industrialization of Canada.

Timber Front (Frank Badgley) 21:00. Conserving Canada's forests and their vital role in reconstructive social planning.

Toilers of the Grand Banks (Stuart Legg) 9:00. The work of fishermen and shipyard workers on the East Coast.

Wings of Youth (Raymond Spottiswoode) 19:00. Canada's contribution to the construction of air fields, machines and equipment required for the Commonwealth air training scheme.

1941

Battle of Brains (Stanley Hawes) 13:00. Emphasizes the work of scientists rather than industrial production workers.

Call for Volunteers (Radford Crawley) 10:00. The role of Winnipeg women in supporting the war effort; emphasis is on women's "support" work for men.

Churchill's Island (Stuart Legg) 22:00. The interrelationship between various forces which contributed to Britain's defence including the merchant seamen and workers in factories.

Heroes of the Atlantic (J.D. Davidson) 15:00. Includes scenes on the role of civilian labour in producing munitions and foodstuffs.

People of Blue Rocks (Produced by Douglas Sinclair & Edward Buckman) 9:00. Fishermen in Nova Scotia and issues of collective community work.

Pipeline Builders (Paul LeBel) 22:00. The construction of the pipelines from Portland, Maine to Montreal. Produced in cooperation with the Imperial Oil Company.

Strategy of Metals (Raymond Spottiswoode) 19:00. The strategic significance of Canadian aluminium in building crank shafts, tanks and planes.

1942

Battle of the Harvests (Stanley Jackson) 18:00. The role of farmers in supporting the war effort.

Empty Rooms Mean Idle Machines (Philip Ragan) 2:00. A character named Plugger helps the war effort by renting out his spare room so that a new worker can be brought in to work an idle machine at the munitions plant.

Ferry pilot (Stuart Legg and Ross McLean) 19:00. Includes footage on workers in the airplanes factories.

Fighting Ships (Robert Edmonds) 24:00. Shipyard workers in the war.

Five For Four (Norman McLaren) 2:52. Animated film on the need to support the wartime savings campaign.

Food, Weapon of Conquest (Stuart Legg) 21:08. Includes an assessment of the role of cooperative farming in the Soviet Union and how it contributes to the country's economic success.

Forward Commandos (Raymond Spottiswoode) 22:00. Includes footage of resistance and the guerrilla tactics used by Soviet Union during the war.

Geopolitik – Hitler's Plan for Empire (Stuart Legg) 20:00. Refers to the rise of fascism in Europe and the struggle against its rise during the Spanish Civil War.

Great Guns (Radford Crawley) 24:00. Industrial production of steel, pulp, and ship building on the Great Lakes.

If (Philip Ragan) 3:00. Inflation and war industrial production.

Inside Fighting Canada (Jane March) 11:00. The role of workers in lumber farming, and shipyard industries. The film also includes visual reference to women farmers and truck drivers.

Inside Fighting China (Stuart Legg) 22:00. The role of the Popular Front in China. Emphasis on the need for unity in fighting fascism and towards achieving economic and social justice. Reference to the link between workers and other sections of society in China.

Inside Fighting Russia (Stuart Legg) 22:00. The role of Soviet men and women workers in building the ingredients for successfully fighting fascism.

Keep 'em Flying (Graham McInnes) 20:00. The aircraft industry and the vital role of workers within it.

National Income (Philip Ragan) 2:00. An illustration of the composition and the spending of national income.

Northland (Ernest Borneman) 20:00. The mining towns and camps of the North and the role of miners.

Prices in Wartime (Philip Ragan) 10:00. The causes and effects of inflation during wartime.

Subcontracting for Victory 24:00. Coordinating the effort between management, labour and government.

Thank You Joe 10:00. The role of workers in producing trucks and tanks.

Voice of Action (James Beveridge) 17:00. The importance of involving labour and farmers in CBC radio's forums and discussions on the economy.

Women are Warriors (Jane March) 14:00. The role of women workers in the war and beyond. Reference to the Soviet experience in incorporating women into all sections of the work force.

1943

Action Stations! (Joris Ivens) 44:00. Ivens' first film at the NFB. This wartime film depicts the struggles of the Canadian Merchant Marine as it organizes its defence against German submarines.

Alexis Trembley: Habitant (Jane March) 37:00. Family farming in Quebec.

Battle is their Birthright (Stuart Legg) 18:00. Contrasting the military obedience of Japanese and Nazi youth, with the practice of citizenship education in the Soviet Union and China.

Before they are Six (Gudrun Parker) 15:00. Support of working mothers and the importance of creating day nurseries.

Bluenose Schooner (Eduard Buchman and Douglas Sinclair) 20:00. East Coast fishery and communities' use of cooperative methods.

Canada-Workshop of Victory 10:00. The development of the war industry.

Canada Communiqué No.1. 12:00. Includes reference to the role of Nova Scotia women workers in the ship-building industry.

Canada Communiqué No.3. 12:00. Includes reference to the role of women workers in West Coast shipyards.

Canada Communiqué No.4. 12:00. Includes reference to the essential role of coal miners.

Canada Communiqué No.6. 12:00. Includes reference to the Gaspé fishing industry.

Coal Face, Canada (Robert Edmonds) 20:00. Coal miners, unions and the role of workers in building a new future for Canada.

Curtailment of Civilian Industries (Philip Ragan) 2:00. Animated film on the different priorities of work and production during the peace and war period.

Coal Miners (Alan Field) 13:30. Coal miners and their role in the war.

Farm Front 20:00. The need to coordinate and centralize the effort to improve farming methods to aid in the war efforts.

The Farm Forum 10:00. A radio program dedicated to discussing the needs and the tasks of farmers during the war.

Film and Radio Discussion Guide 3:00. Discussion forums that deal with post-war social and economic issues.

The Gates of Italy (Tom Daly and Stuart Legg) 21:00. The rise of fascism in Italy and its political manipulation of workers.

Getting Out the Coal 13:00. British coal industry's big cutting and loading methods.

Grand Manan (Robert Crowther) 10:00. Collective effort and cooperative community work in a fishing New Brunswick town.

Handle with Care (George L. George) 20:00. Workers in a publicly owned factory.

He Plants for Victory (Philip Ragan) 2:00. Animated film on the benefits of cooperative gardening and shared farming practices.

Industrial Workers (Ernest Borneman) 20:00. Contributions made by industrial workers of Canada and in other Allied countries.

Labour Front 21:00. Mobilizing of the labour force during WWII. Emphasis on workers' expectations in sharing later opportunities of peace.

A Man and His Job (Alistair M. Taylor) 17:00. Unemployment insurance and its benefits for Canadian workers and for the national economy.

New Horizons (Evelyn Cherry) 31:00. Industrial development and possibilities for post-war benefits for workers and other citizens.

The People's Bank (Gudrun Bjerring) 17:22. A history of the credit union movement and illustration of the steps needed to set up a credit union.

Plowshares into Swords 20:00. Farmers and their role in supporting the war effort.

Prince Edward Island (Margaret Perry) 10:00. Includes dealing with the role of the cooperative and credit union movements among farmers and fishermen.

Proudly She Marches (Jane March) 18:27. Women workers as temporary workers during the war.

Thought for Food (Stanley Jackson) 20:00. Providing soldiers and industrial workers with adequate nutrition to safeguard work performance.

Tomorrow's World (Raymond Spottiswoode) 20:14. Centralized economic and social planning and the involvement of workers in building a better future.

The War for Men's Minds (Stuart Legg) 21:07. Labour, the war, Labour-Management Committees, and building a new world based on the principles of the American and French revolutions.

Wartime Housing (Graham McInnis) 20:00. Dealing with the rising need to provide workers with adequate housing.

Windbreaks on the Prairies (Evelyn Cherry) 21:00. Farming problems in the Prairies.

Wings on her Shoulders (Jane March) 11:07. Emphasis on the role of working women as "supporters to men."

Women Don Slacks and Hair Nets. 1:00. A news clip urging women to work in the factories.

Workers at War No.1. 9:00. Footage on the Toronto Workers' Theatre, the role of workers on assembly lines, and workers in the Saguenay dam in Quebec.

Workers at War No.1A. 5:00. Footage on a fitness class for workers in Vancouver.

Workers at War No.2. 10:00. Nova Scotia working women.

Workers at War No.5. 6:00. Manufacturing in, and laying of underwater mines. Also footage on the textile production industry.

Workers at War No.6. 7:00. Munitions factory and women shipbuilders.

1944

According to Need (Dallas Jones) 11:00. A survey of national local stabilizing controls to ensure an efficient distribution of agricultural equipment among the Allies and the liberated countries.

Balkan Powder Keg (Stuart Legg) 19:00. A depiction of the role of Greek and Yugoslav left-wing resistance against fascism during World War II. The film was extremely controversial and as a result was ordered withdrawn from circulation.

Canadian Labour Meets in Annual Conventions 4:00. A meeting of the Canadian Trade and Labour Congress.

Cost of Living Index 6:00. An animated film illustrating how the Canadian consumer price index was determined during the war.

Children First (Evelyn Cherry) 17:00. Coordinating nutritional policies and priorities during the war.

Coal for Canada 9:00. Workers in the coal mines. The film shows in some detail the process of dynamiting, loading and grading the coal.

Democracy At Work (Stanley Hawes) 20:30. Labour-Management Committees in Britain

Eisenhardt Discussion Preface and Trailer (Stanley Hawes) 5:00. Fitness programs for workers as introduced in two separate films.

Farm Plan 6:00. Farmers are invited to meet for discussions on ways to reach new standards for war agricultural production.

A Friend for Supper (Graham McInnes) 10:00. An appeal for coordinating the priorities of distributing food to war allies.

Gaspé Cod Fishermen (Jean Palardy) 11:00. Cooperative work as an ingredient for "building democracy into the lives of a fishing community." The only film in the period which deals with working-class issues in Quebec that is made from a Quebec filmmaker's perspective.

Getting the Most Out of A Film: No.5. Welcome Soldier (Stanley Hawes) 5:00. The labour representative on the Ontario Social Security and Rehabilitation Committee chairs a discussion on the difficulties faced by veterans returning to the work force.

Getting the Most Out of A Film: Tyneside Story (Stanley Hawes) 8:00. Toronto workers discuss post-war employment.

Getting the Most out of A Film: UNRRA – In the wake of the Armies (Stanley Hawes) 3:00. Trade union representatives discuss the work of UN Relief and Rehabilitation Administration.

Global Air Routes (Stuart Legg) 14:45. Solidifying friendship with the Soviet Union through creating new air routes.

Hands for the Harvests (Stanley Jackson) 22:00. Coordinating the work in the farming Canadian hinterland and the need to incorporate the help of labour from across the country. The film presents a problematic and potentially racist view of Japanese-Canadian internees.

Home Front (Stanley Hawes) 11:00. The role of women in the work force.

How Prices Could Rise (Philip Ragan) 2:00. An animated film on the need to create a government price control system during wartime.

Inside France (Stuart Legg) 21:00. Economic and labour problems and their impact on weakening the resistance to fascism.

Joe Dope Causes Inflation (Jim MacKay) 2:00. An animated film about inflation's effects on the economy.

Lessons in Living (Bill MacDonald) 23:00. A working-class community in Lantzville, British Columbia. The film depicts the community's effort to expand their local school.

Looking for a Job (Nicholas Balla) 4:00. The issue of transferring of soldiers to civilian jobs.

The New Pattern (Stanley Hawes) 14:00. The role played by the labour-Management Production Committees in the construction industry in Britain.

Our Northern Neighbour (Tom Daly) 21:00. Labour, socialism, and the fight against fascism.

Partners in Production (Stanley Hawes) 27:30. Absorption of women into war factories and the setting up of Labour-Management Committees.

Providing Goods for You (Philip Ragan). 4:00. An animated film on the need to curtail the consumption and the rationing of civilian goods during the war.

PX for Rubber (Graham McInnes) 8:00. Workers and production in the publicly owned Polner Corporation factory in Sarnia.

River of Canada (Ross Pitt-Taylor) 22:00. The industrial activity along the St. Lawrence River.

Salt from the Earth 9:00. Mining and processing of salt in the Nova Scotia Malagash mine.

She Speeds the Victory (Philip Ragan). 1:00. An animated film on the need to recruit women for the work force "to free men for battlefront duty."

Ships and Men (Leslie McFarlane) 18:00. Building the merchant ships, and the training of ship seamen.

Six Slices a Day 10:27. Coordinating the distribution and consumption of cereal products.

Trades and Labour Congress Meets At Toronto. 7:00. The Diamond Jubilee of the Trades and Labour Congress.

Trans-Canada Express (Stanley Hawes) 20:00. A historical survey of the building of the Canadian railway tracks and its role in connecting "25000 miles of Canadian territory." The film totally ignores the contribution made by Chinese workers.

When Asia Speaks (Gordon Weisenborn) 19:00. Ending colonialism, and the need for world cooperation.

When Do We Eat 21:00. Ensuring healthy eating for workers as a measure for improving their productivity and strength.

When the Work's All Done this Fall 3:00. An appeal to give temporary help to wartime industries by farmers after the end of the harvesting season.

1945

Atlantic Crossroads (Tom Daly) 10:00. Newfoundland's role during WWII. The films also includes reference to the fishing industry.

Back to Jobs (Nicholas Balla) 9:35. The return of Canadian veterans to the civilian work force.

Behind the Swastika: Nazi Atrocities. 5:00. Nazi crimes and abuses are revealed by liberators.

Building a House (Beth Zirkan) 8:00. Labour input is equated with efficiency of production. Building a house is given as an example.

Canadian Screen Magazine No. 6. 10:00. Includes footage on the manufacturing of aluminium prefabricated houses for Britain.

Canadian Screen Magazine No. 7. 8:00. The film includes footage on retraining veterans in the building trades to help meet the housing shortage.

Early Start (Ernest Reid) 19:00. The organization and work of Boys and Girls Farm Clubs

Fishing Partners (Jean Palardy) 20:00. Scientific research in aid of cod fishermen.

Home to the Land (Graham McInnes) 21:00. The Veteran's Land Act provides low-cost loan for veterans to buy and operate new or existing farms.

Main Street, Canada (Alistair M. Taylor) 10:45. Canadians working together using such measures as rationing, salvage drives and victory gardens to alleviate the problems of food shortage and inflation.

Price Controls and Rationing (Philip Ragan) 10:00. An animated film about the need for price controls and rationing in the immediate post-WWII period.

The Road to Civvy Street (Vincent Paquette) 19:00. Various programs and services available to help veterans re-establish themselves in civilian life.

Salute to a Victory 10:00. Includes a tribute to the role of workers in the war.

Soil for Tomorrow (Lawrence Cherry) 43:00. Farmers in relation to scientific research and the Prairie Farm Rehabilitation act of 1935.

Suffer Little Children (Sydney Newman) 10:00. Post-war hunger in Europe and the role of international cooperation.

This is our Canada (Stanley Jackson) 20:00. Example of the shift away from emphasizing the role of labour. Emphasis is on Canadian unity.

Trees that Reach the Sky (Beth Zinkan) 9:00. The labour process transforms a tree and incorporates it into the construction of a Mosquito bomber.

Vocational Training 4:00. Former Canadian servicemen adapt to working life after the war.

After Work (Stanley Hawes) 11:00. Cooperation between management, civic groups and labour to create recreational centres for workers.

Back to Work (Vincent Pacquette) 13:00. Ex-servicemen and women are equipped for civilian jobs.

Canadian Screen Magazine No. 1. 10:00. Includes footage on vocational training for veterans.

Canadian Screen Magazine No. 7. 8:00. Includes footage on retraining of veterans in the building trades.

Eyes Front No. 28. 10:00. Addresses the issue of the rehabilitation of women who worked in the armed services during the war.

Food: Secret of The Peace (Stuart Legg) 11:00. Strategies to deal with causes of food shortages in Europe, and the measures taken by the Allies to solve these problems.

Gateway to Asia (Tom Daly) 10:00. British Columbia is becoming a vital economic location. Some emphasis on workers and social problems.

Getting the Most Out of A Film No. 10: Now the Peace (Stanley Hawes) 18:00. Features discussion among members of various unions in the Vancouver area. Workers express hope that the newly established United Nations will be able to reduce the threat of war and increase the security and prosperity of workers everywhere.

Getting the Most Out of A Film No. 11: Veterans in Industry (Fred Lasse) 8:00. A discussion film on veterans. Winnipeg Trades and Labour Council members express their opinion about reintegrating veterans into the work force.

Getting the Most Out of A Film No. 12: Second Freedom (Fred Lasse) 5:00. Union members discuss the creation of Canadian Unemployment and Health Insurance plans.

Land for Pioneers (Stanley Hawes) 5:30. Discussion about the industrial development of the Canadian North.

Joint Labour-Management Production Committee [Discussion Preface] 3:00

Joint Labour-Management Production Committee [Discussion Trailer] 3:00

Labour Looks Ahead (Stanley Hawes) 10:00. The role of the labour-management production committees and other official bodies such as the wartime Labour Relations Board and the International Labour Office.

Movies for Workers [Story with two endings and Discussion Trailer] (Stanley Hawes) 17:00. Discussion on the issue of inflation.

The Peace Builders (Alan Field) 11:00. Issues of international cooperation and peace.

Reinstatement in Former Job (Jeff Hurley) 2:00. Veterans return to the work force.

The Three Blind Mice (George Dunning) 5:00. Industrial factory safety rules.

Training Industry's Army (Vincent Pacquette). 18:00. Vocational training and helping workers expand their wartime skills.

Trappers of the Sea (Margaret Perry) 12:00. The lobster fishing industries in Nova Scotia. A brief reference to the cooperative movement and how co-ops are used within communities.

Valley of the Tennessee [Discussion Trailer] (Stanley Hawes) 7:00. A group of farmers and industrial workers discuss issues of interdependence between rural and industrial workers.

Veterans in Industry (Fred Lasse) 18:00. The reintegration of veterans and wartime industrial workers into new skills.

Work and Wages (Guy Glover) 18:00. Canadian organized labour, industry and government work together to control the war stresses through wage control, high production levels and rationing.

Canada-World Trader (Tom Daly) 11:00. Post-war international cooperation.

1946

Canadian Screen Magazine No. 10. 3:00. Includes footage from an annual lumbermen's picnic.

Canadian Screen Magazine No. 11. 7:00. Includes a speech by the labour minister in an International Labour Organization meeting.

The Challenge of Housing (Tom Daly) 10:00. Slum housing conditions are cited as a pretext to develop large scale housing projects. The need for labour and industry's cooperation is stressed.

Everyman's World (Sydney Newman) 10:00. A good example of the shift in post-war NFB films from stressing the role of labour to the focus on the role of government and government officials.

Falls (Don Mulholland) 4:00. Safety at the workplace.

Farm Electrification (Evelyn Cherry) 21:00. Manitoba's rural electrification plan is discussed. Hesitancy of farmers to adapt to new methods and new technologies is emphasized.

Food: Secret of the Peace [discussion Trailer] (Stanley Hawes) 5:00. A group discussion on the social and political implications of post-war starvation.

Getting the Most Out of a Film No. 14: Work and Wages 5:00. Workers discuss inflation and peace.

Getting the Most Out of a Film No. 15: A Place to Live 6:00. Discussion on housing with contributions from the United Auto Workers.

Getting the Most Out of a Film No. 16: Ballot Boxes 15:00. Trade unionists discuss the politics of elections and the role of labour.

Handling (Don Mulholland) 5:58. Safety at the workplace.

Machines (Don Mulholland) 6:52. Safety at the workplace.

Organization (Don Mulholland) 9:35. Safety at the workplace.

Power From Shipshaw (George Lilley) 10:00. The role of workers in building a power dam at Shipshaw, Quebec.

[Racial Unity Discussion Preface and Trailer] (Stanley Hawes) 5:00. Racial harmony and combating prejudice in the workplace.

Rural Health (Ernest Reid) 18:00. Manitoba health plan.

Safe Clothing (David Bairstow) 7:42. Safety at the workplace.

The Safety Supervisor (Ronald Weyman) 10:27. Coordination between management and labour to guarantee workplace safety.

Silicosis (Vincent Pacquette) 26:00. Ways of preventing lung disease among mine workers caused by their exposure to silicate and quartz dust.

The Third Freedom 24:00. Repositioning of amputee veterans in civilian jobs.

To the Ladies (Nicholas Balla) 10:00. The role of working women during the war. Emphasis on women returning to their "natural" role at home.

Who is My Neighbour? 24:00. Emphasis on the role of welfare organizations. The film advocates the coordination between these organizations under the leadership of the Canadian welfare Council.

Workers on the Land (Ernest Reid) 17:00. Farm labour and the need to reorganize work to provide profitable employment during winter.

SELECTED LIST OF KEY FILMS DEALING WITH WORKING-CLASS POLITICS BETWEEN 1929 AND 1949

NFB Series Produced by William Weintaub

The Good Bright Days: 1919–1927 (1960) 28:55. The Winnipeg General Strike, the Red Scare and the Toronto Street Car Strike.

Sunshine and Eclipse: 1927–1934 (1960) 28:57. The Crash of '29, the deepening of the Depression and Prime Minister Bennett's response, and the rise of fascism.

The Twilight of An Era: 1934–1939 (1960) 29:03. The Depression and the rise of fascism in Europe.

Canada Between Two World Wars (1962) 21:33. An overview of the period between the two world wars which incorporates important archival film and still photos.

Bethune (1964) 58:38. Directed by D. Brittain, J. Kemeny and G. Glover. Archival newsreel footage, interviews and other material on the famous Canadian communist doctor.

The Best of Times, The Worst of Times (1973) 56:50. Directed by Brian Nolan. The Depression and the Bennett years. Also some material on the birth of the C.C.F. and the role of played by the Communist Party in Canada during the Depression.

Dreamland: A History of Early Canadian Movies 1895–1939 (1974) 85:53. Directed by Donald Brittain. A general survey of early Canadian films including the Canadian Pacific Railway material.

The Working Class on Film (1975, Susan Schouten) 14:08. John Grierson and his philosophy on using film as a tool for social criticism and change.

Portrait of the Artist As An Old Lady (1982) 27:00. Directed by Gail Singer. Paraskeva Clark, artist, communist, feminist, talks about her art and involvement with working-class cultural activities in the 1930s and 1940s.

Grierson and Gouzenko (1986). Directed by Martin Kinch, written by Rick Salutin, and produced and televised by the CBC, this was among the first films to document aspects of state repression, activism and cultural politics before, during and after the beginning of the Cold War in Canada.

Imperfect Union: Canadian Labour and the Left – Part 1 – International Background – Canadian Roots (1989) 54:30. Directed by Arthur Hammond. The early development of the Canadian labour-socialist alliance mostly in connection with the Industrial Revolution in Great Britain.

Imperfect Union: Canadian Labour and the Left – Part 2 – Born of hard Times (1989) 51:32. Directed by Arthur Hammond. The rise of communist influence within the labour and unemployed workers' movements in the mid-1930s, and the rivalry between the Communists and the C.C.F.

Imperfect Union: Canadian Labour and the Left – Part 3 – Falling Apart and Getting Together (1989) 53:19. Directed by Arthur Hammond. The period immediately following World War II and the rise of influence of the trade union movement during the war.

A Vision in the Darkness (1991). A major document on the labour and political activities in the early part of the twentieth century. Directed by Sophie Bissonnette, the film presents a detailed treatment of the life of labour activist, anti-fascist, communist, and feminist leader Lea Roback.

On to Ottawa (1992). The film is directed by Sara Diamond. It features several stories and cultural activities associated with the major events of the Great Depression, including the communist-led On-to-Ottawa Trek of the mid-1930s.

Defying the Law (1997). Directed by Marta Nielson-Hastings. The film depicts aspects of labour unrest towards the end of World War II. It specifically gives an account of the 1946 strike at the Steel Company of Canada plant in Hamilton.

Rosies of the North (1999). Directed by Kelly Saxberg. The film tells the story of the Canadian Car and Foundry in Fort Williams (now part of Thunder Bay), during World War II the site of Canada's largest aircraft plant. 3000 out of the factory's 7000 work force were women.

Prairie Fire: The Winnipeg General Strike of 1919 (1999). Directed by Audrey Mehler, the film identifies the main stages of the strike. The film includes major collections of photographic images and interviews with historians and eyewitness.

The Idealist: James Beveridge Film Guru (2006). The film is directed by Nina Beveridge, the daughter of one of the leading directors/producers of the NFB during the war period. The director presents a personal look at James Beveridge's professional and political life and its effect on his relationships at home.

BIBLIOGRAPHY

Abella, Irving M. *Nationalism, Communism, and Canadian Congress of Labour, 1935–1956*. Toronto: University of Toronto Press, 1973.

———. *On Strike: Six Key Labour Struggles in Canada 1919–1949*. Toronto: James Lorimer, 1975.

Acland, Charles. "National Dreams, International Encounters: The Formation of Canadian Film Culture in the 1930s," *Canadian Journal of Film Studies* 1 (1994): 3–26.

———. "Mapping the Serious and the Dangerous: Film and the National Council of Education 1920–1939." *Cinema* 6 (1995): 101–18.

Aitken, Ian. *Film and Reform: John Grierson and the Documentary Film Movement*. New York: Routledge, 1990.

———, ed. *The Documentary Film Movement, An Anthology*. Edinburgh: Edinburgh University Press, 1998.

Alexander, William. *Film on the Left: American Documentary Film from 1931 to 1942*. Princeton, 1981.

Allan, Blaine. "Making *Heritage*, a Canadian government Motion Picture." *Prairie Forum* (Spring 2004): 85–102.

Arroyo, Jose. "John Grierson: Years of Decision." *Cinema Canada* 169 (1989): 15–19.

———. "Bordwell Considered: Cognitivism, Colonialism and Canadian Cinematic Culture." *CineAction* 28 (1992): 74–88.

Avakumovic, Ivan. *The Communist Party in Canada: A History*. Toronto: McClelland and Stewart, 1975.

Backhouse, Charles. *The Canadian Government Motion Picture Bureau: 1917–1941*. Ottawa: Canadian Film Institute, 1974

Bailey, Cameron. "What The Story Is: An Interview with Srinivas Krishna." *CineAction* 28 (1992): 38–47.

Banning, Kass. "Rhetorical Remarks Towards the Politics of Otherness." *CineAction* 16 (1989): 14–19.

Barnouw, Erik. *Documentary: A History of the Non-Fiction Film.* New York: Oxford University Press, 1993 [1974].

Barrowclough, Susan, ed. *Jean-Pierre Lefebvre: The Quebec Connection.* London: British Film Institute, 1982.

Baruth-Walsh, Mary E. and G. M. Walsh. *Strike! 99 Days on the Line.* Ottawa: Penumbra Press, 1995.

Beattie, Eleanor. *The Handbook of Canadian Film.* Toronto: Peter Martin Associates Limited, 1977.

Beeching, William C. *Canadian Volunteers: Spain, 1936–1939.* Regina: Canadian Plains Research Center/University Regina, 1989.

Benjamin, Walter. "The Work of Art in the Age of Mechanical Reproduction." In *Film Theory and Criticism.* Edited by Gerald Mast, M. Cohen, and L. Braudy. New York: Oxford University Press, 1992: 682–89.

Bercuson, David. "Through the Looking-Glass of Culture: An Essay on the New Labour History and Working Culture in Recent Historical Writing." *Labour/Le Travail* 7 (Spring 1981): 95–112.

Berton, Pierre. *Hollywood's Canada. The Americanization of Our National Image.* Toronto: McClelland and Stewart, 1975.

Beveridge, James. *John Grierson: Film Master.* New York: Macmillan, 1978.

Bissonnette, Lise. "Denys Arcand and 'Le confort et l'indifference.'" *Cine-Tracts* 4 (1982): 74–76.

Bissonnette, Sophie. "Women and Political Documentary in Quebec: An interview with Sophie Bissonnette. Interview by Barbara Evans and Scott Forsyth." *CineAction* 28 (1992): 66–70.

Blumer, Ronald. "John Grierson: I Derive My Authority from Moses." *Take One* 2:9 (1970): 17.

Browder, Laura. *Rousing the Nation: Radical Culture in Depression America.* Amherst: University of Massachusetts Press, 1998.

Brown, Lorne. *Breaking Down Myths of Peace and Harmony in Canadian Labour History.* Winnipeg, 1975.

Brown, Michael, Randy Martin, Frank Rosengarten, and George Snedeker eds. *New Studies in the Politics of U.S. Communism.* New York: Monthly Review Press, 1993.

Buchsbaum, Jonathan. S. "Left Political filmmaking in France in the 1930s." Ph.D. dissertation, NYU. Ann Arbor: University Microfilms International, 1983.

Buck, Tim. *A National Front for Victory,* 1941.

———. *A Labour Policy for Victory.* Toronto, 1943.

————. *Canada's Choice: Unity or Chaos*. Toronto, 1944.

Buhay, Beckie. "The Struggle for Women's Rights." *National Affairs Monthly* 5:2 (1948): 104–105.

Burnett, Ron. "The Crisis of the Documentary and Fictional film in Quebec." *Cine-Tracts* 4 (1982): 29–35.

Campbell, Russell. *The Cinema Strikes Back: Radical Filmmaking in the United States 1930–1942*. Ann Arbor: UMI Research Press, 1978.

Canada. House of Commons. *Debates*. 1940–1946.

Canada Year Book 1952–53. Ottawa, 1953.

Canadian Chamber of Commerce. *The Communist Threat to Canada*. Montreal, 1947.

Carlsen, John and Jean-Michael Lacroix. *Canadian Society and Culture in Times of Economic Depression – culture et societe au Canada en periodes de crise economique*. Ottawa: Association for Canadian Studies/Association des etudes canadiennes, 1987.

Cavalcanti, Alberto. *Le Mouvement neo-realiste en Angletterre. Le Role intellectuel du cinema* ('The Neo-Realist Movement in England' in The Intellectual Role of Cinema). Paris: Institut international de cooperation intellectuelle, 1937: 235–41.

Cine-Tracts. Editorial 1 (1977): 3.

Clandfiel, David. *Canadian Film*. Toronto: Oxford University Press, 1987.

Clarion, The. 29 June 1937.

————. 5 February 1938.

————. 16 September 1939.

Communist Party of Canada. *Canada's Party of Socialism: History of the Communist Party of Canada*. Toronto: Progress Books, 1982.

Cox, Kirwan. "The Grierson Files." *Cinema Canada* 56 (1979): 16–24.

Crowdus, Gary, ed. *The Political Companion to American Film*. Chicago: Lake View Press, 1994.

Curran, James and Vincent Porter, eds. *British Cinema History*. London: Weidenfield and Nicolson, 1983.

Davies, Gwendolyn. *Myth and Milieu: Atlantic Literature and Culture 1918–1939*. Fredericton: Acadiensis Press, 1993.

Denning, Michael. *The Cultural Front: The Laboring of American Culture in the Twentieth Century*. New York: Verso, 1996.

Department of Labour. *Labour Organization in Canada*. Ottawa, 1937.

Dimitrov, Georgi. *The United Front against War and Fascism*. New York, 1936.

————. *The United Front*. New York: International Publishers, 1938.

Dion, Robert. *Crimes of the Secret Police*. Montreal: Black Rose Books, 1982.

Doherty, Thomas. *Projections of War: Hollywood, American Culture, and World War II*. New York: Columbia University Press, 1993.

Dorland, Michael. "Thesis On Canadian Nationalism: In Memoriam George P. Grant." *CineAction* 16 (1989): 3–5.

———. *So Close to the State/s: the emergence of Canadian film policy*. Toronto: University of Toronto Press, 1998.

Eagleton, Terry. *Literary Theory: An Introduction*. Minneapolis: University of Minnesota Press, 1983.

Eamon, Greg. "Farmers, Phantoms and Princes. The Canadian Pacific Railway and Filmmaking from 1899–1919." *Cinemas* 6 (1995): 11–31.

———. *Image and Identity, Reflections on Canadian Film and Culture*. Toronto: Wilfrid Laurier University Press, 1989.

Ellis, Jack C. *The Documentary Idea, a critical history of English-language documentary film and video*. New Jersey: Prentice-Hall, 1989.

———. *John Grierson, Life, Contributions, Influence*. Carbondale and Edwardsville: Southern Illinois University Press, 2000.

Endres, Robin. Introduction. *Eight Men Speak and Other Plays*. Edited by Richard Wright and Robin Endres. Toronto: New Hogtown Press, 1976: xi–xxxvi.

Euvrard, Michel, and Pierre Véronneau. "Direct Cinema." In *Self Portrait, Essays on the Canadian and Quebec Cinemas*. Edited by Pierre Veronneau. Ottawa: Canadian Film Institute, 1980: 78–93.

Evans, Barbara, and Scott Forsyth. "Women and Political Documentary in Quebec, an interview with Sophie Bissonnette." *CineAction* 28 (1992): 66–70.

Evans, Gary. "The Politics of Propaganda." *Cinema Canada* 56 (1979): 12–15.

———. *John Grierson and the National Film Board: The Politics of Wartime Propaganda*. Toronto: University of Toronto Press, 1984.

———. *In the National Interest: A Chronicle of the National Film Board of Canada from 1994 to 1989*. Toronto: University of Toronto Press, 1991.

———. *John Grierson: Trailblazer of Documentary Films*. Montreal: XYZ Publishers, 2005.

Feldman, Seth, ed. *Take Two*. Toronto: Irwin Publishing, 1984.

Feldman, Seth, and Joyce Nelson, eds. *Canadian Film Reader*. Toronto: Peter Martin Associates Limited, 1977.

———. "The Silent Subject in English Canadian Film." In *Words & Moving Images. Essays on Verbal and Visual Expression in Film and Television*. Edited by William C. Wees and Michael Dorland. Montreal: Mediatexte Publications, 1984.

Femia, Joseph V. "Hegemony and Consciousness in the Thought of Antonio Gramsci." *Political Studies* 23 (1975).

————. *Gramsci's Political Thought: Hegemony, Consciousness, and the Revolutionary Process.* Oxford: Clarendon Press, 1981.

Fetherling, Douglas, ed. *Documents in Canadian Film.* Peterborough: Broadview Press, 1988.

Filewod, Alan. *Collective Encounters: Documentary Theatre in English Canada.* Toronto: University of Toronto Press, 1987.

Financial Post. "Film Board Monopoly Facing Major Test." 19 November 1949: 17.

Forsyth, Hardy. *John Grierson: A Documentary Biography.* London, 1979.

Forsyth, Scott. "Grierson and Canadian Nationalism." *CineAction* 16 (1989): 77–79.

————. "The Failures of Nationalism and Documentary: Grierson and Gouzenko." *Canadian Journal of Film Studies* 1 (1990): 74–82.

————. "Communists, Class, and Culture." In *Working on Screen: Representations of the Working Class in Canadian Cinema.* Edited by Malek Khouri and Darrell Varga. Toronto: University of Toronto Press, 2006: 46–72.

Frank, David. "Short Takes: The Canadian Worker on Film." *Labour/le Travail* 46 (Fall 2000): 417–37.

Frye, Northrop. *Anatomy of Criticism: Four Essays.* Princeton, NJ: Princeton University Press, 1957.

Gasher, Mike. "Decolonizing the Imagination: Cultural Expression as Vehicle of Self-Discovery." *Canadian Journal of Film Studies* 2–3 (1993): 95–105.

Genovese, Michael, A. *The Political Film: An Introduction.* Neeham Heights, MA: Simon & Shuster, 1998.

Gramsci, Antonio. *Selections from the Prison Notebooks.* Edited by Q. Hoare and G. Nowell Smith. New York: International Publishers, 1971.

————. *Selection from the Cultural Writings.* Edited by D. Forgacs and G. Nowell Smith. Cambridge: Cambridge University Press, 1984.

Gray, C. W. *Movies for the People: The Story of the National Film Board of Canada's Unique Distribution System.* Montreal: National Film Board, 1973.

Grierson, John. "Flaherty-Naturalism-and the Problem of English Cinema." *Artwork* 7 (Autumn 1931): 210–15.

————. "Documentary (1)," *Cinema Quarterly* 1 (Winter 1932): 67–72.

————. *Grierson on Documentary.* University of California Press, 1966.

————. *Grierson on Documentary.* Edited by Forsyth Hardy. London: Faber, 1979.

————. *Grierson on the Movies.* London: Faber, 1981.

Hackett, Yvette. "The National Film Society of Canada, 1935–1951: Its Origins and Development." *Flashback: People and Institutions in Canadian Film History.* Montreal: Mediatext Publications, 1986: 135–165.

Hall, Stuart. "In praise of the Particular." *Marxism Today* 31 (1987): vii.

Handling, Piers. "Censorship and Scares." *Cinema Canada* 56 (1979): 25–30.

———. "The National Film Board of Canada: 1939–1959." *Self Portrait: Essays on the Canadian and Quebec cinemas*. Ottawa: Canadian Film Institute, 1980: 42–53

Harcourt, Peter. *Towards a National Cinema, Movies & Mythologies*. Toronto: Canadian Broadcasting Corporation, 1977.

———. "The Canadian Nation – An Unfinished Text." *Canadian Journal of Film Studies* 2–3 (1993): 5–26.

———. "Imaginary Images: An Examination of Atom Egoyan's Films." *Film Quarterly* 3 (1995): 2–14.

Hardy, Forsyth, ed. *Grierson On Documentary*. London: Faber & Faber, 1946.

———. *John Grierson: A Documentary Biography*. London: Faber and Faber, 1979.

Hawes, Stanley. An interview within the Stanley Hawes Papers, ScreenSound, Canberra, Australia, Box 52 (14–15 February 1980).

Hebdige, Dick. "From Culture to Hegemony." In *The Cultural Studies Reader*. Edited by Simon During. New York: Routledge, 1994: 357–67.

Herf, Jeffrey. *Reactionary Modernism: Technology, Culture and Politics in Weimar and the Third Reich*. Cambridge: Cambridge University Press, 1984.

Heron, Craig. *The Canadian Labour Movement: a brief history*. Toronto: J. Lorimer, 1996.

Hofsess, John. *Inner View: Ten Canadian Film-Makers*. Toronto: McGraw-Hill Ryerson Limited, 1975.

Hogenkamp. Bert. *Deadly Parallels: Film and the Left in Britain, 1929–1939*. London, 1986.

Horn, Michiel. *The League for Social Construction: Intellectual Origins of the Democratic Left in Canada, 1930–1942*. Toronto: University of Toronto Press, 1980.

———. *The Great Depression of the 1930s in Canada*. New Brunswick: Canadian Historical Association, 1984.

Houle, Michel. "Some Ideological and Thematic Aspects of the Quebec Cinema." In *Self Portrait: Essays on the Canadian and Quebec Cinemas*. Edited by Pierre Veronneau and Piers Handling. Ottawa: Canadian Film Institute, 1980: 159–181.

Howard, Victor. *We were the salt of the Earth! : a narrative of the On-to-Ottawa trek and the Regina Riot*. Regina: University of Regina/Canadian Plains Research Center, 1985.

Izod, John, Richard Kilborn, and Matthew Hibberd, eds. *From Grierson to the Docu-Soap: Breaking the Boundaries*. Luton: University of Luton Press, 2000.

James, Rodney. *Film as a National Art: NFB of Canada and the Film Board Idea*. New York: Arno Press, 1977.

Jameson, Fredric. "Class and Allegory in Contemporary Mass Culture: Dog Day Afternoon as a Political Film." In *Movies and Methods* (volume II). Edited by Bill Nichols. Los Angeles: University of California Press, 1985: 715–33.

John Grierson Project, The. *John Grierson and the NFB*. Toronto: ECW Press, 1984.

Jones, D. B. *Movies and Memoranda: An Interpretive History of the National Film Board of Canada*. Ottawa: Canadian Film Institute, 1981.

———. *The Best Butler in the Business: Tom Daly of the National Film Board of Canada*. Toronto: University of Toronto Press, 1996.

Jones, Stephen G. *The British Labour Movement and Film, 1918–1939*. New York: Routledge & Kegan Paul, 1987.

Kealey, Linda. *Enlisting women for the cause: women, labour, and the left in Canada, 1890–1920*. Toronto: University of Toronto Press, 1998.

Kealey, S. Gregory. *Workers and Canadian History*. Buffalo: McGill University Press, 1995.

Kelly, Merrill, John J. Pitney, Jr., Craig R. Smith, and Herbert E. Gooch III. *Reelpolitik. Political Ideologies in '30s and '40s Films*. Westport: Paeger, 1998.

Kern, Robert W., ed. *Historical Dictionary of Modern Spain, 1700–1988*. New York: Greenwood, 1990.

Khouri, Malek. "John and the Missus: Progress, Resistance, and 'Common Sense.'" *CineAction* 49 (1999): 2–11.

Khouri, Malek and Darrell Varga, eds. *Working on Screen: Representations of the Working Class in Canadian Cinema*, Toronto: University of Toronto Press, 2006.

Klingender, F.D. and Stuart Legg. *Money Behind the Screen*. London: Lawrence & Wishart, 1937.

Knelman, Martin. *This is Where We Came In: The Career and Character of Canadian Film*. Toronto: McClelland and Stewart, 1977.

Leach, Jim. "The Body Snatchers: Genre and Canadian Cinema." *Cinema Canada* (May 1987): 18–21.

Lee, John Alan and Edward Mann. *RCMP Versus the People: inside Canada's security service*. Don Mills, Ontario: General, 1979.

Lindsay, Shelley Stamp. "Toronto's 'Girl Workers.' The Female Body and Industrial Efficiency in Her Own Fault." *Cinemas* 6 (1995): 81–99.

Liversedge, Ronald. *Recollections of the On-to-Ottawa Trek*. Cowichan Lake, 1963.

Loiselle, Andre. "Novel, Play, Film: The Three Endings of Gordon Pinsent's John and the Missus." *Canadian Journal of Film Studies* 1 (1994): 67–82.

Magder, Ted. *Canada's Hollywood: The Canadian State and Feature Films*. Toronto: University of Toronto Press, 1993.

Mandel, Ernest. *The Meaning of the Second World War*. London: Verso, 1986.

Matthews, Ralph. *There's No Better Place Than Here*. Toronto: Peter Martin Associates, 1976.

May, Lary. *Screening out the Past: The Birth of Mass Culture and the Motion Picture Industry*. New York, 1980.

McCullough, John. "*Rude*; or the Elision of Class in Canadian Movies." *CineAction* 49 (1999): 19–25.

McInnes, Graham and Gene Walz. *One Man's Documentary: A Memoir of the Early Years of the National Film Board.* Toronto: University of Toronto Press, 2005.

McKay, Ian. "Helen Creighton and the Politics of Antimodernism." In *Myth and Milieu: Atlantic Literature and Culture 1918–1939.* Edited by Gwendolyn Davies. Fredericton: Acadiensis Press, 1993: 1–16.

———. ed. *For a Working-Class Culture in Canada: a selection of Colin McKay's writings on sociology and political economy, 1897–1939.* St. John's: Canadian Committee on Labour History, 1996

———. "For a New Kind of History: A Reconnaissance of 100 Years of Canadian Socialism." *Labour/LeTravail* 46 (Fall 2000): 69–125

McKay, Marjorie. *History of the National Film Board.* Unpublished and undated manuscript, NFB Archives, Montreal.

McMillan, Robert. "Ethnology and the N.F.B.: The Laura Boulton Mysteris." *Canadian Journal of Film Studies* 1:2 (1991): 67–82.

Morris, Lesley. T. *The Big Ford Strike.* Toronto, 1947.

Morris, Peter. *The National Film Board of Canada: The War Years.* Ottawa: Canadian Film Institute, 1971.

———. *Embattled Shadows, A History of Canadian Cinema 1895–1939.* Kingston: McGill-Queen's University Press, 1978.

———. "Objects of History." *Cinema Canada* 56 (1979): 10–11.

———. "Re-Thinking Grierson: The Ideology of John Grierson." Speech delivered to the FSAC/AQEC Conference, Montreal, 1986.

———. "Defining a (Canadian) Art Cinema in the Sixties." *CineAction* 16 (1989): 7–13.

———. "Praxis into Process: John Grierson and the National Film Board of Canada." *Historical Journal of Film, Radio and Television* 9:3 (1989): 269–82.

———. "In Our Own Eyes: the Canonizing of Canadian Film." *Canadian Journal of Film Studies* 1 (1994): 27–44.

Mouffe, Chantal. "Hegemony and ideology in Gramsci." In *Gramsci and Marxist Theory.* Edited by Chantal Mouffe. Boston: Routledge and Kegan Paul, 1979: 168–204.

Muenzenberg, Willi. "Capture the Film!" *Daily Worker* (New York). 23 July 1925: 3.

Nash, M. Teresa. "Images of Women in National Film Board of Canada Films During World War II and the Post-War Years (1939–1949)." Ph.D. Dissertation, McGill University, 1982.

National Film Board of Canada. *Seeing Ourselves: Films for Canadian Studies.* 1979.

Nelson, Joyce. *The Colonized Eye: Rethinking the Grierson Legend.* Toronto: Between the Lines, 1988.

Neve, Brian. *Film and Politics in America: A Social Tradition.* New York: Routledge, 1992.

One Big Union Bulletin. 10 March 1927.

Ory, Pascal. *La belle illusion: culture et politique sous le signe du front populaire 1935–1938.* Paris: Plon, 1994.

Pallister, Janis L. *The Cinema of Quebec: Masters in Their Own House.* Mississauga, Ontario: Associated University Presses, 1995.

Parker, Douglas Scott. "Women in Communist Culture in Canada: 1932 to 1937." Masters Thesis, McGill University, 1994.

Parsons, Brenda M. "A Dramatic Interpretation of Reality for Democratic Purposes: John Grierson's Drifters." Ph.D. Dissertation, McGill University, 1983.

Pendakur, Manjunath. *Canadian Dreams and American Control: The Political Economy of the Canadian Film Industry.* Detroit: Wayne State University Press, 1990.

———. On the Brink. *CineAction* 28 (1992): 34–36.

———. "Ghost Busting: 100 Years of Canadian Cinema." *Take One* 12 (1996): 6–13.

Pierson, Ruth Roach. *Canadian Women and the Second World War.* Ottawa: Canadian Historical Association, 1983.

Piva, Michael J. *The Condition of the Working Class in Toronto, 1900–1921.* Ottawa: University of Ottawa Press, 1979.

Pollard, Juliet. "Propaganda for Democracy: John Grierson and Adult Education During the Second World War." In *Knowledge for the People: the Struggle for Adult Learning English-speaking Canada, 1828–1973.* Edited by Michael R. Welton. 132–45. Toronto: Ontario Institute for Studies in Education, 1987.

Purdy, Sean. *Radicals and Revolutionaries.* Toronto: University of Toronto Press, 1998.

Radforth, Ian. "Political Prisoners: The Communist Internees." In Franca Iacovetta, Roberto Perin and Angelo Principe eds., *Enemies Within: Italian and Other Internees in Canada and Abroad*, Toronto: University of Toronto Press, 2000.

Ramsay, Christine. "Canadian Narrative Cinema from the Margins; 'The Nation' and Masculinity in *Goin' Down The Road.*" *Canadian Journal of Film Studies* 2–3 (1993): 27–49.

Reilly, Sharon. *Robert Kell and the Art of the Winnipeg General Strike. Labour/Le Travail* 20 (1987): 185–92.

Repka, William and Kathleen. *Dangerous Patriots: Canada's Unknown Prisoners of War.* Vancouver: New Star Books, 1982.

Report of the Proceedings of the Ninth Annual Convention of British Columbia Federation of Labour. 10–13 March 1919.

Ross, Steven J. "Beyond the Screen: History, Class, and the Movies." In *The Hidden Foundation; Cinema and the Question of Class.* Edited by David E. James and Rick Berg. Minneapolis: University of Minnesota Press, 1996: 26–55.

———. *Working-Class Hollywood: silent film and the shaping of class in America.* Princeton: Princeton University Press, 1998.

Rotha, Paul. *Documentary Film.* Third edition. London: Faber, 1966.

Rush, Maurice. *We Have a Glowing Dream.* Vancouver: Centre for Socialist Education, 1996.

Ryan, Toby Gordon. *Stage Left: Canadian Workers Theatre, 1929–1940.* Toronto: Simon and Pierre, 1985.

Ryerson, Stanley. "By Way of a Birth Certificate." *National Affairs* I (April 1944).

Safarian, A.E. *The Canadian Economy in the Great Depression.* Toronto: McClelland and Stewart, 1970.

Salsberg, J.B. *The War Situation and Canadian Labour.* Toronto, 1940.

Salutin, Rick. "The NFB Red Scare." *Weekend Magazine,* 23 September 1978: 29.

———. "It Happened Here. Earlier and Worse." *Marginal Notes.* Toronto: Lester & Orpen Dennys, 1984.

Sangster, Joan. *Dreams of Equality: women on the Canadian left, 1920–1950.* Toronto: McClelland and Stewart, 1989.

Scher, Len. *The Un-Canadians. True Stories of the Blacklist Era.* Toronto: Lester Publishing Limited, 1992.

Sheils, J. Evans, and B. Swankey. *Work and Wages.* Vancouver, 1977.

Smith, Albert Edward. *All My Life.* Toronto: Progress Books, 1977.

Stead, Peter. *Film and The Working Class.* New York: Routledge, 1991.

Steedman, Mercedes. "The Promise: Communist Organizing in the Needle Trades, The Dressmakers Campaign, 1928 to 1937." *Labour/Le Travail* 34 (1994): 37–73.

———. *Angels of the workplace: women and the construction of gender relations in the Canadian clothing industry, 1890–1940.* Toronto: Oxford University Press, 1997.

Steven, Peter, ed. *Jump Cut. Hollywood, Politics and Counter-cinema.* Toronto: Between the Lines, 1985.

Stukator, Angela. "Critical Categories and the Logic of Identity." *Canadian Journal of Film Studies* 2–3 (1993): 117–28.

Sussex, Elizabeth. *The Rise and Fall of British Documentary: The Story of the Film Movement Founded by John Grierson.* Berkeley: University of California Press, 1975.

Sykes, A.R. "Believe Suspicion Will Kill Film Board's Bid for Independence." *Ottawa Journal,* 25 November 1949.

"TimeLines." *Take One* 5:12 (1996): 16–54.

Tippett, Maria. "The Writing of English-Canadian Cultural History, 1970–1985." *Canadian Historical Review* LXVII (1986): 548–61.

———. *The Making of English-Canadian Culture, 1900–1939: The External Influences*. Toronto: York University, 1987.

———. *Making Culture; English-Canadian Institutions and the Arts before the Massey Commission*. Toronto: University Press, 1990.

Urquhart, Peter. "The Glace Bay Miners' Museum/*Margaret's Museum*: Adaptation and Resistance." *CineAction* 49 (1999): 12–18.

Véronneau, Pierre, ed. *Self-portrait: essays on the Canadian and Quebec Cinema*. Ottawa: Canadian Film Institute, 1980.

———. *L'Histoire du cinema au Quebec; III. Resistance et affirmation: la production francophone a l'ONF – 1939–1946*. Montreal: Cinematheque Québécoise, 1987.

———. *L'Histoire du cinema au Quebec*. 3 vols. Montreal: Cinematheque Québécoise, 1969–88.

Vulpe, Nicola, and Maha Albari, eds. *Sealed in Struggle. Canadian Poetry & the Spanish Civil War*. Madrid: Centre for Canadian Studies, 1995.

Walz, Gene, ed. *Flashback. People and Institutions in Canadian Film History*. Montreal: Mediatexte Publications Inc., 1986.

Waugh, Tom. "Action Stations! Joris Ivens and The National Film Board." In *Flashback. People and Institutions in Canadian Film History*. Montreal: Mediatexte Publication Inc., 1986.

Watt, F.W. "Literature of Social Protest." In *Literary History of Canada: Canadian Literature in English*. Edited by Carl Klinck. Toronto: University Press, 1976: 473–89.

Wees, William C., and Michael Dorland, eds. Words & Moving Images. *Essays on Verbal and Visual Expression in film and Television*. Montreal: Mediatexte Publications Inc., 1984.

Weisbord, Merrily. *The Strangest Dream*. Montreal: Vehicule Press, 1994.

Whitaker, Reginald and Gary Marcuse. *Cold War Canada: the making of a national insecurity state 1945–1957*. Toronto: University of Toronto Press, 1994.

———. "Origins of the Canadian Government's Internal Security System, 1946–52." *Canadian Historical Review* 65 (1984).

Whynot, Chris. "The NFB and Labour, 1945–1953." *Journal of Canadian Studies* 1 (1981).

Wilden, Anthony. "Culture and Identity: The Canadian Question, Why." *Cine-Tracts* 2 (1979): 1–22.

Wilden, Tony. *The Imaginary Canadian: An Examination for Discovery*. Vancouver: Pulp Press, 1980.

Willemen, Paul. "The National." In *Fields of Vision*. Edited by L. Devereaux and R. Hillman. Los Angeles: University of California Press, 1995: 21–34.

Williams, Raymond. *The Country and the City*. London: Ghatto and Windus, 1973.

———. *Marxism and Literature*. London: Oxford University Press, 1977.

———. *Problems in Materialism and Culture: Selected Essays*. London: New Left Books, 1980.

———. *Culture*. London: Fontana, 1981.

———. *The Sociology of Culture*. New York: Schocken Books, 1982.

———. "Base and Superstructure in Marxist Cultural Theory." *New Left Review* 82 (1983): 6–33.

Winston, Brian. *Claiming the Real, The Griersonian Documentary and its Legitimations*. London: British Film Institute, 1995.

Wood, Robin. "Towards A Canadian (Inter)National Cinema." *CineAction* 16 (1989): 59–63.

The Worker. 1 April 1922.

———. 30 May 1923.

———. 31 May 1930.

———. 28 June 1930.

Workers' Unity League. *Constitution of the Workers' Unity League*. Montreal, 1931.

———. *Workers' Unity League: Policy – Tactics – Structure – Demands*. Toronto, 1932.

———. "Final Statement of the WUL Executive Board to those Trade Unionists Who constituted Its Membership, and Who have Now Merged within the Unions of the AFL, 18 June 1936." CPC Archives.

Yamaguchi, Joanne. "Who is the American Cousin?" *CineAction* 16 (1989): 70–72.

Zaritsky, Donna. *Gramsci's Theory of Hegemony*. Ph.D. dissertation, McGill University, 1982.

NOTES

INTRODUCTION

1   S. Gregory Kealey, *Workers and Canadian History* (Buffalo: McGill University Press, 1995), 104.

2   Ian McKay, "For a New Kind of History: A Reconnaissance of 100 Years of Canadian Socialism," *Labour/Le Travail* 46 (2000): 107.

3   Ibid., 96.

4   Ibid., 97.

5   Ibid., 100. McKay here is referring to a document titled *Make This Your Canada*, authored in 1943 by David Lewis and Frank Scott (both leaders in the CCF at the time).

6   Ibid., 103.

7   Ibid., 102.

8   Janis L. Pallister, *The Cinema of Quebec: Masters in Their Own House* (Mississauga: Associated University Presses), 25–26.

9   Editorial, *Cine-Tracts* 1 (1977): 3.

10   Steven J. Ross, "Beyond the Screen: History, Class, and the Movies," in *The Hidden Foundation; Cinema and the Question of Class*, ed. David E. James and Rick Berg (Minneapolis: University of Minnesota Press, 1996), 28.

11   Raymond Williams, *Marxism and Literature* (London: Oxford U.P., 1977), 140.

12   For a detailed assessment and consideration of Foucault's approach, particularly his concept of "governmentality," refer to Michael Dorland's *So Close to the State/s: the emergence of Canadian film policy* (Toronto: University of Toronto Press, 1998).

13   Antonio Gramsci, *Selections from the Prison Notebooks* (New York: International Publishers, 1971), 377.

14   Chantal Mouffe, "Hegemony and Ideology in Gramsci," in *Gramsci and Marxist Theory*, ed. Chantal Mouffe (Boston: Routledge and Kegan Paul, 1979): 168–204.

15   Gramsci, *Selections from the Prison Notebooks*, 366–67

16   Ibid., 367

17   Ibid., 377.

18   Terry Eagleton, *Literary Theory: An Introduction* (Minneapolis: University of Minnesota Press, 1983), 15.

19   Two major programs of films were made by the NFB between 1939 and 1946. The first was titled "Canada Carries On" and included sixty-two films that were primarily concerned with Canada's role in the war. The second series, entitled "World in Action," included thirty films that concentrated on international topics. Many of the other films produced by the Board contained footage recycled from these two series. This was part of a "compilation film" practice that dominated the NFB during this period, and corresponded with a model that Grierson favoured; it involved compilation footage used in conjunction with newly shot material allowing the production of larger number of films to be made more quickly and inexpensively. A huge number of films were made this way and were eventually used under numerous titles.

20   Michael Denning, *The Cultural Front: The Laboring of American Culture in the Twentieth Century* (New York: Verso, 1996), xx.

21   Scott Forsyth in *Working on Screen: Representations of the Working Class in Canadian Cinema*, ed. Malek Khouri and Darrell Varga (Toronto: University of Toronto Press, 2006).

22   Reginald Whitaker and Gary Marcuse, *Cold War Canada: the making of a national insecurity state 1945–1957* (Toronto: University of Toronto Press, 1994), 229.

CHAPTER 1

1   *Working on Screen: Representation of the Working Class in Canadian Cinema*, ed. Malek Khouri and Darrell Varga (Toronto: University of Toronto Press, 2006) is the first book to comprehensively deal with the issue of class in Canadian cinema.

2   Important work in this regard has been published over the years in the journals *Labour/Le Travaille, Journal of Canadian Studies, Prairie Forum*, and *Atlantis*, among others.

3   Robert Fothergill, "Coward, Bully or Clown," in *Canadian Film Reader*, ed. Seth Feldman and Joyce Nelson (Toronto: Peter Martin Associates, 1977), 235.

4   The book began as a series of CBC radio broadcasts, and mainly attempted to demonstrate the link between nationalist-inflected criticism and dominant media outlets.

5   Peter Harcourt, *Towards a National Cinema: Movies & Mythologies* (Toronto: Canadian Broadcasting Corporation, 1977), 5.

6   Ibid., 166.

7   Ibid., 161.

8   Peter Harcourt, "Politics or Paranoia," in *Documents in Canadian Film*, ed. Douglas Fetherling (Peterborough: Broadview Press, 1988), 298.

9   Mike Gasher, "Decolonizing the Imagination: Cultural Expression as Vehicle of Self-Discovery," *Canadian Journal of Film Studies* 2–3 (1993), 96.

10   Ibid., 104

11   Jim Leach, "Second Images: Reflections on Canadian Cinema(s) in the Seventies," in *Take Two*, ed. Seth Feldman (Toronto: Irwin Publishing, 1984), 19.

12   Joanne Yamaguchi, "Who is the American Cousin?" *CineAction* 16 (1989), 72.

13   Ibid.

14   Robin Wood, "Towards A Canadian (Inter)National Cinema," *CineAction* 16 (1989), 60.

15   John Hofsess, *Inner View: Ten Canadian Film-Makers* (Toronto: McGraw-Hill Ryerson, 1975), 68.

16   Ibid.

17   Michel Euvrard and Pierre Veronneau, "Direct Cinema," in *Self Portrait, Essays on the Canadian and Quebec Cinemas*, ed. Pierre Veronneau (Ottawa: Canadian Film Institute, 1980), 92–93.

18   Seth Feldman, "The Silent Subject in English-Canadian Film," in *Words & Moving Images. Essays on Verbal and Visual Expression in Film and Television*, ed. William C. Wees and Michael Dorland (Montreal: Mediatexte Publications Inc., 1984), 211.

19   Susan Barrowclough, ed., *Jean-Pierre Lefebvre: The Quebec Connection* (London: British Film Institute, 1982), 13.

20   Ibid., 23.

21   Euvrard and Véronneau, 87–88.

22   Ibid., 90.

23   Ibid., 90.

24   Piers Handling, "The National Film Board of Canada: 1939–1959," in *Self Portrait: Essays on the Canadian and Quebec cinemas* (Ottawa: Canadian Film Institute, 1980), 53.

25   Leach, "Second Images," 106.

26   Ibid.

27   Bruce Elder, "The Cinema We Need," in *Documents In Canadian Film*, ed. Douglas Fetherling (Peterborough: Broadview Press, 1988), 264.

28   See Christine Ramsay, "Canadian Narrative Cinema from the Margins; 'The Nation' and Masculinity in Goin' Down The Road," *Canadian Journal of Film Studies* 2–3 (1993), 27–49.

29   Joyce Nelson, *The Colonized Eye: Rethinking the Grierson Legend* (Toronto: Between the Lines, 1988), 146–49.

30   Stephen G. Jones, *The British Labour Movement and film, 1918–1939* (New York: Routledge & Kegan Paul, 1987), 27.

31   Raymond Williams, *The Sociology of Culture* (New York: Schocken Books, 1982), 12–13.

32   Barbara Halpern Martineau, "Before the Guerillieres: Women's Films at the NFB During World War II," in Feldman, ed., *Canadian Film Reader*, 60.

CHAPTER 2

1   See Ted Magder, *Canada's Hollywood: The Canadian State and Feature Films* (Toronto: University of Toronto Press, 1993), 39.

2   Greg Eamon, "Farmers, Phantoms and Princes. The Canadian Pacific Railway and Filmmaking from 1899–1919," *Cinemas* 6 (1995), 14.

3   See Manjunath Pendakur, *Canadian Dreams and American Control: The Political Economy of the Canadian Film Industry* (Detroit: Wayne State University Press, 1990), Chapters 1 and 2.

4   Eamon, "Farmers, Phantoms and Princes," 14.

5   David Frank, "Short Takes: The Canadian Worker on Film," in *Labour/le Travail* 46 (Fall 2000), 421–22.

6   Peter Morris, *Embattled Shadows, A History of Canadian Cinema 1895–1939* (Kingston: McGill-Queen's University Press, 1978), 30–44.

7   Ibid., 30–31.

8   Magder, *Canada's Hollywood*, 48.

9   "TimeLines," *Take One*, 5:12 (1996), 20.

10 David Frank, "Short Takes: The Canadian Worker on Film," in *Labour/le Travail* 46 (Fall 2000), 427.

11 Ibid.

12 Morris, *Embattled Shadows*, 67–69.

13 Ibid., 68.

14 David Frank, "Short Takes: The Canadian Worker on Film." *Labour/le Travail* 46 (Fall 2000), 427.

15 Magder, *Canada's Hollywood*, 30.

16 Ibid., 30.

17 Shelly Stamp Lindsay, "Toronto's 'Girl Workers': The Female Body and Industrial Efficiency in Her Own Fault," *Cinemas* 6 (1995): 84.

18 Ibid., 96.

19 Ibid., 95.

20 Charles Backhouse quoted in David Clandfiel, *Canadian Film* (Toronto: Oxford University Press, 1987), 9.

21 Yvette Hackett, "The National Film Society of Canada, 1935–1951: Its Origins and Development," in *Flashback: People and Institutions in Canadian Film History* (Montreal: Mediatext Publications, 1986), 135.

22 Charles Acland, "National Dreams, International Encounters: The Formation of Canadian Film Culture in the 1930s," *Canadian Journal of Film Studies* 1 (1994), 4.

23 Ibid., 5.

24 Ibid., 7.

25 Maria Tippett, *The Making of English-Canadian Culture, 1900–1939: The External Influences* (Toronto: York University, 1987), 3.

26 Ian McKay, "Helen Creighton and the Politics of Antimodernism," in *Myth and Milieu: Atlantic Literature and Culture 1918–1939*, ed. Gwendolyn Davies (Fredericton: Acadiensis Press, 1993), 5.

27 Ibid., 7.

28 Charles Acland, "Mapping the Serious and the Dangerous: Film and the National Council of Education 1920–1939," *Cinema* 6 (1995), 103.

29 Ibid., 107.

30 According to Avakumovic, "The fact that the principal strike leaders were not among the pioneers of the Communist movement [in Canada], but merely sympathetic to many of the aspirations of the Soviet regime, could be and was explained away by drawing attention to the large number of East European strikers who appeared to be the very pro-soviet." Ivan Avakumovic, *The Communist Party in Canada: A History* (Toronto: McClelland and Stewart, 1975), 14.

31 Acland, "Mapping the Serious and the Dangerous," 106–7.

32 Ibid., 110.

33 Ibid., 115.

34 Tippett, *The Making of English-Canadian Culture*, 15.

CHAPTER 3

1 For a detailed account of the dynamics that contributed to the radicalization of the industrial working-class movement in Canada between 1917 and the 1920s in particular, see Avakumovic, *The Communist Party in Canada*, 1–53.

2 Ian McKay, "For a New Kind of History," 82.

3 Ibid., 83.

4 Ibid., 87–88.

5 *Report of the Proceedings of the Ninth Annual Convention of British Columbia Federation of Labour* (10–13 March 1919), 24. The document can be consulted at the private library of the Communist Party of Canada in British Colombia.

6 *One Big Union Bulletin* (10 March 1927).

7 A.E. Safarian, *The Canadian Economy in the Great Depression* (Toronto, 1970), 75.

8 Ibid., 86.

9 For an excellent account of the situation in Canada during the Great Depression see Michiel Horn, *The Great Depression of the 1930s in Canada* (New Brunswick: Canadian Historical Association, 1984).

10 Maurice Rush, *We Have a Glowing Dream* (Vancouver: Centre for Socialist Education, 1996), 39–40.

11 Ibid., 40.

12 *The Worker* (28 June 1930).

13 *Constitution of The Workers' Unity League* (Montreal, 1931).

14 Rush, *We Have a Glowing Dream*, 16–17.

15 Ibid., 16–17.

16 These numbers were taken from the documents of the Workers Unity League itself. Nevertheless, no contradictory numbers were found in any of the sources of the two rival unions.

17 *The Worker* (31 May 1930).

18 For additional and first-hand information on the Trek movement see Victor Howard, *We were the salt of the Earth!: A narrative of the On-to-Ottawa trek and the Regina Riot* (Regina: University of Regina/Canadian Plains Research Centre, 1985).

19 J. Evans Sheils and B. Swankey, *Work and Wages* (Vancouver, 1977), 180, 227.

20 Robin Endres, Introduction, *Eight Men Speak and Other Plays*, ed. Richard Wright and Robin Endres (Toronto: New Hogtown Press, 1976), xx.

21 Willi Muenzenberg, "Capture the Film!" *Daily Worker* (New York, 23 July 1925), 3.

22 Russell Campbell, *Cinema Strikes Back: Radical Filmmaking in The United States 1930–1942* (Ann Arbor, Michigan: UMI Research Press, 1978), 124.

23 Ross, *Working-Class Hollywood*, 7.

24 Ibid., 7.

25 Ibid., 7.

26 Ibid., 9.

27 Campbell, *Cinema Strikes Back*, 123–25.

28 Gary Crowdus, ed., *The Political Companion to American Film* (Chicago: Lake View Press, 1994).

29 Michiel Horn, *The League for Social Construction: Intellectual Origins of the Democratic Left in Canada, 1930–1942* (Toronto: University of Toronto Press, 1980), 11.

30 Ibid., 6, 13.

31 *The Worker* (1922–1923).

32 Communist Party of Canada, *Canada's Party of Socialism: History of the Communist Party of Canada* (Toronto: Progress Books, 1982), 29.

33 See the Introduction in Endres and Wright, *Eight Men Speak*.

34 For a concise overview of cultural activism in the 1930s check the introduction to Endres and Wright, *Eight Men Speak* and Sean Purdy, *Radicals and Revolutionaries* (Toronto: University of Toronto Press, 1998), 45–51. For explicit assessment of the role played by women in the cultural field during this period see Joan Sangster, *Dreams of Equality: women on the Canadian left, 1920–1950* (Toronto: McClelland and Stewart, 1989), 155–57.

35 Avakumovic, *The Communist Party in Canada*, 126–27.

36   Ibid., 127.

37   Endres, "Introduction," xxiv.

38   Ibid., xxiv.

39   Douglas Scott Parker, "Women in Communist Culture in Canada: 1932 to 1937" (masters thesis, McGill University, 1994), 34.

40   Ibid., 45.

41   Alan Filewod, *Collective Encounters: Documentary Theatre in English Canada* (Toronto: University of Toronto Press, 1987).

42   Albert Edward Smith, *All My Life* (Toronto: Progress Books, 1977), 165, 180.

43   Communist Party of Canada, *Canada's Party of Socialism*, 77–78.

44   This term was used by Michael Denning in his book *The Cultural Front: The Labouring of American Culture in the Twentieth Century* to indicate the evolvement of a working-class discourse in the U.S. around the same period of time.

45   Rush, *We Have a Glowing Dream*, 44.

46   Georgi Dimitrov, *The United Front* (New York: International Publishers, 1938), 31.

47   Georgi Dimitrov, *The United Front against War and Fascism* (New York, 1936), 8.

48   Canada, House of Commons, *Debates*, 1944, 94.

49   Rush, *We Have a Glowing Dream*, 41–42, and *Daily Clarion* 1937, 1938.

50   Workers Unity League, "Final Statement of the WUL Executive Board to those Trade Unionists Who constituted Its Membership, and Who have Now Merged within the Unions of the AFL," 18 June 1936, CPC Archives, 9.

51   Communist Party of Canada, *Canada's Party of Socialism*, 104–5. For a brief non-partisan account of the history of the labour movement in Canada see Craig Heron, *The Canadian Labour Movement: a brief history* (Toronto: J. Lorimer, 1996).

52   Irving M. Abella, *Nationalism, Communism, and Canadian Congress of Labour, 1935–1956* (Toronto: University of Toronto Press, 1973), v.

53   Mercedes Steedman, "The Promise: Communist Organizing in the Needle Trades, The Dressmakers Campaign, 1928 to 1937," *Labour/Le Travail* 34 (1994), 72.

54   Robert W. Kern, ed., *Historical Dictionary of Modern Spain, 1700–1988* (New York: Greenwood, 1990), 267.

55   Merrily Weisbord, *The Strangest Dream* (Montreal: Vehicule Press, 1994), 94.

56   Rush, *We Have a Glowing Dream*, 33.

57   Weisbord, *The Strangest Dream*, 64.

58   Nicola Vulpe and Maha Albari, eds., *Sealed in Struggle. Canadian Poetry & the Spanish Civil War* (Madrid: Centre for Canadian Studies, 1995), 32.

59   Weisbord, *The Strangest Dream*, 91.

60 Ibid., 91–92.

61 Michael J. Piva, *The Condition of the Working Class in Toronto, 1900–1921* (Ottawa: University of Ottawa Press, 1979), 17.

62 Among the more elaborate critical readings on the role of women during this period are Linda Kealey, *Enlisting women for the cause: women, labour, and the left in Canada, 1890–1920* (Toronto: University of Toronto Press, 1998) and Mercedes Steedman, *Angels of the workplace: women and the construction of gender relations in the Canadian clothing industry, 1890–1940* (Toronto: Oxford University Press, 1997).

63 Parker, "Women in Communist Culture in Canada," 79.

64 Ibid., 45.

65 Ibid., 45.

CHAPTER 4

1 Magder, *Canada's Hollywood*, 51.

2 Allan Blaine, "Making Heritage, a Canadian Government Motion Picture," *Prairie Forum* 1 (Spring 2004), 99.

3 D.B. Jones, *The Best Butler in the Business: Tom Daly of the National Film Board of Canada* (Toronto: University of Toronto Press, 1996), 9.

4 Ibid., 9.

5 The John Grierson Project, *John Grierson and the NFB* (Toronto: ECW Press, 1984), 104.

6 "Timelines," *Take One* 5:12 (1996), 28.

7 See Magder, *Canada's Hollywood*, 49–61.

8 John Grierson, "A Film Policy for Canada," in *Documents in Canadian Film*, ed. Douglas Fetherling (Peterborough: Broadview Press, 1988), 55–56.

9 Reprinted in John Grierson, *Grierson on Documentary* , ed. Forsyth Hardy (London: Faber and Faber, 1946), 110.

10 Alberto Cavalcanti, *Le Mouvement neo-realiste en Angletterre. Le Role intellectuel du cinema*, (The Neo-realist Movement in England, in The Intellectual Role of Cinema) (Paris: Institut international de cooperation intellectuelle, 1937), 236.

11 James Beveridge, *John Grierson: Film Master* (New York: Macmillan, 1978), 44.

12 *The John Grierson Project*, 104.

13 Beveridge, *John Grierson: Film Master*, 18.

14 Beveridge, *John Grierson: Film Master*, 43.

15 Filewod, *Collective Encounters*, 14.

16 The British Communist *Daily Worker*, quoted in Stephen Jones, *The British Labour Movement and film*, 170.

17 Grierson (1966), 52.

18 Whitaker and Marcuse, *Cold War Canada*, 230.

19 Beveridge, *John Grierson: Film Master*, 238.

20 Gary Evans, "The Politics of Propaganda," *Cinema Canada* 56 (1979), 13.

21 The John Grierson Project, *John Grierson and the NFB*, 43.

22 Ian Aitken, ed., *The Documentary Film Movement, An Anthology* (Edinburgh: Edinburgh University Press, 1998), 27.

23 Beveridge, *John Grierson: Film Master*, 183.

24 Ibid., 182.

25 Ibid., 237.

26 Len Scher, *The Un-Canadians. True Stories of the Blacklist Era* (Toronto: Lester Publishing Limited, 1992), 89. Scher's view on how Grierson tended to hire people because of their social-activist sensibilities (rather than their production experience) is set against the standard view of some, which claims that he hired inexperienced filmmakers simply to maintain control over them.

27 Ibid., 92.

28 C.W. Gray, *Movies for the People: The Story of the National Film Board of Canada's Unique Distribution System* (Montreal: National Film Board, 1973), 14.

29 Ibid., 27.

30 Whitaker and Marcuse, *Cold War Canada*, 232.

31 Ibid., 232.

32 Evans, "The Politics of Propaganda," 14. Both Morris and Nelson contend on several occasions that when it comes to rural screenings, the NFB's own statistics were exaggerated.

33 Ibid., 14.

34 Aitken, *The Documentary Film Movement*, 28.

35 Ibid., 29.

36 The John Grierson Project, *John Grierson and the NFB*, 35.

37 Ibid., 35.

38 Evans, "The Politics of Propaganda," 14.

39 Gray, *Movies for the People*, 50–52.

40 The John Grierson Project, *John Grierson and the NFB*, 35.

41 Rush, *We Have a Glowing Dream*, 55.

42 Scher, *The Un-Canadians*, 85.

43 Ernst Borneman, "Documentary Films: World War II," in Feldman, ed., *Canadian Film Reader*, 58.

44 Buchanan quoted in Beveridge, *John Grierson:0 Film Master*, 151.

45 Evans, "The Politics of Propaganda," 14.

46 Ibid., 14.

47 Magder, *Canada's Hollywood*, 59–61.

48   Evans, "The Politics of Propaganda," 14–15.

49   Waugh, 37–38.

50   Martineau, " Before the Guerillieres," 58–67.

51   Ibid., 58–67.

52   Raymond Williams, "Base and Superstructure in Marxist Cultural Theory," *New Left Review* 82 (1983), 8–9.

CHAPTER 5

1   Allan, "Making *Heritage*," 86.

2   Ibid., 99.

3   Workers' Unity League, *Constitution*.

4   Ross, *Working-Class Hollywood*, 8.

5   Malek Khouri, "John and the Missus: Progress, Resistance, and 'Common Sense'," *CineAction* 49 (1999), 2–11, and Peter Urquhart, "The Glace Bay Miners' Museum/Margaret's Museum: Adaptation and Resistance," *CineAction* 49 (1999), 12–18.

6   Rush, *We Have a Glowing Dream*, 48.

7   Ibid., 48.

8   *The Clarion*, 16 September 1939.

9   J.B. Salsberg, *The War Situation and Canadian Labour* (Toronto, 1940), 6–8.

10   Scott Forsyth, "Communists, Class, and Culture in Canada" in *Working on Screen: Representations of the Working Class in Canadian Cinema*, ed. Malek Khouri and Darrell Varga (Toronto: University of Toronto Press, 2006), 59-60.

11   For more information on the CPC and the treaty between the Soviet Union and Nazi Germany and issues of inter-imperialist, colonialist, anti-colonialist, anti-capitalist and anti-fascist dimensions of the war see Ernest Mandel, *The Meaning of the Second World War* (London: Verso, 1986). Of particular interest regarding the repression of Communists after the Stalin-Hitler Pact see Ian Radforth, "Political Prisoners: The Communist Internees," in Franca Iacovetta, Roberto Perin and Angelo Principe, eds., *Enemies Within: Italian and Other Internees in Canada and Abroad* (Toronto: University of Toronto Press, 2000), 194–223.

12   Communist Party of Canada, *Canada's Party of Socialism*, 136–41.

13   Rush, *We Have a Glowing Dream*, 53.

14   Nielsen was not officially a member of the Communist Party. Her election to the Parliament on 26 March 1940 was on a "Unity" ticket. Nielsen was originally prominent in the local CCF organization in the rural riding of North Battleford in Saskatchewan. The local itself was dissolved because Neilsen eventually chose to run on the pro-communist "Unity" ticket. Yet the

support for Nielsen "included Social Crediters, CCFers as well as those who had sympathized with the CPC." Avakumovic, *The Communist Party of Canada*, 144–45.

15   Ibid., 145.

16   For an excellent discussion on the dynamics of using war-machine images as "high art" and its implications for early twentieth-century politics see Walter Benjamin's seminal essay: "The Work of Art in the Age of Mechanical Reproduction," in *Film Theory and Criticism*, ed. Gerald Mast, M. Cohen, and L. Braudy (New York: Oxford University Press, 1992), 682–89.

CHAPTER 6

1   Communist Party of Canada, *Canada's Party of Socialism*, 141.

2   Canada, House of Commons, *Debates*, 1944, 2770.

3   Peter Morris, *The National Film Board of Canada: The War Years* (Ottawa: Canadian Film Institute, 1971), 1.

4   Evans, "The Politics of Propaganda," 13.

5   Rush, *We Have a Glowing Dream*, 48.

6   Jack C. Ellis, *John Grierson, Life, Contributions, Influence* (Carbondale and Edwardsville: Southern Illinois University Press, 2000),154.

7   Evans, "The Politics of Propaganda," 13.

8   Trotskyists generally rejected the notion of Popular Front alliances, and favoured a more militant and clearly recognizable socialist program. Trotskyists also rejected the notion of alliance with the west, and considered the war itself as basically an inter-imperialist war in which both its initiators in the west were bent on destroying the worker's state in Russia.

9   Whitaker and Marcuse, *Cold War Canada*, 230–31.

10   Ibid., 230–31.

11   Tim Buck, *A National Front for Victory* (1941), 9–13.

12   Tim Buck, *A Labour Policy for Victory* (1943), 3

13   Canada, House of Commons, *Debates*, 1942, 467

14   Ellis, *John Grierson, Life, Contributions, Influence*, 154.

15   Canada, House of Commons, *Debates*, 1942, 466.

16   Canada, House of Commons, *Debates*, 1941, 1698.

17   Martineau, " Before the Guerillieres," 62.

18   Ibid., 63.

19   Piers Handling, "Censorship and Scares," *Cinema Canada* 56 (1979), 27.

20   *Rebel Girls* was made for Media Resources at Capilano College by producer T.J. Roberts.

CHAPTER 7

1 While these films never used the terms "corporate" or "corporation," references to "private interests" clearly implicated the capitalist mode of production particularly as it relates to big industries.

2 Canada, House of Commons, *Debates*, 1944, 96.

3 See Nelson, *The Colonized Eye*.

4 Canada, House of Commons, *Debates*, 1942, 463.

5 Beveridge, *John Grierson: Film Master*, 151.

6 Ibid., 151.

7 See Abella, *Nationalism, Communism, and Canadian Congress of Labour, 1935-1956*.

8 Ibid.

9 Canada, House of Commons, *Debates*, 1944, 97.

10 Tim Buck, *Canada's Choice: Unity or Chaos* (Toronto, 1944), 23–24.

11 Evans, "The Politics of Propaganda," 14.

12 Buck, *Canada's Choice*, 14–15.

13 Canada, House of Commons, *Debates*, 1945, 99.

14 Canada, House of Commons, *Debates*, 1945, 99.

15 Buck, *Canada's Choice*.

16 Canada, House of Commons, *Debates*, 1944, 2769

17 Canada, House of Commons, *Debates*, 1945, 100.

18 Canada, House of Commons, *Debates*, 1945, 100.

19 Canada, House of Commons, *Debates*, 1942, 465. ·

CHAPTER 8

1 Whitaker and Marcuse, *Cold War Canada*, 231.

2 Ellis, *John Grierson, Life, Contributions, Influence*, 37.

3 Ibid., 37.

4 Grierson cited in Ellis, *John Grierson, Life, Contributions, Influence*, 38.

5 John Grierson, "Flaherty-Naturalism-and the Problem of English Cinema," *Artwork* 7 (Autumn 1931), 210–15.

6 For a sense of what Grierson's documentary influence instigated within debates on documentary cinema, see Ian Aitken, *Film and Reform: John Grierson and the Documentary Film Movement* (New York: Routledge, 1990), 5–15.

7 John Grierson, "Documentary (1)," *Cinema Quarterly* 1 (Winter 1932), 67–72.

8 Grierson from the article "The Documentary Idea 1942," cited in Ellis, *John Grierson, Life, Contributions, Influence*, 203.

9 Aitken, *Film and Reform*, 7.

10   Aitken, *The Documentary Film Movement*, 27.

11   Applebaum quoted in Aitken, *The Documentary Film Movement*, 27.

12   Aitken, *The Documentary Film Movement*, 28.

13   Ibid., 29.

14   Beveridge, *John Grierson Film Master*, 29.

15   Brian Winston, *Claiming the Real, The Griersonian Documentary and its Legitimations* (London: British Film Institute, 1995), 99.

16   Grierson, John, "Putting Punch in a Picture," *Motion Picture News* (27 November 1926) as quoted in Aitken, *The Documentary Film Movement*, 69.

17   Ibid., 69

18   Ibid., 69–70.

19   Ellis, *John Grierson, Life, Contributions, Influence*, 204.

20   Euvrard and Véronneau, "Direct Cinema," 92–93.

21   1970s NFB program *Challenge for Change* stressed the use of film as a tool for discussing issues of social justice.

22   Feldman, "The Silent Subject in English-Canadian Film," 211.

23   See Erik Barnouw, *Documentary: A History of the Non-fiction Film* (New York: Oxford University Press, 1993), 240.

24   Ellis, *John Grierson, Life, Contributions, Influence*, 27.

25   Beveridge, *John Grierson Film Master*, 43.

26   Aitken, *Film and Reform*, 75, 77.

27   Ibid., 76.

28   Ibid., 76.

29   Beveridge, *John Grierson: Film Master*, 237.

30   Winston, *Claiming the Real*, 166.

31   Rotha quoted in Winston, *Claiming the Real*, 166.

32   Grierson quoted in Winston, *Claiming the Real*, 166.

33   For various versions of Grierson's theorizations of "reality" in connection with the role of film and propaganda, see Forsyth Hardy, ed., *Grierson On Documentary* (London: Faber & Faber, 1946), 237–48.

34   Ellis, *John Grierson, Life, Contributions, Influence*, 153.

35   Ibid., 153–54.

36   From Denning, *The Cultural Front*, 118–19.

37   Ibid., 120.

38   Ibid., 122.

39   Anstey cited in Ellis, *John Grierson, Life, Contributions, Influence*, 154.

40   Ellis, *John Grierson, Life, Contributions, Influence*, 155.

41 For details on both *Cine-Liberte* and *L'Equipe*, see Jonathan S. Buchsbaum, "Left Political Filmmaking in France in the 1930s," Ph.D. dissertation, NYU (Ann Arbor: University Microfilms International, 1983), *passim* and Pascal Ory, *La belle illusion: culture et politique sous le signe du front populaire 1935–1938* (Paris: Plon, 1994), Chapter 8.

42 Hawes quoted by Ian Lockerbie, "Grierson in Canada: The peak of his creative career?" in *From Grierson to the Docu-Soap: Breaking the Boundaries*, ed. John Izod, Richard Kilborn and Matthew Hibberd (Luton: University of Luton Press, 2000), 26.

43 Filewod, *Collective Encounters*, 14.

44 Grierson, *Grierson on Documentary*, 13.

45 Stanley Hawes interview, 14–15 February 1980, Stanley Hawes Papers, ScreenSound, Canberra, Australia, Box 52.

CHAPTER 9

1 Kealey, *Workers and Canadian History*, 436.

2 For an elaborate account of the development of the labour strike movement in Canada during this period, see Kealey, *Workers and Canadian History*, 345–411.

3 Ibid., 345–411.

4 Mary E. Baruth-Walsh and G. M. Walsh, *Strike! 99 Days on the Line* (Ottawa: Penumbra Press, 1995), 29–30.

5 Kealey, *Workers and Canadian History*, 437.

6 Ibid., 436.

7 Rush, *We Have a Glowing Dream*, 55–56.

8 Communist Party of Canada, *Canada's Party of Socialism*, 145–46.

9 McKay, "For a New Kind of History," 96. McKay's ground-breaking article presents a unique and a detailed re-assessment of continuities, parallels and divergences between the CPC and CCF views during this period.

10 Ibid., 100. McKay is quoting here a document called *Make This Your Canada*, authored in 1943 by David Lewis and Frank Scott (both leaders in the CCF at the time).

11 Ibid.

12 Magder, *Canada's Hollywood*, 60.

13 Kirwan Cox, "The Grierson Files," *Cinema Canada* 56 (1979), 17.

14 Ibid., 19.

15 Magder, *Canada's Hollywood*, 59.

16 More than 800,000 files were kept by the RCMP on "suspect" Canadians up to the time of the McDonald Commission in the late 1970s. For more details consult Robert Dion, *Crimes of the Secret Police* (Montreal: Black Rose Books, 1982) or John Alan Lee and Edward Mann, *RCMP Versus the People: inside Canada's security service* (Don Mills, Ontario: General, 1979).

17 Dick Hebdige, "From Culture to Hegemony," in *The Cultural Studies Reader*, ed. Simon During (New York: Routledge, 1994), 367.

18 Beckie Buhay, "The Struggle for Women's Rights," *National Affairs Monthly* 5:2 (1948), 102.

19 Canada, House of Commons, *Debates*, 1943, 146.

20 For an excellent and detailed account of events related to the Cold War in Canada including a discussion of the NFB and Grierson see Whitaker and Marcuse, *Cold War Canada*.

21 Magder, *Canada's Hollywood*, 60.

22 Scher, *The Un-Canadians*, 8–9.

23 *Canada Year Book 1952–53* (Ottawa, 1953), 734.

24 Communist Party of Canada, *Canada's Party of Socialism*, 154–68.

25 Canada, House of Commons, *Debates*, 1945, 839

26 Weisbord, *The Strangest Dream*, 188–89.

27 Ibid., 188.

28 For further discussion of the Cold War and the NFB see also Scott Forsyth, "The Failures of Nationalism and Documentary: Grierson and Gouzenko," *Canadian Journal of Film Studies* 1 (1990), 74–82.

29 Canadian Chamber of Commerce, *The Communist Threat to Canada* (Montreal, 1947), 5.

30 "Film Board Monopoly Facing Major Test," *Financial Post*, 19 November 1949, 17.

31 Scher, *The Un-Canadians*, 91.

32 *Ottawa Citizen*, 4 February 1950.

33 Whitaker and Marcuse, *Cold War Canada*, 255.

34 Handling, "The National Film Board of Canada," 48.

35 Scher, *The Un-Canadians*, 12.

36 Rick Salutin, "The NFB Red Scare," *Weekend Magazine*, 23 September 1978, 29.

37 A. R. Sykes, "Believe Suspicion Will Kill Film Board's Bid for Independence," *Ottawa Journal*, 25 November 1949.

38 Salutin, "The NFB Red Scare," 21.

39 Magder, *Canada's Hollywood*, 81.

40 Peter Morris, "After Grierson: The National Film Board 1945–1953," in Feldman, *Take Two*, 190.

41 Ibid., 190.

42 Whitaker and Marcuse, *Cold War Canada*, 232.

43 Ibid., 233.

44 Piers Handling, quoted in Whitaker and Marcuse, *Cold War Canada*, 243.

45 Salutin, "The NFB Red Scare," 21.

46 Ibid., 21.

47 Clandfield, *Canadian Film*, 19.

48   Aitken, The Documentary Film Movement, 31.

49   Ibid., 31.

50   D.B. Jones, *The Best Butler in the Business: Tom Daly of the National Film Board of Canada* (Toronto: University of Toronto Press, 1996), 27.

51   Raymond Williams, *Culture* (London: Fontana, 1981), 85–86.

52   Tom Waugh, "Action Stations! Joris Ivens and The National Film Board," *Flashback. People and Institutions in Canadian Film History* (Montreal: Mediatexte Publication Inc., 1986), 59.

INDEX

CINEMAS OFF CENTRE SERIES

Malek Khouri, general editor

The Cinemas Off Centre series highlights bodies of cinematic work that, for various reasons, have been ignored, marginalized, overlooked, and/or obscured within traditional and dominant canons of film and cinema studies. The series presents cutting edge research that provokes and inspires new explorations of past, present, and emerging cinematic trends by individuals and groups of filmmakers from around the world.

Filming Politics: Communisim and the Portrayal of the Working Class at the National Film Board of Canada, 1939–46 by Malek Khouri · No. 1